By the same author

HOUSING AND LOCAL GOVERNMENT (*George Allen & Unwin*)
HOUSING IN TRANSITION (*Heinemann*)
HOUSING NEEDS AND PLANNING POLICY (*Routledge*)
ENGLISH HOUSING TRENDS (*Bell*)
A PROFILE OF GLASGOW HOUSING (*Oliver & Boyd*)
HOUSING AND LABOUR MOBILITY (*OECD*)
PROBLEMS OF AN URBAN SOCIETY (3 vols: *George Allen & Unwin*)
ENVIRONMENTAL PLANNING: VOLUME I:
Reconstruction and Land Use Planning (*HMSO*)

The New Local Government Series
No. 8

TOWN AND COUNTRY PLANNING IN BRITAIN

The New Local Government Series

Series Editor: Professor Peter G. Richards

TOWN AND COUNTRY PLANNING IN BRITAIN

BY

J. B. CULLINGWORTH

Sixth Edition

London
GEORGE ALLEN & UNWIN LTD
RUSKIN HOUSE   MUSEUM STREET

First published 1964
Second edition 1967
Second impression 1969
Third edition 1970
Fourth edition 1972
Fifth edition 1974
Sixth edition 1976

ISBN 0 04 352060 X hardback
0 04 352061 8 paperback

Jacket and cover illustration:
Courtesy of
Milton Keynes Development Corporation

*Printed in Great Britain
in 10 on 11 pt Times type*
BY T. AND A. CONSTABLE LTD.,
HOPETOUN STREET, EDINBURGH

PREFACE

This is the sixth edition of a book originally written in 1963. The changes which have taken place in town and country planning policies – and in the problems for which they are designed – are dramatic. Indeed they now justify a separate historical volume. The major themes of such a volume would be the increasing social content of planning, a growing awareness of the political nature of planning, and repeated attempts to make the planning machine more sensitive and responsive to the needs which it exists to serve. Some of these issues are discussed in the author's *Problems of an Urban Society*. That work was conceived as being complementary to the present volume, with much greater emphasis on problems and the social policy context. Here the objective is to set out the machinery of British planning.

That machinery has undergone drastic – and accelerating – change in recent years. As a result, major revisions have been made in the current edition. At the same time more space has been devoted to the Scottish scene, not simply to justify the title, but because developments in machinery and policy north of the Border are of particular interest. The reference is not to North Sea Oil (which, indeed, is one of the subjects which is omitted, both because there is a continuing spate of writings on this and because there is insufficient space to deal with it); the reference is to the new organisation of Scottish local government and its emerging planning role.

Despite the revisions, the basic framework of the book remains the same. Chapter I provides a background account of the evolution of town and country planning, the inadequacies of the embryonic instruments of the inter-war years, and the now largely forgotten enthusiasm and confidence of the architects of post-war planning. Chapter II describes how this idealism battled against the facts of political and administrative life: a battle which is still unresolved – if it ever can be.

Chapters III to VI give an account of the structure of the planning machine and the general powers at its disposal. Chapter III deals with central government while Chapter IV gives a succinct account of the reorganised machinery of local government. The latter sheds the lengthy accounts of plans for reorganisation which appeared in previous editions: the reorganisation is now a fact, though perhaps less stable than might have been expected. Chapter V now focuses on the 'new' planning system and omits much of the earlier account of 'old-style' development plans. Chapter VI, though boasting a new title – the control of development – is an up-dated version of material previously forming part of another chapter, but it includes an extended account of the Dobry Reports (which may well have a greater influence on administrative processes than they have had on statutory procedures).

Chapter VII, on planning and land values, has been revised to include a short discussion of the Community Land Act. Here the account is likely to be out of focus since the text had to be written as the Bill staggered through its final parliamentary stages. This chapter ends on a note of optimism which hopefully does not, in retrospect, painfully display the vicissitudes which attend this complex and highly political issue.

A short Chapter VIII outlines traffic planning but is purposely 'light' on policy – thus truly reflecting the contemporary situation.

Previous editions contained a separate chapter on amenity. This has now been incorporated in Chapter IX on 'planning the environment'. The shorter treatment now seems justified in the light of changed public attitudes and a much greater concern for environmental quality – on which the avid reader has a surfeit of alternative readings. Similarly with Chapter X on leisure which, at one time, was a very lengthy chapter.

Chapter XI attempts a summary of policy and achievements in relation to new and expanding towns. Chapter XII deals in greater detail than previously with slum clearance and house improvement policies where changes in approach are particularly striking.

Regional planning – still a promise rather than an actuality (except in Scotland where it is premature to make judgements) – forms the subject matter of Chapter XIII. Here it is sad to have to state again that disappointingly little fundamental revision has been appropriate.

The final chapter, on the other hand, has been subject to substantial amendment. 'Planning and the public' is no longer seen as a matter for public relations on finalised plans: it is of the essence of government in a democratic society.

All references and suggestions for further reading have been collated (and expanded) in an Appendix. It is hoped that this will prove more useful than the precise referencing given at the end of each chapter in the previous edition. Where appropriate, sufficient indication is given in the text to enable particular references to be identified.

Grateful acknowledgement is made to the many people, mostly within the planning profession, who have assisted in various ways in the writing of this book. Though anonymity must be preserved in accordance with convention, my debt is great – and, to the discerning, obvious. Thanks are due to the Controller of HM Stationery Office for permission to quote extensively from official publications. My largest debt, as always, is to my wife, who has borne a large part of the social cost of this composition.

J. B. Cullingworth

December 1975

CONTENTS

Chapter I

THE EVOLUTION OF TOWN AND COUNTRY PLANNING

THE PUBLIC HEALTH ORIGINS

Town and country planning as a task of government has developed from public health and housing policies. The nineteenth-century increase in population and, even more significant, the growth of towns led to public health problems which demanded a new role for government. Together with the growth of medical knowledge, the realisation that overcrowded insanitary urban areas resulted in an economic cost (which had to be borne at least in part by the local ratepayers) and the fear of social unrest, this new urban growth eventually resulted in an appreciation of the necessity for interfering with market forces and private property rights in the interest of social well-being. The nineteenth-century public health legislation was directed at the creation of adequate sanitary conditions. Among the measures taken to achieve these were powers for local authorities to make and enforce building by-laws for controlling street widths and the height, structure and layout of buildings. Limited and defective though these powers proved to be, they represented a marked advance in social control and paved the way for more imaginative measures. The physical impact of by-law control on British towns is depressingly still very much in evidence; and it did not escape the attention of contemporary social reformers. In the words of Unwin:

'. . . much good work has been done. In the ample supply of pure water, in the drainage and removal of waste matter, in the paving, lighting and cleansing of streets, and in many other such ways, probably our towns are as well served as, or even better than, those elsewhere. Moreover, by means of our much abused building bye-laws, the worst excesses of overcrowding have been restrained; a certain minimum standard of air-space, light and ventilation has been secured; while in the more modern parts of towns a fairly high degree of sanitation, of immunity from fire, and general stability of construction have been maintained, the importance of which can hardly be exaggerated. We have, indeed, in all these matters laid a good foundation and have secured many of the necessary elements for a healthy condition of life; and yet the remarkable fact remains that there are growing up around our big towns vast districts, under these very bye-laws, which for dreariness and sheer ugliness it is difficult to match anywhere, and compared with which many of the old unhealthy slums are, from the point of view of picturesqueness and beauty, infinitely more attractive.'

It was on this point that public health and architecture met. The enlightened experiments at Saltaire (1853), Bournville (1878), Port Sunlight (1887) and elsewhere had provided object lessons. Ebenezer Howard and the Garden City Movement were now exerting considerable influence on contemporary thought. The National Housing Reform Council (later the National Housing and Town Planning Council) were campaigning for the introduction of town planning. Even more significant was a similar demand from local government and professional associations such as the Association of Municipal Corporations, the Royal Institute of British Architects, the Surveyors' Institute and the Association of Municipal and County Engineers. As Ashworth has pointed out, in *The Genesis of Modern British Town Planning*, 'the support of many of these bodies was particularly important because it showed that the demand for town planning was arising not simply out of theoretical preoccupations but out of the everyday practical experience of local administration. The demand was coming in part from those who would be responsible for the execution of town planning if it were introduced.'

THE FIRST PLANNING ACT

The movement for the extension of sanitary policy into town planning was uniting diverse interests. These were nicely summarised by John Burns, President of the Local Government Board, when he introduced the first legislation bearing the term 'town planning' – the Housing, Town Planning, Etc., Act, 1909:

'The object of the Bill is to provide a domestic condition for the people in which their physical health, their morals, their character and their whole social condition can be improved by what we hope to secure in this Bill. The Bill aims in broad outline at, and hopes to secure, the home healthy, the house beautiful, the town pleasant, the city dignified and the suburb salubrious.'

The new powers provided by the Act were for the preparation of 'schemes' by local authorities for controlling the development of new housing areas. Though novel, these powers were logically a simple extension of existing ones. It is significant that this first legislative acceptance of town planning came in an Act dealing with health and housing. And, as Ashworth has pointed out, the gradual development and the accumulated experience of public health and housing measures facilitated a general acceptance of the principle of town planning. 'Housing reform had gradually been conceived in terms of larger and larger units. Torrens' Act (Artizans and Labourers Dwellings Act, 1868) had made a beginning with individual houses; Cross's Act (Artizans and Labourers Dwellings Improvement Act, 1875) had introduced an element of town planning by concerning itself with the reconstruction of insanitary areas; the framing of bye-laws in accordance with the Public Health Act of 1875 had accustomed local authorities to the imposition of at least a minimum of regulation on new building, and such a measure as the London Building Act of 1894 brought into the scope of public control the formation and widening of streets, the lines of buildings frontage, the extent of open space around buildings, and the height of buildings. Town planning was therefore not altogether a leap in the dark, but could be represented as a logical extension, in accordance with changing aims and conditions, of earlier legislation concerned with housing and public health.' The 'changing conditions' were predominantly the rapid growth of suburban development – a factor which increased in importance in the following decades.

'In fifteen years 500,000 acres of land have been abstracted from the agricultural domain for houses, factories, workshops and railways. . . . If we go in the next fifteen years abstracting another half a million from the agricultural domain, and we go on rearing in green fields slums, in many respects, considering their situation, more squalid than those which are found in Liverpool, London and Glasgow, posterity will blame us for not taking this matter in hand in a scientific spirit. Every two and a half years there is a County of London converted into urban life from rural conditions and agricultural land. It represents an enormous amount of building land which we have no right to allow to go unregulated.'

The emphasis was entirely on raising the standards of *new* development. The Act permitted local authorities (after obtaining the permission of the Local Government Board) to prepare town planning schemes with the general object of 'securing proper sanitary conditions, amenity and convenience', but only for land which was being developed or appeared likely to be developed.

Strangely it was not at all clear what town planning involved. Aldridge, writing in 1915, noted that it certainly did not include 'the remodelling of the existing town, the replanning of badly planned areas, the driving of new roads through old parts of a town – all these are beyond the scope of the new town planning powers'. The Act itself provided no definition: indeed, it merely listed nineteen 'matters to be dealt with by General Provisions Prescribed by the Local Government Board'. The restricted and vague nature of this first legislation was associated in part with the lack of experience of the problems involved: Nettleford even went so far as to suggest that 'when this Act was passed, it was recognized as only a trial trip for the purpose of finding out the weak spots in local government with regard to town and estate development so that effective remedies might be later on devised'.

Nevertheless the cumbersome administrative procedure devised by the Local Government Board – in order to give all interested parties 'full opportunity of considering the proposals at all stages' – might well have been intended to deter all but the most ardent of local authorities. The land taxes threatened by the 1910 Finance Act, and then the First World War, added to the difficulties. It can be the occasion of no surprise that very few schemes were actually completed under the 1909 Act.

INTER-WAR LEGISLATION

The first revision of town planning legislation which took place after the First World War (the Housing and Town Planning Act of 1919) did little in practice to broaden the basis of town planning. The preparation of schemes was made obligatory on all borough and urban districts having a population of 20,000 or more, but the time limit (1 January 1926) was first extended (by the Housing Act, 1923) and finally abolished (by the Town and Country Planning Act, 1932). Some of the procedural difficulties were removed, but no change in concept appeared. Despite lip-service to the idea of town planning, the major advances made at this time were in the field of housing rather than in planning. It was the 1919 Act which began what Marion Bowley has called 'the series of experiments in State intervention to increase the supply of working-class houses'. The 1919 Act accepted the principle of State subsidies for housing and thus began the nation-wide growth of council house estates. Equally significant was the entirely new standard of working-class housing provided: the three-bedroom house with kitchen, bath and garden,

built at the density recommended by the Tudor Walters Report of
not more than twelve houses to the acre. At these new standards
development could generally take place only on virgin land on the
periphery of towns, and municipal estates grew alongside the
private suburbs – 'the basic social products of the twentieth
century', as Asa Briggs has termed them.

This suburbanisation was greatly accelerated by rapid developments in transportation – developments with which the young
planning machine could not keep pace. The ideas of Howard and
the Garden City Movement, of Geddes and of those who, like
Warren and Davidge, saw town planning not just as a technique for
controlling the layout and design of residential areas, but as part of a
policy of national economic and social planning, were receiving
increasing attention, but in practice town planning often meant
little more than an extension of the old public health and housing
controls.

Various attempts were made to deal with the increasing difficulties. Of particular significance were the Town and Country Planning
Act of 1932, which extended planning powers to almost any type of
land, whether built-up or undeveloped, and the Restriction of
Ribbon Development Act, 1935, which, as its name suggests, was
designed to control the spread of development along major roads.
But these and similar measures were inadequate. For instance,
under the 1932 Act planning schemes took about three years to
prepare and pass through all their stages. Final approval had to be
given by Parliament and schemes then had the force of law – as a
result of which variations or amendments were not possible except
by a repetition of the whole procedure. 'Interim development
control' operated during the time between the passing of a resolution to prepare a scheme and its date of operation (as approved by
Parliament). This enabled – but did not require – developers to
apply for planning permission. If they did not obtain planning
permission, and the development was not in conformity with the
scheme when approved, the planning authority could require the
owner (without compensation) to remove or alter the development.
But all too often developers preferred to take a chance that no
scheme would ever come into force, or that if it did no local
authority would face pulling down existing buildings. The damage
was therefore done before the planning authorities had a chance to
intervene. Once a planning scheme was approved, on the other
hand, the local authority ceased to have any planning control over
individual developments. The scheme was in fact a zoning plan:
land was zoned for particular uses – residential, industrial, and so on
– though provision could be made for limiting the number of

buildings, the space around them, etc. In fact, so long as the developer did not try to introduce a non-conforming use he was fairly safe. Furthermore, most schemes in fact did little more than accept and ratify existing trends of development, since any attempt at a more radical solution would have involved the planning authority in compensation they could not afford to pay. In most cases the zones were so widely drawn as to place hardly more restriction on the developer than if there had been no scheme at all. Indeed in the half of the country covered by draft planning schemes in 1937 there was sufficient land zoned for housing to accommodate 350 million people.

ADMINISTRATIVE SHORTCOMINGS

A major weakness was, of course, the administrative structure itself. At the local level the administrative unit outside the county boroughs was the district council. Such authorities were generally small and weak. This was implicitly recognised as early as 1919, for the Act of that year permitted the establishment of joint planning committees. The 1929 Local Government Act went further, by empowering county councils to take part in planning, either by becoming constituent members of joint planning committees or by undertaking powers relinquished by district councils. A number of regional advisory plans were prepared, but these were generally ineffective and, indeed, conceived as little more than a series of suggestions for controlling future development, together with proposals for new main roads. The noteworthy characteristic of a planning scheme was its regulatory nature. It did not secure that development would take place: it merely secured that if it did take place in any particular part of the area covered by the scheme it would be controlled in certain ways. Furthermore, as the Uthwatt Report stressed, the system was 'essentially one of local planning, based on the initiative and financial resources of local bodies (whether individual local authorities or combinations of such authorities) responsible to local electorates. . . . The local authorities naturally consider questions of planning and development largely with a view to the effect they will have on the authorities' own finances and trade of the district. Proposals by landowners involving the further development of an existing urban area are not likely in practice to be refused by a local authority if the only reason against the development taking place is that from the national standpoint its proper location is elsewhere, particularly when it is remembered that the prevention of any such development might not only involve the authority in liability to pay heavy compensation but would, in addition, deprive them of substantial increases in rate income.'

The central authority – the Ministry of Health – had no effective powers of initiation and no power to grant financial assistance to local authorities. Indeed their powers were essentially regulatory and seemed to be designed to cast them in the role of a quasi-judicial body to be chiefly concerned with ensuring that local authorities did not treat property owners unfairly.

The difficulties were not, however, solely administrative. Even the most progressive authority were greatly handicapped by the inadequacies of the law relating to compensation. The compensation paid either for planning restrictions or for compulsory acquisition had to be determined in relation to the most profitable use of the land, even if it was unlikely that the land would be so developed, and without regard to the fact that the prohibition of development on one site usually resulted in the development value (which had been purchased at high cost) shifting to another site. Consequently, in the words of the Uthwatt Committee, 'an examination of the Town Planning maps of some of our most important built-up areas reveals that in many cases they are little more than photographs of existing users and existing lay-outs, which, to avoid the necessity of paying compensation, become perpetuated by incorporation in a statutory scheme irrespective of their suitability or desirability'.

These problems increased as the housing boom of the thirties developed; 2,700,000 houses were built in England and Wales between 1930 and 1940. At the outbreak of war one-third of all the houses in England and Wales had been built since 1918. The implications for urbanisation were obvious, particularly in the London area. Between 1919 and 1939 the population of Greater London rose by about three-quarters of a million on account of natural increase but by over one and a quarter million by migration. This growth of the metropolis was a force which existing powers were incapable of halting, despite the large body of opinion favouring some degree of control.

THE DEPRESSED AREAS

The crux of the matter was that the problem of London was closely allied to that of the declining areas of the north and of South Wales – and both were part of the much wider problem of industrial location. In the south-east the insured employed population rose by 44 per cent between 1923 and 1934, but in the north-east it fell by 5·5 per cent and in Wales by 26 per cent. In 1934, 8·6 per cent of insured workers in Greater London were unemployed, but in Workington the proportion was 36·3 per cent, in Gateshead 44·2 per cent and in Jarrow 67·8 per cent. In the early stages of political action these two problems were divorced. For London, various advisory committees were set up and a series of reports issued – the Royal Commission on the Local Government of Greater London (1921–3); the London and Home Counties Traffic Advisory Committee (1924); the Greater London Regional Planning Committee (1927); the Standing Conference on London Regional Planning (1937); as well as *ad hoc* committees and inquiries, e.g. on Greater London Drainage (1935) and a Highway Development Plan (the Bressey Report, 1938). For the depressed areas, attention was first concentrated on encouraging migration, on training schemes and on schemes for establishing the unemployed in smallholdings. Increasing unemployment accompanied by rising public concern (especially after hunger marches on the one hand and articles in *The Times* on the other) necessitated further action. Government 'investigators' were appointed and, following their reports, the Depressed Areas Bill was introduced in November 1934 – to pass (after the Lords had amended the title) as the Special Areas Act. Under the Act a Special Commissioner for England and Wales, and one for Scotland, were appointed, with very wide powers for 'the initiation, organisation, prosecution and assistance of measures designed to facilitate the economic development and social improvement' of the Special Areas. The areas were defined in the Act and included the north-east coast, west Cumberland, industrial South Wales – and, in Scotland, the industrial area around Glasgow. By September 1938, the Commissioners had spent, or approved the spending of, nearly £21 million, of which £15 million was for the improvement of public and social services, £3 million for smallholdings and allotment schemes, and £½ million on amenity schemes such as the clearance of derelict sites. Physical and social amelioration, however, was intended to be complementary to the Commissioners' main task: the attraction of new industry. Appeals to industrialists proved inadequate; in his second report, Sir Malcolm Stewart, the Commissioner for England and Wales, concluded 'there is little prospect of the Special Areas being assisted by the spontaneous action of industrialists now located outside these Areas'. On the other hand, the attempt actively to attract new industry by the development of trading estates achieved considerable success, which at least warranted the comment of the Scottish Commissioner that there had been 'sufficient progress to dispel the fallacy that the Areas are incapable of expanding their light industries'. Nevertheless there were still 300,000 unemployed in the Special Areas at the end of 1938, and though 123 factories had been opened between

1937 and 1938 in the Special Areas, 372 had been opened in the London area. Sir Malcolm Stewart concluded, in his third annual report, that 'the further expansion of industry should be controlled to secure a more evenly distributed production'. Such thinking might have been in harmony with the current increasing recognition of the need for national planning, but it called for political action of a character which would have been sensational. Furthermore, as Neville Chamberlain (then Chancellor of the Exchequer) pointed out, even if new factories were excluded from London it did not follow that they would forthwith spring up in South Wales or west Cumberland. The immediate answer of the Government was to appoint the Barlow Commission.

THE BARLOW REPORT

The Barlow Report is of significance not merely because it is an important historical landmark, but also because some of its major policy recommendations have been accepted by all post-war governments as a basis for planning policy. Only recently have these policies been questioned.

The terms of reference of the Commission were 'to inquire into the causes which have influenced the present geographical distribution of the industrial population of Great Britain and the probable direction of any change in that distribution in the future; to consider what social, economic or strategic disadvantages arise from the concentration of industries or of the industrial population in large towns or in particular areas of the country; and to report what remedial measures if any should be taken in the national interest'.

These very wide terms of reference represented, as the Commission pointed out, 'an important step forward' in contemporary thinking. Reviewing the history of town planning they noted that:

'Legislation has not yet proceeded so far as to deal with the problem of planning from a *national* standpoint; there is no duty imposed on any authority or Government Department to view the country as a whole and to consider the problems of industrial, commercial and urban growth in the light of the needs of the entire population. The appointment, therefore, of the present Commission marks an important step forward. The evils attendant on haphazard and ill-regulated town growth were first brought under observation; then similar dangers when prevalent over wider areas or regions; now the investigation is extended to Great Britain as a whole. The Causes, Probable Direction of Change and Disadvantages mentioned in the Terms of Reference are clearly not concerned with separate localities or local authorities, but with England, Scotland and Wales collectively: and the Remedial Measures to be considered are expressly required to be in the national interest.'

After reviewing the evidence, the Commission concluded that 'the disadvantages in many, if not in most of the great industrial concentrations, alike on the strategical, the social and the economic side, do constitute serious handicaps and even in some respects dangers to the nation's life and development, and we are of opinion that definite action should be taken by the Government towards remedying them'. The advantages of concentration were clear – proximity to market, reduction of transport costs and availability of a supply of suitable labour. But these, in the Commission's view, were accompanied by serious disadvantages such as heavy charges on account mainly of high site values, loss of time through street traffic congestion, and the risk of adverse effects on efficiency due to long and fatiguing journeys to work. The Commission maintained that the development of garden cities, satellite towns and trading estates could make a useful contribution towards the solution of these problems of urban congestion.

The London area, of course, presented the largest problem, not simply because of its huge size, but also because 'the trend of migration to London and the Home Counties is on so large a scale and of so serious a character that it can hardly fail to increase in the future the disadvantages already shown to exist'. The problems of London were thus in part related to the problems of the depressed areas:

'It is not in the national interest, economically, socially or strategically, that a quarter, or even a larger, proportion of the population of Great Britain should be concentrated within 20 to 30 miles or so of Central London. On the other hand, a policy:

(i) of balanced distribution of industry and the industrial population so far as possible throughout the different areas or regions in Great Britain;

(ii) of appropriate diversification of industries in those areas or regions;

would tend to make the best national use of the resources of the country, and at the same time would go far to secure for each region or area, through diversification of industry and variety of employment, some safeguard against severe and persistent depression, such as attacks an area dependent mainly on one industry when that industry is struck by bad times.'

Such policies could not be carried out by the existing administrative machinery: it was no part of statutory planning to check or to encourage a local or regional growth of population. Planning was essentially on a local basis; it did not, and was not intended to, influence the geographical distribution of the population as between one locality and another. The Commission unanimously agreed that the problems were national in character and required a central authority to deal with them. They argued that the activities of this authority ought to be distinct from and extend beyond those of any existing government department. They should be responsible for formulating a plan for dispersal from congested urban areas – determining in which areas dispersal was desirable; whether and where dispersal could be effected by developing garden cities or garden suburbs, satellite towns, trading estates or the expansion of existing small towns or regional centres. They should be given the right to inspect town planning schemes and 'to consider, where necessary, in co-operation with the Government Departments concerned, the modification or correlation of existing or future plans in the national interest'. They should study the location of industry throughout the country with a view to anticipating cases where depression might probably occur in the future and encouraging industrial or public development before a depression actually occurred.

But though the Commission were agreed on the 'objectives of national action' and on the necessity for a central authority, they were not agreed on the powers to be given to this authority. The majority recommended that it should be a National Industrial Board consisting of a chairman and three other members appointed by the President of the Board of Trade after consultation with the Ministers of Health, Labour and Transport, and the Secretary of State for Scotland. This board should have research, advisory and publicity functions, but also (in view of the necessity for immediate action in the London area) executive powers to regulate additional industrial building in London and the Home Counties. These 'negative powers' should be extendable by Order in Council to other areas. Finally the board should be required to decide what additional powers they needed to carry out their functions.

Three members of the Commission (Professor J. H. Jones, Mr George W. Thomson and Sir William E. Whyte), though signing the majority report, prepared a 'note of reservations'. They argued that the control of industrial development in the London area was an inadequate measure to achieve the 'objectives of national action'. Such controls needed to be operated over the whole country.

Furthermore, they believed that it was even more important for the Government 'to create more favourable conditions of life and work in other parts of the country and thereby weaken the inducement to seek work in or near London'. In their view the powers of the Commissioners for the Special Areas should be largely transferred to the new board which would be given powers to enable them to offer such inducements as they thought necessary to make effective the policy of securing a better balance and a greater diversification of industry throughout the country. Regional administration was essential, and a series of divisional boards should be set up as an integral part of the new authority.

A minority of the Commission (Professor Patrick Abercrombie, Mr H. H. Elvin and Mrs H. Hichens) felt unable to put their signatures to the main recommendations. They went even further in their criticisms of the inadequacy of these than the three members who signed the 'note of reservations'. In their view the problems were of immediate urgency, particularly since an unprecedented amount of new factory building was under way in connection with the rearmament programme. They felt that the majority report seemed to imply that there was ample time for preparation and research, whereas in fact the problem was an immediate one. The urgency of the situation demanded the setting up of a powerful body with executive powers. The board proposed by the majority was not strong enough: what was required was a new ministry exercising full executive powers. This ministry would 'nccd to be fitted into the scheme of central and local government if it is to function properly'. It would obviously have to take over the planning functions of the Ministry of Health (and possibly some of their housing functions), as well as some of the planning powers of the Ministry of Transport. The work of the Commissioners for the Special Areas should be transferred to it – and at the same time extended to the whole country.

The differences between the three sets of recommendations were less striking than their unanimous condemnation of the existing situation and the inadequacy of both policy and machinery for dealing with it. All were agreed that a far more positive role for government was required, that control should be exercised over new factory building at least in London and the Home Counties, that dispersal from the larger urban concentrations was desirable, and that measures should be taken to anticipate regional economic depression. The differences centred largely on how such policies should be translated into terms of administrative machinery.

THE IMPACT OF WAR

The Barlow Report was published in January 1940 – some four months after the start of the Second World War. The problem which precipitated the decision to set up the Barlow Commission – that of the depressed areas – rapidly disappeared. The unemployed of the depressed areas now became a powerful national asset. A considerable share of the new factories built to provide munitions or to replace bombed factories were located in these areas. By the end of 1940 'an extraordinary scramble for factory space had developed'; and out of all this 'grew a war-time, an extempore, location of industry policy covering the country as a whole'. This emergency war-time policy – paralleled in other fields, such as hospitals – not only provided some 13 million square feet of munitions factory space in the depressed areas which could be adapted for civilian industry after the end of the war; it also provided experience in dispersing industry and in controlling industrial location which showed the practicability (under war-time conditions at least) of such policies. The Board of Trade became a central clearing-house of information on industrial sites. During the debates on the Distribution of Industry Bill, their spokesman stressed:

'We have collected a great deal of information regarding the relative advantage of different sites in different parts of the country, and of the facilities available there with regard to local labour supply, housing accommodation, transport facilities, electricity, gas, water, drainage and so on. . . . We are now able to offer to industrialists a service of information regarding location which has never been available before.'

Hence, though the Barlow Report (to use a phrase of Dame Alix Meynell) 'lay inanimate in the iron lung of war', it seemed that the conditions for the acceptance of its views on the control of industrial location were becoming very propitious: there is nothing better than successful experience for demonstrating the practicability of a policy.

The war thus provided a great stimulus to the extension of town and country planning into the sphere of industrial location. And this was not the only stimulus it provided. The destruction wrought by bombing transformed 'the rebuilding of Britain' from a socially desirable but somewhat visionary and vague ideal into a matter of practical and defined necessity. Nor was this all: the very fact that rebuilding was clearly going to take place on a large scale provided an unprecedented opportunity for comprehensive planning of the bombed areas and a stimulus to overall town planning. In the Exeter Plan, Thomas Sharp urged that 'to rebuild the city in the old lines . . . would be a dreadful mistake. It would be an exact repetition of what happened in the rebuilding of London after the Fire – and the results, in regret at lost opportunity, will be the same. While, therefore, the arrangements for rebuilding to the new plan should proceed with all possible speed, some patience and discipline will be necessary if the new-built city is to be a city that is really renewed.' In Hull, Lutyens and Abercrombie argued that 'there is now both the opportunity and the necessity for an overhaul of the urban structure before undertaking this second refounding of the great Port on the Humber. Due consideration, however urgent the desire to get back to working conditions, must be given to every aspect of town existence.' The note was one of optimism of being able to tackle problems which were of long standing. In the metropolis (to quote from the *County of London Plan*) 'London was ripe for reconstruction before the war; obsolescence, bad and unsuitable housing, inchoate communities, uncorrelated road systems, industrial congestion, a low level of urban design, inequality in the distribution of open spaces, increasing congestion of dismal journeys to work – all these and more clamoured for improvement before the enemy's efforts to smash us by air attack stiffened our resistance and intensified our zeal for reconstruction.'

This was the social climate of the war and early post-war years. There was an enthusiasm and a determination to undertake social reconstruction on a scale hitherto considered utopian. The catalyst was, of course, the war itself. At one and the same time war occasions a mass support for the way of life which is being fought for and a critical appraisal of the inadequacies of that way of life. Modern total warfare demands the unification of national effort and a breaking down of social barriers and differences. As Titmuss noted, it 'presupposes and imposes a great increase in social discipline; moreover, this discipline is tolerable if – and only if – social inequalities are not intolerable'. On no occasion was this more true than in the Second World War. A new and better Britain was to be built. The feeling was one of intense optimism and confidence. Not only would the war be won: it would be followed by a similar campaign against the forces of want. That there was much that was inadequate, even intolerable, in pre-war Britain had been generally accepted. What was new was the belief that the problems could be tackled in the same way as a military operation. What supreme confidence was evidenced by the setting up in 1941 of committees to consider post-war reconstruction problems – the Uthwatt Committee on Compensation and Betterment, the Scott Committee on Land Utilization in Rural Areas and the Beveridge Committee on Social Insurance and Allied Services. Perhaps it was Beveridge who most clearly summed up the spirit of the time – and the philosophy which was to underlie post-war social policy:

'The Plan for Social Security is put forward as part of a general programme of social policy. It is one part only of an attack upon five great evils: upon the physical Want with which it is directly concerned, upon Disease which often causes Want and brings many other troubles in its train, upon Ignorance which no democracy can afford among its citizens, upon the Squalor which arises mainly through haphazard distribution of industry and population, and upon Idleness which destroys wealth and corrupts men, whether they are well fed or not, when they are idle. In seeking security not merely against physical want, but against all these evils in all their forms, and in showing that security can be combined with freedom and enterprise and responsibility of the individual for his own life, the British community and those who in other lands have inherited the British tradition, have a vital service to render to human progress.'

It was within this framework of a newly acquired confidence to tackle long-standing social and economic problems that post-war town and country planning policy was conceived. No longer was this to be restricted to town planning 'schemes' or regulatory measures. There was now the same breadth in official thinking as had permeated the Barlow Report. The attack on Squalor was conceived as part of a comprehensive series of plans for social amelioration. To quote the 1944 White Paper *The Control of Land Use*:

'Provision for the right use of land, in accordance with a considered policy, is an essential requirement of the Government's programme of post-war reconstruction. New houses, whether of permanent or emergency construction; the new layout of areas devasted by enemy action or blighted by reason of age or bad living conditions; the new schools which will be required under the Education Bill now before Parliament; the balanced distribution of industry which the Government's recently published proposals for maintaining active employment envisage; the requirements of sound nutrition and of a healthy and well-balanced agriculture; the preservation of land for national parks and forests, and the assurance to the people of enjoyment of the sea and countryside in times of leisure; a new and safer highway system better adapted to modern industrial and other needs; the proper provision of airfields – all these related parts of a single reconstruction programme involve the use of land, and it is essential that their various claims on land should be so harmonized as to ensure for the people of this country the greatest possible measure of individual well-being and national prosperity.'

THE NEW PLANNING MACHINERY

This broad historical approach must now give way to a series of discussions on particular issues – administration, planning powers and policies, the problem of land values, and so on. Before embarking upon this, however, it is useful to provide a brief outline of the new planning machinery. This will provide a general background which will be detailed and brought up to date in later chapters.

The pre-war machinery of planning was defective in several ways. It was optional on local authorities; planning powers were essentially regulatory and restrictive; such planning as was achieved was purely local in character; the central government had no effective powers of initiative, or of co-ordinating local plans; and the 'compensation bogey' – with which local authorities had to cope without any Exchequer assistance – bedevilled the efforts of all who attempted to make the cumbersome planning machinery work.

By 1942, 73 per cent of the land in England and 36 per cent of the land in Wales had become subject to 'interim development control', but only 5 per cent of England and 1 per cent of Wales was actually subject to operative schemes; and there were several important towns and cities as well as some large country districts for which not even the preliminary stages of a planning scheme had been carried out. Administration was highly fragmented and was essentially a matter for the lower-tier authorities: in 1944 there were over 1,400 planning authorities. Some attempt to solve the problems to which this gave rise was made by the (voluntary) grouping of planning authorities in joint committees for formulating schemes over wide areas, but, though an improvement, this was not sufficiently effective.

The new conception of town and country planning underlined the inadequacies. It was generally (and perhaps uncritically) accepted that the growth of the large cities should be restricted. Regional plans for London, Lancashire, the Clyde Valley and South Wales all stressed the necessity of large-scale overspill to new and expanded towns. Government pronouncements echoed the enthusiasm which permeated these plans. Large cities were no longer to be allowed to continue their unchecked sprawl over the countryside. The explosive forces generated by the desire for better living and working conditions would no longer run riot. Suburban dormitories were a thing of the past. Overspill would be steered into new and expanded towns which could provide the conditions people wanted – without the disadvantages inherent in satellite suburban development. When the problems of reconstructing blitzed areas, redeveloping blighted areas, securing a 'proper distribution' of industry, developing national parks, and so on, are added to the list, there was a clear need for a new and more positive role for the central government, a transfer of powers from the smaller to the larger authorities, a considerable extension of these powers and – most difficult of all – a solution to the compensation-betterment problem.

The necessary machinery was provided in the main by the Town and Country Planning Acts, the Distribution of Industry Acts, the National Parks and Access to the Countryside Act, the New Towns Act and the Town Development Act.

The 1947 Town and Country Planning Act brought almost all development under control by making it subject to planning permission. But planning was to be no longer merely a regulative function. Development plans were to be prepared for every area in the country. These were to outline the way in which each area was to be developed or, where desirable, preserved. In accordance with the wider concepts of planning, powers were transferred from district councils to county councils. The smallest planning units thereby became the counties and the county boroughs. Co-ordination of local plans was to be effected by the new Ministry of Town and Country Planning. Development rights in land and the associated development values were nationalised. All owners were thus placed in the position of owning only the existing (1947) use rights and values in their land. Compensation for development rights was to be paid 'once and for all' out of a national fund, and developers were to pay a 'development charge' amounting to 100 per cent of the increase in the value of land resulting from the development. The 'compensation bogey' was thus at last to be completely abolished: henceforth development would take place according to 'good planning principles'.

Responsibility for securing a 'proper distribution of industry' was given to the Board of Trade. New industrial projects (above a minimum size) would require the board's certification that the development would be consistent with the proper distribution of industry. More positively, the board were given powers to attract industries to development areas by loans and grants, and by the erection of factories.

New towns were to be developed by *ad hoc* development corporations financed by the Treasury. Somewhat later (in 1952) new powers were provided for the planned expansion of towns by local authorities. The designation of national parks and 'areas of outstanding natural beauty' was entrusted to a new National Parks Commission, and local authorities were given wider powers for securing public access to the countryside. A Nature Conservancy was set up to provide scientific advice on the conservation and control of natural flora and fauna, and to establish and manage nature reserves. New powers were granted for preserving amenity, trees, historic buildings and ancient monuments. Later controls were introduced over river and air pollution, litter and noise. Indeed, the flow of legislation has been unceasing.

It would, however, be misleading even in a brief sketch to give an impression of continued progress. Certainly there have been some remarkable achievements (which the social commentator tends to forget in his analysis of shortcomings and needed reforms), but many of the problems for which this wealth of legislation was designed have themselves changed in character and become more difficult. Experience of dealing with industrial location, urban growth, amenity, and so on, has shown that they present far greater problems than was originally anticipated. Above all, instead of having to plan for a static or slowly growing population, the planners have had to wrestle with the problem created by an unexpected population increase: between 1951 and 1971 the population of England and Wales increased by 5 million. (In Scotland the increase during this period was a mere 130,000.) Even more problematic has been the forecasting of the future population. In the mid-fifties it was anticipated that, by the turn of the century, the population of England and Wales would be less than 50 million; a decade later the forecast had risen *to 66 million*; in recent years the forecast has been steadily reduced. Nothing is more eloquent of the difficulty of long-term planning than these figures:

Projected Population for England and Wales

Base year of projection	Year for projection	Population projected Millions
1955	1995	46·3
1958	1998	52·0
1961	2001	58·3
1965	2001	66·4
1967	2001	62·9
1969	2001	58·6
1971	2001	55·5
1973	2001	52·4
1974	2001	52·2

Chapter II

THE AGENCIES OF PLANNING

THE CENTRAL AUTHORITY

The new conception of town and country planning raised the difficult problem as to how the extended responsibilities were to be fitted into the organisation of central government. Were the Ministry of Health – the department responsible for housing and other local government matters – to retain their existing executive powers in relation to town and country planning, and, at the same time, expand their activities into the broad policy fields of regional and national planning? Should there be a separate Ministry of Town and Country Planning and, if so, should they be responsible both for the framing of policies and for their implementation? Would it be preferable to leave the latter with the Ministry of Health and set up a separate National Planning Authority which could also have certain responsibilities in the field of industrial location and transport? Should Scotland be dealt with in the same way as England and Wales?

Such questions were not quickly answered. Indeed, the problems they pose are still with us, and it is doubtful whether any ideal solution exists. Town and country planning in its wider sense embraces a large part of the activities of government. A separate all-embracing ministry is a contradiction in terms. An all-powerful 'grand co-ordinating' ministry does not square with the facts of administrative and political life. There must be some division of responsibilities and, at the same time, some means of co-ordination which is acceptable to the individual ministries. The *modus operandi* devised at any one point of time will reflect not only the particular urgencies of the existing situation, but also the views and personalities of the politicians and administrators whose task it is to interpret them. The importance of these factors is highlighted by the story of the setting up of the Ministry of Town and Country Planning.

The new town and country planning was born in the ancient Office of Works – a department which had become increasingly active with government building since the rearmament programme started. In September 1940 this office became the Ministry of Works and Buildings – responsible for 'the proper co-ordination of building work, the carrying out of Government building programmes, the control of building materials, and research into building and conservation of materials'. At the invitation of Ernest Bevin, then Minister of Labour, Sir John (later Lord) Reith became the first minister of this department – an appointment which exercised considerable influence on later developments in the organisation of planning. Reith was not only enthusiastic about the new post; as he records in his autobiography *Into the Wind*, he was already 'looking beyond the war to the problems of planning and reconstruction', and was hoping that however much responsibility the Ministry of Works and Buildings might initially be given, 'it would acquire still more – by doing things that had not been thought of and for which no one else had staked claims'. Indeed, almost immediately he proposed that his ministry 'should be ready to take up responsibility for . . . planning and reconstruction arising out of the war and post-war period'. This met with objection from the Ministry of Health (the department then responsible for town and country planning). This dispute was settled only after the Lord Privy Seal (Mr Attlee) had acted as arbiter. The outcome was that the Ministry of Health retained their normal town and country planning functions while Lord Reith was to plan for the future. This he did by means of a Reconstruction Group in his department, as well as by setting up two committees – the Uthwatt Committee on Compensation and Betterment and the Scott Committee on Land Utilization in Rural Areas. The reports of these committees together with that of the Barlow Commission constituted the famous trilogy which had a great influence on post-war planning.

Relationships between Lord Reith and Mr Arthur Greenwood (who had been appointed Minister without Portfolio with special responsibility for all post-war reconstruction problems) and the Ministry of Health were not easy. The boundaries between town and country planning on the one hand and general social and economic planning were not always clear. Lord Reith, however, was authorised to proceed on three assumptions which he announced in the House of Lords in February 1941:

'(1) That the principle of planning will be accepted as national policy and that some central planning authority will be required;
(2) that this authority will proceed on a positive policy for such matters as agriculture, industrial development and transport;

(3) that some services will require treatment on a national basis, some regionally and some locally.'

For a while Lord Reith retained his personal responsibility for long-term planning while the Minister of Health retained his statutory planning functions. Following an interim report of the Uthwatt Committee, and 'to ensure that the administration of the Town and Country Planning Act and any legislation implementing the recommendations made in the first report of the Uthwatt Committee shall proceed in conformity with long-term planning policy as it is progressively developed', a Committee of the Privy Council was appointed: Lord Reith (as chairman), the Minister of Health and the Secretary of State for Scotland.

The next development was the fusion of Lord Reith's Reconstruction Group and the Town and Country Planning Division of the Ministry of Health. This created some misgivings, particularly on the part of the Minister without Portfolio. A proposal to create both a new department for town and country planning and a new executive council for policy and development was rejected by the Cabinet: instead all the town and country planning functions of the Ministry of Health were transferred to a reorganised Ministry of Works and Planning. Lord Reith's apparent victory proved to be a hollow one: within a fortnight of the Cabinet decision he was asked to resign. With the exit of Lord Reith (and his replacement by Lord Portal who, according to Reith, 'disliked planning') the sands shifted. Furthermore, the Ministry of Health were now overburdened. The alternatives were now to create a new department or a non-departmental body. The latter proposal – on which a four-man committee set up under Lord Samuel's chairmanship could not agree – was rejected by the Cabinet on the ground that planning policy was essentially political and could not be removed from parliamentary control. Furthermore, experience which had been gained with the Ministry of Works and Planning showed that the subject required the full-time services of a front-rank minister and also that this minister 'should not only be, but should also appear to be, entirely impartial in his judgment as to the right use of any particular piece of land: if he can be regarded as a Minister already predisposed by reason of his other Ministerial duties to lean to a particular type of land use he will for that very reason be less able to exercise his influence'.

In short, the decision was taken to set up a separate Ministry of Town and Country Planning.

The decision was not unanimously applauded, especially since the legislation merely dealt with machinery: 'the way in which it will be used will depend on the powers which the House confers on the Minister hereafter'. Greenwood was particularly concerned about what he considered to be the implicit assumption that town and country planning could neatly be made the responsibility of a single department. In the debates on the Minister of Town and Country Planning Bill, he said:

'I cannot overemphasize what I think Government inquiries and enlightened public opinion . . . have undoubtedly proved, namely the complexities of the issues involved and the paramount importance of collective responsibility for policy by the Ministers whose departments will have to take a hand in carrying the plans into effect. You cannot make a super-department which will take the life blood of the Ministry of Agriculture, the Board of Trade and the Ministry of Health and so on.'

But the general discussion was inconclusive – as it had to be, since the legislation did little more than establish the new department, with a minister charged with the duty of 'securing consistency and continuity in the framing and execution of a national policy with respect to the use and development of land throughout England and Wales'.

The new ministry had responsibilities only for England and Wales. In Scotland central responsibility remained with the Department of Health for Scotland. Neither of these two departments was responsible for the location of industry. The 'Barlow policy' for industrial location was accepted, as was the Beveridge principle of full employment but, to quote from the 1944 White Paper on *Employment Policy*:

'no single department could undertake the responsibility for formulating and administering the policy for the distribution of industry . . . This is essentially a policy of the Government as a whole, and its application in practice will involve action by a number of different departments, each of which will adapt its administration to conform with the general government policy. The main responsibility will rest with the Board of Trade, the Ministry of Labour and National Service, the Ministry of Town and Country Planning and the Scottish Office. Standing arrangements will be made for supervising and controlling, under the Cabinet and as part of the central government machinery, the development and execution of the policy as a whole . . . It is necessary, however, that there should be a single channel through which government policy on the distribution of industry can be expressed. . . . [This] shall be the Board of Trade.'

In short, the Ministry of Town and Country Planning were to be responsible for town and country planning, the Ministry of Health for housing and the Board of Trade for industrial location, but there would be 'standing arrangements' for co-ordination where necessary.

LOCAL PLANNING AUTHORITIES

The shaping of a local government structure to meet new needs raises problems of an acute nature. There are inherent problems of devising units which are viable in terms of size and financial resources for the administration of different services. But of even greater practical importance is the problem of securing political agreement for change – at the level of both national and local politics. The need for reform at any one point of time may be clear to the reformers, but to demonstrate and prove the beneficial effects (which are often of a long-term nature) is quite a different matter. Usually local government reform is a matter of real interest only to academics, politicians and local government officers. Since these cannot agree (even on the necessity for change) the result is commonly a deadlock. Local government may then be bypassed, and services transferred to government departments or *ad hoc* authorities – as has happened, for example, with the licensing of passenger road services, trunk roads, hospitals, public assistance, valuation for rating and the major public utilities of gas and electricity.

Post-war attempts to reorganise local government have generally been abortive and it is only in the last few years that the problem has been tackled. The tone was set in 1944 when the then Minister of Health stated that it was clear from the views put forward by the various local authority associations and 'other authoritative sources' that there was no general desire to disrupt the existing structure of local government: in the view of the Government no case had been made out for any drastic change. However, there was scope for improvements, and a White Paper (*Local Government in England and Wales during the Period of Reconstruction*) published the following year outlined the Government's proposals for a Local Government Boundary Commission. This was set up in the same year, but in fact achieved nothing more than the publication of three annual reports. The Commission was set up to consider the *boundaries* of local authorities – in spite of the general agreement that the question of boundaries could be usefully considered only in relation to *functions*. In their second report, the Commission argued cogently that they could not, within their terms of reference, make proposals which would result in 'effective and convenient units of local government administration'. Such units 'cannot everywhere be produced without a fresh allocation of functions among the various types of local authorities, particularly where the larger towns are concerned'. They therefore had to decide whether to make second-best alterations to the existing structure (i.e. boundary adjustments) within the limits of their powers or to outline the case for radical reorganisation in the hope that this would be followed by legislation widening their powers. They chose the latter.

Briefly, the plan envisaged three types of local authorities. The whole of England and Wales *including the areas of existing county boroughs* would be divided into new counties. These would be formed on the basis of existing counties (combined or divided where necessary) and county boroughs (combined or extended as necessary). The smaller of the new counties would be administered on the one-tier system and the larger on the two-tier system. Second-tier authorities would be either 'new county boroughs' ('most-purpose' authorities) or county districts ('minor-purpose' authorities).

So far as town and country planning was concerned, responsibility for preparing overall development plans would rest with the counties. They would thus be responsible for general policy issues such as determining main lines of communication, and the location of new developments, green belts and major open spaces. Within the framework of the county plan, the new most-purpose authorities would be responsible for the preparation of the detailed plans for their areas.

To the advocates of local government reform these proposals were regarded as a step forward, but the absence of a 'regional outlook' was criticised. Robson, for example (in *The Development of Local Government*), complained that 'the Commissioners never for a moment turned their eyes towards the regional movement which has wrought havoc with local government. They did not ask why responsibility for electricity and gas supply, civil airfields, hospitals, trunk roads, passenger road services, and other services, has recently been taken away from local authorities and given to regional or central bodies; or under what conditions it might be practicable for these functions to be restored to the realm of local self-government.'

Though the proposals did 'abolish the fatal separation of town and country in watertight compartments which was made in 1888', they gave too little attention to the size of areas and types of authorities needed to carry out services which required large-scale planning and administration.

But to the Government of the day the proposals were either too radical or too embarrassing. There was little political support for them, and the Government took the easy way out by simply abolishing the Commission.

Since local government was not to be reorganised, the question of the local administration resolved itself into a choice between giving responsibility to the existing local government units or setting up *ad hoc* planning bodies on the lines followed in the case of hospitals or the nationalised utilities. The latter would have had the advantage of allowing the boundaries of planning authorities to be drawn on a rational basis, but in fact it was never seriously entertained. The 1947 Town and Country Planning Act gave responsibility to the major authorities – the counties and county boroughs. This reduced the number of local planning authorities from 1,441 to 145 – a reduction of 90 per cent. This obviously greatly enlarged the area over which local planning was to be effected, but two further steps were required.

First, as the Scott Committee pointed out:

'the local planning authority should be the same authority or combination of authorities as executes the principal local government functions involving the use of land. Within this framework the extremely important functions will devolve on the smaller authorities of affording the county planning authorities the benefit of their local knowledge in the formulation of plans, and the county authorities must consult the district councils accordingly; whilst in due course the responsibility for the execution of works within the approved scheme may fall on the district councils.'

Accordingly, the 1947 Act required county councils to consult with district authorities in the preparation of their plans and enabled them to delegate powers of controlling development to district councils (or to decentralise these powers to sub-committees charged with responsibility for certain areas).

Secondly, though the Act enlarged the areas over which planning powers were to be exercised by single authorities, the need still existed in some parts of the country (particularly in the case of conurbations) for larger planning areas. The Act therefore gave the minister power to set up joint planning boards for combined areas. This could be done either with the agreement of the local authorities concerned or, following a local inquiry, by the minister. In fact this power has never been used. A similar power to establish joint advisory committees, on the other hand, has been used.

REGIONAL ADMINISTRATION

Within the new structure there was no formal place for regional authorities. The need for wider planning areas was recognised in the provision made for joint planning boards and joint advisory committees, but these constituted a typical English compromise which excited little enthusiasm. Bevan, when Minister of Health, echoed the general feeling: a joint board, he said, 'has no biological content; it has no mother and it has no progeny; it is a piece of paper work'. In the absence of a formal creation of executive, financially responsible, organs of regional government, it was left to the ministry themselves to undertake such regional planning as was to be effected – by co-ordinating the efforts of the separate planning authorities and reconciling and amending the plans prepared by them and submitted to the ministry for approval. This, indeed, was one of the functions implied by the duty with which the ministry were charged of 'securing consistency and continuity in the framing and execution of a national policy with respect to the use and development of land throughout England and Wales'.

What might at first sight have been regarded as a clear advance towards regionalism was the war-time establishment of civil defence regions and the appointment of regional commissioners. These were set up to deal with the conditions which might have arisen had communications been disrupted. This organisation – into eleven regions – was retained after the war, but the regions were (and still are) 'no more than civil service creations, established for the dispatch of business; they are not, in any sense, "organic" units'. The Ministry of Town and Country Planning appointed regional planning officers as early as 1943. As the scope and complexity of planning legislation grew, the regional machinery was expanded. By 1948 there was an office in each region under the control of a regional controller. The initial object of the regional offices was to give advice to local authorities, but the establishment of regional controllers marked a new step towards solving the increasing number of conflicting claims over land use from government departments. The regional controllers presided over regional planning committees composed of representatives from the various other government departments in the region. But this was simply an administrative device to cope with inter-departmental frictions.

In view of the absence of regional machinery in the final outcome it is interesting to note Reith's original proposals (submitted to Churchill in 1940 and quoted in Reith's autobiography) for:

'a central authority to frame and be responsible for the execution of a national plan covering the basic objectives; to lay down the general principles of planning; to supervise planning, design, finance, execution; regional machinery to apply the national plan and to co-ordinate and control the work of local authorities; Exchequer assistance to supplement local funds in approved development'.

Since there was now no middle tier, it followed that the central authority would be greatly concerned with the day-to-day work of local authorities (and the time-consuming business of appeals against local authorities), and thus face the danger of paying insufficient attention to 'basic objectives' and 'general principles' – a point to which we return in later chapters.

Chapter III

THE ROLE OF CENTRAL GOVERNMENT

CENTRAL GOVERNMENT ORGANISATION

In *Beyond the Stable State*, Donald Schon argues that 'if government is to learn to solve new public problems, it must also learn to create the systems for doing so and to discard the structure and mechanisms grown up around old problems. The need is not merely to cope with a particular set of new problems, or to discard the organizational vestiges of a particular form of governmental activity which happen at present to be particularly cumbersome. It is to design and bring into being the institutional processes through which new problems can continually be confronted and old structures continually discarded.'

How far recent years have seen the development of really new and relevant 'institutional processes' is a big question which cannot be examined adequately here, but certainly there have been a remarkable number of organizational changes. In this chapter, attention is focused on changes in the structure of central government, though the reader is warned that these take place at a rate which defeats the chronicler who attempts to provide an up-to-date picture.

Throughout the fifties, town and country planning was the responsibility of the Ministry of Housing and Local Government – the central department also responsible (as the name suggests) for housing and a range of local government services. These included water and sewerage, refuse collection and disposal, burial grounds and crematoria, clean air and river pollution, together with the general structure (including reorganisation) and finance of local government. In April 1965, certain functions (e.g. in relation to water resources, national parks and responsibility for the Land Commission and Leasehold Enfranchisement Bills) were transferred to a new Ministry of Land and Natural Resources. This ministry was, however, short-lived: its functions were returned to the Ministry of Housing and Local Government in February 1967.

Of rather longer life was the Department of Economic Affairs (October 1964 to October 1969). This was responsible for the new regional economic planning system (which, at the time of writing, is still in existence but faces major uncertainties while decisions on regional devolution are awaited).

In October 1969, the Labour Government created an 'overlord' for local government and regional planning with major responsibilities for local government reorganisation and 'environmental pollution in all its forms'. The overlord – the Secretary of State for Local Government and Regional Planning – had federal powers in relation to the Ministry of Housing and Local Government and the Ministry of Transport, together with direct responsibility for the regional planning councils and boards (discussed in Chapter XIII) which were transferred to him from the Department of Economic Affairs. At the same time, the Board of Trade's responsibilities in the field of regional economic development went to another super-ministry: the Ministry of Technology. This had responsibility for industrial development certificates (but not office development permits, which were transferred to the Ministry of Housing and Local Government), industrial estates in development areas, building grants and loans. The rationale here was that the ministry which was responsible for dealing with the greater part of private and public industry should also be responsible for executive decisions concerning the location of industry.

THE DEPARTMENT OF THE ENVIRONMENT

This organisation of central government functions had a life of only one year before the Conservative Government (elected June 1970) carried the process one stage further (see the 1970 White Paper, *The Reorganization of Central Government*). So far as the subject matter of this book is concerned, most of the relevant functions are now organised in a huge Department of the Environment under a Secretary of State for the Environment. Except in Scotland and Wales, where the Scottish and Welsh Offices have major responsibilities, the DoE are responsible for 'the whole range of functions which affect people's living environment'.

The Secretary of State has final responsibility for all the functions of the department (including all statutory powers). He is, however, concerned primarily with strategic issues of policy and priority, including public expenditure, which determine the operations of the department as a whole. The department has three functional parts – Planning and Local Government, Housing and Construction and Transport, each with a separate minister with the status (but not

the legal position) of a minister in charge of a separate department
not represented in the Cabinet.

Minister of Housing and Construction

Housing programmes and finance; housing improvement; building
regulations; relations with the building and civil engineering industry; building research and development; and the Property Services
Agency (PSA), which provides nearly all government common
services relating to land, property, building and furnishings.

Minister for Transport

Ports; general transport policy, including transport grants to local
authorities; railways; inland waterways; freight haulage; international aspects of inland transport; and road and vehicle safety and
licensing.

Minister for Planning and Local Government

Land use and regional planning; compensation and betterment;
new towns; minerals; local government structure and finance; and
countryside policy.

Additionally there are two ministers of state and three parliamentary under-secretaries of state. One minister has special responsibilities for sport and recreation, and water, sewage and pollution
policy. The other minister is responsible for urban planning problems, historic towns and conservation.

SCOTLAND AND WALES

In Scotland somewhat similar changes were made as long ago as
1962, when town and country planning and environmental services
were transferred from the Department of Health to the Scottish
Development Department which at the same time took over all the
local government, electricity, roads and industry functions of the
Scottish Home Department.

In 1973, a major change was made with the establishment of the
Scottish Economic Planning Department. This is concerned with
industrial and economic development in Scotland, including the
Scottish aspects of regional policies both in a UK and an EEC
context. It has a major concern with North Sea Oil and has also
taken over responsibility (from the Department of Industry) for
direct support to industry, factory building and industrial estates.
Its responsibilities also extend to new towns (because of their
essential function in Scotland of facilitating economic development) and the new Scottish Development Agency.

In Wales, increasing responsibilities over a wide field have in recent years been transferred to the Welsh Office. So far as town and country planning is concerned they are unaffected by the new changes, though other important functions in relation to primary and secondary education, and child care, have been transferred to the Secretary of State for Wales.

In the following account the term 'Secretary of State' is used for the sake of simplicity, but it should be interpreted to refer to the Secretaries of State for the Environment, for Scotland and for Wales. Similarly, references to the Department of the Environment should be read as applying, *mutatis mutandis*, to the Scottish Office and the Welsh Office.

CENTRAL-LOCAL RELATIONSHIPS

The Secretary of State is charged with the duty of 'securing consistency and continuity in the framing of a national policy with respect to the use and development of land'. The powers are very wide and, in effect, give the department the final say in all policy matters (subject, of course, to parliamentary control). The extent of these powers is too wide to permit an adequate summary: they are discussed in detail at appropriate points in other chapters. For many matters the Secretary of State is required or empowered to make regulations; this delegated legislation covers a wide field. For example, one Order (the Use Classes Order) classifies industrial and commercial uses and permits 'changes of use' within each of the categories without the need for planning permission. Similarly, the advertisement regulations specify certain types of advertisement for which permission is 'deemed' to be given, and the General Development Order provides a detailed list of types of development which do not require planning permission. One function of the department is thus (within the limits laid down by Parliament) to make legislation.

In a wide range of matters, approval is necessary for proposals made by a local authority. A development plan (and the new-style structure plan), for example, does not become operative until it has been approved by the Secretary of State. This approval can stipulate modifications in the plan; the Secretary of State has great discretionary powers here, since he is acting administratively and quasi-judicially. If a local planning authority fail to produce a plan (or a plan 'satisfactory to the Secretary of State'), he can act in default. Decisions of a local planning authority on applications for planning permission can, on appeal, be modified or revoked – even if the development proposed is contrary to the development plan.

Proposals which the Secretary of State regards as being sufficiently important can be 'called in' for his decision.

In spite of all these powers, it is not the function of the Secretary of State to decide detailed planning policies. This is the business of local planning authorities. The Secretary of State's function is to co-ordinate the work of individual local authorities and to ensure that their development plans and development control decisions are in harmony with broad planning policies. That this often involves rather closer relationships than might *prima facie* be supposed follows from the nature of the governmental and administrative processes. The line dividing policy from day-to-day administration is a fine one. Policy has to be translated into decisions on specific issues, and a series of decisions can amount to a change in policy. This is particularly important in the British planning system, where a large measure of administrative discretion is given to central and local government bodies. This is a distinctive feature of the planning system. There is virtually no provision for external judicial review of local planning decisions: instead, there is the system of appeals to the Secretary of State. A foreign observer (Daniel Mandelker) sees the position clearly:

'The absence of a written constitution makes the statute controlling in England. External review of the merits of local planning decisions is afforded by the Minister of Housing and Local Government. His Ministry is a national agency exercising a supervisory power over local government and having no exact counterpart in the United States. Appeals are taken to the Minister from local refusals of planning permission and from permissions with onerous conditions. English courts can review Ministerial decisions, but their role in the determination of planning policy is peripheral.

'The area of discretion in English planning administration is enlarged further by the lack of separation of function which is traditional to American government. In America, the zoning ordinance is enacted by the local legislative body but is usually administered by the executive department and by nonelective boards created for this purpose. In England the local elected council which adopts the development plan also administers it. The failure to separate function in English planning has the healthy effect of forcing attention to the relationship between the individual decision and the general objectives to which, in a small way, it contributes. But this institutional framework blurs the distinction between policy making and policy applying and so enlarges the role of the administrator who has to decide a specific case.'

It is this broad area of discretion which brings the department in close contact with local planning authorities (though, as is explained later, it is not the only factor). The department in effect operate both in a quasi-judicial capacity and as developers of policy.

The department's quasi-judicial role stems in part from the vagueness of planning policies. Even if these policies are precisely worded, their application can raise problems. Since a local authority have such a wide area of discretion, and since the courts have only very limited powers of action, the department have to act as arbiter over what is fair and reasonable. This is not, however, simply a judicial process. A decision is not taken on the basis of legal rules as in a court of law: it involves the exercise of a wide discretion in the balance of public and private interest within the framework of planning policies. The procedure basically consists of the lodging of objections either to proposals in a draft development plan or to the decision of a local authority on a planning application. Such objections (or appeals, as the latter are called) are made to the Secretary of State, who then holds an inquiry in public. These inquiries are carried out by inspectors of the department but the final decision is the formal responsibility of the Secretary of State. There is no appeal against his decision except on a question of law.

The department's role in policy formulation is not easy to summarise. Policies are usually couched in very general terms – preservation of amenity, restraining urban sprawl, and so on – which give local authorities considerable leeway. Formal guidance (circulars, memoranda, bulletins, etc.) often does not provide a clear indication of the action which should be followed in any particular case. Proposals have to be considered 'on their merits' within the broad framework of a set of principles. These principles can – and do – change, at least in emphasis. Usually the change is gradual, perhaps even coming without a conscious step. And the motivating power may well be the local authorities themselves rather than the department. All this makes it very difficult to present a clear-cut picture of central-local relationships. The truth is that the position is not clear-cut. What is clear is that there is little approaching a situation in which the central department determine policy while local governments carry the policy into effect as agents. As Miller has nicely put it, the larger authorities 'have built up local administrations that can properly be regarded as citadels of local power'. Though central government may lay down national policies, 'it is in the twists and emphases which councils give to central policies, and the degree of co-operation or unwillingness which they show, that their own power lies. They do not have the paper guarantees of local sovereignty which states in a federal system possess, but they have some of the reality of power which comes from being on the spot, knowing the special qualities and demands of the local people, and being costly and difficult to replace if the central government finds them unsatisfactory.'

It is common to talk of central-local government relationships as constituting a 'partnership', and, though any such single term must oversimplify the situation, the description is apposite. Certainly there is no pressure (at least so far as town and country planning is concerned) for a take-over of functions by the department. The positive powers and functions of the department should not, however, be minimised. Reference has already been made to the way in which they can override the decisions of a local authority on particular cases. It is worth examining this in more detail.

PLANNING APPEALS

An unsuccessful planning applicant can appeal to the Secretary of State and a large number in fact do so. Appeals* decided during 1973 numbered 11,393 of which 22 per cent were allowed (many subject to conditions) and 78 per cent dismissed. Here the Secretary of State has very wide powers. He may reverse the local authority's decision or subject it to conditions. He may quash or modify conditions which they have imposed. He may make those conditions more onerous, or he may even go to the extent of refusing planning permission altogether if he decides that the local authority should not have granted it even with the conditions imposed.

Though each planning appeal is considered and determined on its merits, the cumulative effect is an emergence of the department's views on a wide range of planning matters. These have been made more explicit in 'statements of policy' published in the *Bulletin of Selected Planning Appeals, Selected Enforcement and Planning Appeals* and in the *Development Control Policy Notes.* The effect of these on the policy of individual authorities may be difficult to assess, but clearly they are likely to have a very real influence. Local planning authorities are unlikely to refuse planning consents for a

---

* This discussion relates particularly to appeals under Section 36 of the Town and Country Planning Act, 1971. It does not deal specifically with advertisement appeals, appeals against enforcement notices, appeals to determine whether in doubtful cases planning permission is required, or appeals in respect of a local authority's failure to give a planning decision within prescribed time limits – though the principles discussed are generally the same.

Section 36 of the 1971 Act covers appeals against a decision of a local planning authority to refuse planning permission, or against conditions imposed on a grant of permission.

particular type of development if they are convinced that the department would uphold an appeal.

It is not, of course, every planning application that raises an issue of policy. Yet, until 1969, all had to be dealt with by the department's inspectorate. Nearly half of all appeals are settled by correspondence after an informal visit to the site and without a local inquiry. (This is termed 'the written representations procedure'.) The Franks Committee on Administrative Tribunals and Inquiries argued that it was not satisfactory 'that a Government Department should be occupied with appeal work of this volume, particularly as many of the appeals relate to minor and purely local matters, in which little or no departmental policy entered'. An analysis of the subject matter of appeals undertaken by the department (and reported in the 1967 White Paper *Town and Country Planning*) confirmed this. About 60 per cent concerned small-scale development; many of these raised issues of purely local significance. They included such matters as minor residential development, small groups of shops, small caravan sites, betting shops, garages and minor changes of use. Rather more than a quarter related to single houses. Another relevant point was that, of all appeals made during the five years 1962 to 1967, 97·5 per cent were decided as the inspector recommended.

In view of the delay which is inevitable in this appeals system and the huge administrative burden it has placed on the department, considerable thought has been given to possible alternatives. The solution adopted by the 1968 Planning Act is for the determination of certain classes of appeals by inspectors. The classes are determined by the regulation and can thus be amended in the light of experience. The 1972 regulations (SI 1972, No. 1652) provide for appeals broadly relating to such proposals as residential development of sixty houses or less (or, if the application does not specify a number, development for residential purposes on not more than 2 hectares of land); and certain developments of a non-residential character subject to limits of maximum floor area and site area. These classes are further limited in the detailed regulations (e.g. development affecting trunk and special roads, and hotels in London, are excluded). Furthermore, the Secretary of State can 'call in' appeals within these classes if he sees good grounds for so doing, for example in controversial cases. (Further details are to be found in the Statutory Instrument and in MHLG Circulars 68/68 and 76/70 and DoE Circular 110/72.)

The objectives of this innovation are to speed up the appeal procedure and to relieve the central government of detailed work which has taken up far too much of their effort, thereby prejudicing the work which they should be doing on, for example, major issues of policy. In short, the intention is that the department will be better able to fulfil their essential role. In 1973, 8,825 of the total 11,393 appeals were decided by inspectors – three-quarters by written representation. (Statistics are published in an annual *Miscellaneous Local Government and Planning Statistics*, obtainable from the DoE.) Further discussion of appeals is to be found in Chapter XIV.

'CALL-IN' OF PLANNING APPLICATIONS

The power to 'call in' a planning application for decision by the Secretary of State is quite separate from that of determining an appeal against an adverse decision of a local planning authority. This power is not circumscribed: the Secretary of State may call in any application, and his decision is final. Though there is no general statement of policy as to which applications will normally be called in, there are several categories which are particularly liable. In the first place, all applications for development involving a substantial departure from the provisions of a development plan which the local planning authority intend to grant must be sent to the Secretary of State, together with a statement of the reasons why they wish to grant the permission. This procedure enables the Secretary of State to decide whether the development is sufficiently important to warrant its being called in for his own determination. Secondly, mineral workings often raise problems of more than local importance and the national need for particular minerals has to be balanced against planning issues. Such matters cannot be adequately considered by local planning authorities and, in any case, involve technical considerations requiring expert opinion of a character more easily available to the department. For these reasons, large numbers of applications for permission to work minerals have been called in. Furthermore, there is a general direction calling in all applications for the winning and working of ironstone in certain counties where there are large-scale ironstone workings. Thirdly, the power of call-in is generally used when the matter at stake is (as in the case of minerals) of more than local importance or interest.

Dobry's *Review of the Development Control System, Final Report* notes that in recent years, the call-in procedure has tended to be used only for the following kinds of applications:

(a) cases raising issues of national, regional, or otherwise more than local importance;
(b) cases which arouse more than local opposition; e.g. the redevelopment of the Monico site in Shaftesbury Avenue;

(c) cases which, for any reason, it might be unreasonable to ask the
local planning authority to decide, e.g. involving development
proposed by foreign governments (the decision on which could
be diplomatically sensitive), or development raising unfamiliar
problems on which adequate technical advice was not available
to the local planning authority, e.g. the first application for a
processing plant for North Sea Gas;
(d) cases associated with a different issue which can be decided only
by the Secretary of State, e.g. applications for town centre
redevelopment associated with a compulsory purchase order.

In 1973, 160 planning applications were called in – out of a total of
two-thirds of a million.

When an application is called in, the Secretary of State must, if
either the applicant or the local planning authority so desire, hold
a hearing or public inquiry. The public inquiry is more usual,
particularly in important cases.

Since 1968 the Secretary of State has had power to refer development proposals of a far-reaching or novel character to an *ad hoc*
Planning Inquiry Commission. This power has not yet been used:
the Roskill Commission on the third London airport was set up
under non-statutory powers, while the Greater London Development Plan Inquiry was established under the *general* powers to hold
local inquiries provided by the Town and Country Planning Act
(now Section 282 of the 1971 Act).

Further reference must also be made to the circulars, bulletins
and handbooks published by the department, and the studies on
which some of them are based. Quite apart from straightforward
statements of broad policies, these contain a great deal of technical
guidance. It needs to be stressed that planning policies often raise
technical issues which are beyond the competence of local authority
staffs, or at least need a wider background of experience than is
always to be found in a planning authority.

Then again, there are the controls operated by the department
over capital expenditure. These controls have tended to increase as
economic and regional planning tools have gradually developed.

It must be repeated, however, that local planning authorities are
not agents of the department. Though the department can – and do
– exercise many direct controls, they prefer (in accordance with
British traditions) to wield their power in a gentlemanly fashion by
way of exhortation, advice and informal contacts. This is particularly important at officer level. The chief planning officers of local
authorities are not strangers to the department's officials: on the
contrary, relationships between them are close. And they are

members of a small (but active) profession in which policy issues are constantly being discussed.

(For a recent statement of central-local relationships, see Buxton, R., *Local Government*, Chapter 3. A detailed account and valuable discussion of the role of the central department in relation to local planning authorities is given in Griffith, J. A. G., *Central Departments and Local Authorities*, Chapter 5.)

TRANSPORT

Transport is, of course, inseparable from town planning. The volume, nature and even mode of transport is governed by land use. Permitted densities and the type of development which is allowed affect the demand and nature of transport. Indeed, it is the closeness of the relationship between town planning and transport which led to the amalgamation of the two functions in the DoE.

This was preceded, in the Town and Country Planning Act of 1968, by an emphasis on structure plans which are intended to bring about a greater integration of transport and land use planning. Until the amalgamation, the Ministry of Transport were consulted by the Ministry of Housing and Local Government on the highway proposals in development plans, and agreement was reached before the plans were approved. Furthermore, the Planning Acts require local planning authorities to consult the central department responsible for transport before they grant permission for development which will affect trunk roads. After this consultation, the local planning authorities must comply with any direction given concerning the restriction of development. Under administrative arrangements made before the amalgamation, appeals made under the Planning Acts could be referred by the Ministry of Housing and Local Government to the Ministry of Transport where one of the issues on the appeal was the effect of the development on the use and safety of an actual or proposed highway.

Transport planning is, of course, far more than the control of applications and the design of plans. One major positive aspect is the designation of the lines of trunk roads and motorways. This is a central government responsibility. The DoE also have a major influence in determining road priorities by means of grants to local authorities for road construction and improvement.

Both trunk roads and classified roads have been the subject of investigation by the Estimates Committee (and, more recently, by the Expenditure Committee) to which the reader in search of a wealth of detail is referred. The subject of transport planning is discussed in a later chapter. Here attention is concentrated on providing a summary of the organisation of the central department's road functions in so far as they relate to town and country planning.

It is important at the outset to make clear the distinction between trunk and other roads. Trunk roads form a national system of routes for through traffic. The 'highway authority' for these roads is the Secretary of State. It is his responsibility to keep under review the national system of routes for through traffic in Great Britain. (Responsibility for road administration in Scotland and Wales now rests with the respective Secretaries of State.) He can construct new trunk roads and designate existing roads as trunk roads. Motorways are 'special' trunk roads. Most new constructional work and improvement schemes are designed and supervised by local authorities acting as agents for the department. All expenditure on trunk roads is met by the department.

The programming of trunk road schemes is the responsibility of the central department. To quote from the Estimates Committee's 1969 Report on *Motorways and Trunk Roads:*

'The road programme should be thought of as a continuous process extending over a number of years. Trunk road schemes take a long time to prepare up to contract letting stage, perhaps three or four years in the case of large schemes, and the detailed planning of schemes is normally commenced some four years in advance of the time it is expected that constructional work on these will start. A provisional selection of schemes for several years ahead is also made, so that a certain amount of preliminary work, such as making orders setting out the line of route, can be undertaken. Looking even further ahead, there is a special planning section in the Department with the task of working out in the light of the latest information about traffic trends, what the country's long-term road requirements are likely to be.'

In short, so far as trunk roads are concerned, the department are the policy-making body. They determine the programme, approve estimates and allocate money to individual authorities. The local authorities are merely the agents for carrying out the department's policy.

For other roads a different system operates. The responsibility for these lies with local authorities, and the department's position is largely dependent upon their power to make grants. Until 1975, grants were payable for the construction of principal roads (as well as for public transport infrastructure schemes, and in support of rural bus services). All other grant aid was given through the Rate

Support Grant which is a non-specific revenue grant for (nearly) all local government services. This grant took into account both the mileage of highways and expenditure on improvement and maintenance.

Since April 1975 specific grants have been replaced by a new Transport Supplementary Grant (which is 'supplementary' to the Rate Support Grant). This is a unified grant for all local transport services and is determined on the basis of the new TPPs (Transport Policies and Programmes) which are outlined in Chapter VIII.

INDUSTRIAL LOCATION CONTROL

Policies relating to industrial location control can be divided into two categories. Firstly, there are the negative controls operated via the Industrial Development Certificate (IDC) scheme, under which any industrial building or extension above a certain size requires the certification by the central government that it is consistent with the 'proper distribution of industry'. Secondly, there are the positive powers to attract industries to areas of high unemployment.

Until October 1969, the central department responsible for industrial location was the Board of Trade. At that date these responsibilities were transferred to a new Ministry of Technology together with those of the Department of Economic Affairs in relation to regional economic development. This left the Board of Trade with functions relating to external commercial policy and such matters as civil aviation, shipping, tourism, hotels and insurance. In October 1970, the Ministry of Technology and the Board of Trade were merged in a large Department of Trade and Industry (DTI), but further reorganisation in 1974 brought matters full circle, and it is now the Department of Industry who are responsible for industrial location and industrial aspects of regional policy.

The control of industrial location is entirely a central government responsibility. Though certain local authorities have appointed industrial development officers and many act in concert through industrial development associations, they have no statutory responsibility for industrial location policy. This may appear to be an overstatement, since an important part of a local authority's development plan will be concerned with industrial sites. Nevertheless, the powers here are limited and in practice are much more concerned with siting than with general issues of location. The distinction is important. Though local authorities can erect factories in an attempt to encourage industrial growth, and can buy up existing factories in order to reduce the level of employment, their real power lies in approving or rejecting planning applications for industrial development on particular sites. The question as to whether this industrial development should take place at all in the area is a matter for the Department of Industry. In short, the department are responsible for the *location* of industry, whereas local authorities are responsible for the *siting* of industrial developments. It follows that the Department of Industry have an extremely important role to play: they are an executive as well as a policy-making body.

The general policy of the Department of Industry is to encourage industrial expansion in areas of high unemployment and to restrict it in congested areas. This has been the interpretation of 'the proper distribution of industry' – a phrase which is nowhere defined in the legislation, though the department are required (when considering whether an IDC should be granted) to have 'particular regard to the need for providing appropriate employment in development districts'.

Until 1972 no application for planning permission for the erection of an industrial building exceeding a certain floor area could be made unless it was accompanied by an IDC. Following the 1972 White Paper *Industrial and Regional Development* (Cmnd 4942), IDCs were dispensed with in Development Areas. At the same time the exemption limit was fixed at 15,000 square feet except in the South East Economic Planning Region where the limit became 10,000 square feet.

IDCs form a negative control and, furthermore, are limited in extent. There is no control over existing buildings. A firm which is refused permission for development in, say, the London area, may be able to purchase a vacated factory and thus create the very increase in employment which it was the department's objective to prevent. This stems from the fact that the control is applied to buildings and not directly to employment. Under current powers the only alternative is the purchase by the local authority of the property – an extremely costly undertaking.

An IDC is generally made valid for the area of a local authority. The department do not inquire whether the proposed site – if one has been chosen – is suitable. This is an issue of land use which falls within the scope of the local planning authority's functions. It thus follows that the granting of a certificate by the department does not guarantee that the authorised development will – or can – take place.

During the sixties legislation was directed towards a tightening up of the controls. Thus, the Control of Office and Industrial Development Act, 1965, extended the meaning of 'related development' to effect greater control over the creation of a substantial area of floor space by the accumulation of individual pieces of development, each of which is below the exemption limit. Similarly, the Industrial Development Act, 1966, extended the meaning of 'industrial building', thereby bringing under IDC control all buildings used or designed for use for scientific research. ('Scientific research' is defined as 'any activity in the fields of natural or applied science for the extension of knowledge'.) This Act also provided powers which ensure that planning permission is needed before space approved for 'ancillary purposes' such as storage can be converted to production use.

During the seventies, however, economic performance was so poor that a major change in policy began to emerge. While special incentives were still maintained (and increased) in the areas of high unemployment, wider measures were needed to stimulate growth nationally. The 1972 White Paper *Industrial and Regional Development* set out a range of proposals, and the 1972 Industry Act followed.

Preferential assistance is given to three types of 'assisted area': Special Development Areas where the need for new employment is most acute (e.g. Clydeside and Tyneside); Development Areas (including the whole of Scotland, Wales and the north, most of the north-west, Yorkshire & Humberside and parts of the south-west and east midlands regions); and Intermediate Areas (covering the remaining parts of the north-west and Yorkshire & Humberside regions, and the Nottinghamshire-Derbyshire coalfield area).

General incentives (e.g. depreciation allowances for investment in machinery and tax allowances for new industry building) are supplemented in the assisted areas by regional development grants, selective financial assistance and the provision of advance factories.

OFFICE DEVELOPMENT PERMITS

Pressures for the control of office development were resisted throughout the late fifties and early sixties on the ground that it would be impracticable. The 1963 White Paper *London – Employment: Housing: Land* (Cmnd 1952) argued the case well:

'The machinery for controlling the issue of industrial development certificates depends on knowledge of the firm which occupies the factory and on an assessment of the need for that firm to carry on its manufacture in a particular area. Many new factories are purpose-built and have heavy machinery installed; occupiers do not change often. New office blocks, on the other hand, are more often than not built for letting; this is, indeed, often the only way in which modern accommodation can be provided in units of a suitable size for small and medium-sized firms. Consequently, when the developer seeks planning permission he may not know how many tenants he will have or who his tenants will be; and these tenants may change at frequent intervals. A Government Department trying to administer a control of this sort would, therefore, be without the basic information needed for the purpose. Even when a tenant was known it would be extremely difficult to judge the case put forward in support of an office in the central area by a commercial or professional firm. The Government do not believe that it would be practical to administer a system of control of office occupation either effectively or equitably.'

Action along three lines was proposed and carried into effect. Firstly, planning controls over new office building were tightened. The issue here was a complicated legal one. In brief, the existing legislation allowed a 10 per cent increase in cubic capacity to owners rebuilding their premises. Since new buildings have lower ceilings and less circulation space, a 10 per cent increase in cubic capacity could involve as much as 40 per cent increase in floor space. Attempts by local planning authorities to restrict this involved the risk of paying heavy compensation. The Town and Country Planning Act, 1963, removed any compensation liabilities which might arise when permission is refused for an increase in *floor space* of more than 10 per cent.

Secondly, an attempt was made to disperse more government offices. It had been government policy for many years to disperse headquarters departments and self-contained branches which could function away from London without loss of administrative efficiency. In 1962, of the total headquarters staff of 125,000, some 25,000 already worked outside London, and there were plans for moving a further 7,000. It was felt, however, that it was time for a thorough re-examination of the situation. A review was undertaken by Sir Gilbert Flemming. His (unpublished) report recommended the transfer of some 18,000 jobs from central London. (A further examination of this issue was announced in the 1970 White Paper on *The Reorganization of Central Government* (Cmnd 4506): this one was published in 1973 under the title *The Dispersal of Government Work from London* (Cmnd 5322), though it is better known as the Hardman Report.)

Thirdly, the Location of Offices Bureau was set up to encourage the decentralisation of office employment from central London. The bureau's main function is to provide an information and publicity service. Its operations are summarised in its annual reports.

The return of the Labour Government in 1964 was followed by the introduction of direct controls over office building through Office Development Permits. The legislation (Control of Office and Industrial Development Act, 1965 – now consolidated in the 1971 Town and Country Planning Act) applied the control only in the metropolitan region, but provided for its extension by Order to any other part of Great Britain. In August 1965, it was extended to the Birmingham conurbation and in July 1966, to major parts of southern England and the east and west midlands. Currently (1975) it applies to the South East Economic Planning Region only.

The controls are very similar in form to the Industrial Development Certificate system (though they are administered by the Department of the Environment). In the areas to which the Act applies, an Office Development Permit (like the Industrial Development Certificate) must be obtained for development over 10,000 square feet before planning permission can be given. In deciding whether to grant such a permit, the DoE 'shall have particular regard to the need for promoting the better distribution of employment in Great Britain'. The department have complete discretion and there is no right of appeal or compensation if a permit is refused.

Within the general objective, there are three main considerations which influence the examination of applications for Office Development Permits. 'These are, first, whether the activity for which new office accommodation is sought could feasibly be carried out outside the area in which the proposed development is situated; second, whether there is any suitable alternative accommodation available; and third, whether the development accords with the public interest.' Details and statistics of the operation of the control are given in an annual report published as a House of Commons Paper.

EMPLOYMENT POLICIES

Employment is, of course, one of the principal economic considerations in town and country planning, and the new-style development plans (and the Scottish regional reports) are intended to put much greater emphasis on this than has been the case with the typical old-style development plans. It cannot be said that employment policies are, as yet, very successfully integrated with physical planning policies. At least in part, this is due to organisational separatism and the fact that local authorities have little responsibility for employment policies: they are essentially a function of central government.

Until 1974, employment policies were the direct responsibility of the Department of Employment. In that year, the Employment and Training Act of 1973 came into operation, and the Manpower Services Commission was set up to manage the Government's employment and training services. The main purpose of this change was to transfer direct control from central government to representatives of employers, employees, local government and educational interests (who form the Commission). The Secretary of State for Employment retains responsibility for such matters as general manpower policy, manpower aspects of regional policy and regional economic planning, and the department's unit for manpower studies. The Commission discharge their functions through two agencies. the Employment Service Agency (ESA) and the Training Services Agency (TSA). The ESA run the nationwide network of employment exchanges (which are being replaced by JobCentres) and also the various schemes of financial assistance to facilitate the mobility of labour. These schemes were considerably expanded in 1975–6. There are now two major schemes – the Employment Transfer Scheme and the Job Search Scheme. These provide grants and allowances to help with travel and subsistence expenses in finding a new job, and in moving house to take up a job.

The TSA are responsible for managing and developing training programmes. There are twenty-three industrial training boards which are financed in part by levies on employers' payrolls. An independent Industrial Training Service (ITS) – sponsored by the Commission – helps firms, employers' associations and industrial training boards to identify training needs and to formulate training policy. A Government Training Opportunities Scheme (TOPS) supplements training given by industry by providing courses at some fifty 'skillcentres'. There is also a Training Within Industry Scheme (TWIS) for training supervisors.

The Commission also administer the Job Creation Programme, established towards the end of 1975, 'to help the unemployed and the community they live in'. A sum of £30 million has been allocated for schemes sponsored by local authorities, nationalised and private industries, voluntary organisations, community groups and others. The sponsors must provide any necessary materials and equipment, but the Commission will meet labour costs. The scheme covers such work as the clearing of derelict land and environmental improvement.

This rapid sketch of the major functions of the Department of Employment and their agencies might suggest that they play a more important planning role than is in fact the case. Far more attention has been paid by central government to attempting to correct regional imbalances in unemployment by distribution of industry policies (which is a responsibility of the Department of Industry) than to the marked shortages of particular types of skills, the labour shortages of the service sector, the widespread need for training and retraining, the need for job creation programmes and, above all, the relationship between manpower policies and urban and regional planning policies. There are, however, indications of a major shift in thinking – of which the establishment of the Manpower Services Commission and the greatly improved assistance for geographic mobility are particularly important. Also noteworthy are the study carried out for the Commission by S. Mukherjee (published by HMSO in 1974 under the title *There's Work To Be Done*) and the joint study of *The Manning of Public Services in London* (DoE, 1975).

Chapter IV

THE LOCAL PLANNING MACHINE

LOCAL GOVERNMENT REORGANISATION

The map of local government areas in Britain has been radically redrawn in recent years. London government was reorganised by an Act of 1963, English and Welsh local government by an Act of 1972, and Scottish local government by an Act of 1973.

LONDON

The London Government Act, 1963, came into operation in 1965. In brief, the Act established a Greater London Council covering an area of about 620 square miles and a population of nearly 8 million; and thirty-two new London boroughs (plus the unmolested ancient City of London). These replaced the London County Council, twenty-eight metropolitan boroughs, the county council of Middlesex, and the county boroughs of Croydon, East Ham and West Ham. Considerable parts of Essex, Hertfordshire, Kent and Surrey were transferred to the new Greater London area.

In this area the London boroughs are the main local authorities, but the Greater London Council has important functions in relation to strategic planning and services which need to be planned and administered over a wider area – overall planning, main highways, traffic control, overspill housing and the fire and ambulance services.

The GLC have the responsibility of preparing the strategic development plan (now technically a 'structure plan') for the whole of the Greater London area. (This was published in 1969.) It lays down the policies relating to population, housing, employment, transport and, indeed, all major issues which come within the compass of strategic planning. Within this 'strategic framework', the London borough councils each produce their own local development plans. Originally it was intended that these would also be structure plans, but this was changed in 1972. The change was necessitated by the length of time required to process the Greater

London Development Plan. As the Minister for Local Government and Development stated in the House of Commons (10 November 1970): 'the processing thereafter of a further 33 Borough structure plans will be so time-consuming that there is every prospect that the strategic plan itself will have required further modification in the light of changing circumstances before the last structure plan has been approved and local plans adopted'. The boroughs will therefore be required only to prepare local plans within the framework of the GLC structure plan.

The position in London is unique. The relationship between the GLC and the London borough councils is not the same as that between a county and a county district. The boroughs are large authorities with major responsibilities in their areas: indeed, they are *the* local authorities for their areas. The GLC are the local planning authority for Greater London *as a whole*: the boroughs are the planning authorities for their areas – though there is a complex web of interrelationships. In certain areas, such as Covent Garden, and in relation to certain types of development of strategic importance such as transport terminals, university development, major places of public assembly, the GLC themselves are the local planning authority. Planning applications for other developments of 'strategic significance' have to be referred by the borough councils concerned to the GLC, and there is a wide range of provisions for consultations.

A convenient summary of the situation in relation to the development plan and the 'partnership' of the GLC and the boroughs is to be found in the *Statement* of the Greater London Development Plan. This underlines the fact that the GLDP is intended to form the 'context' for the borough plans which will follow it; but in practice a hard and fast division of functions is neither possible nor desirable. Indeed, it is possible (to say the least) that, as the borough plans are prepared within the 'context', issues will emerge that require a revision of this context. The GLDP is therefore essentially a conceptual plan at this stage. It states a set of principles for the future development of Greater London which will have to undergo a 'process of validation' over a number of years.

The *Statement* couches the issues very much in technical terms, but in reality the crucial problems are policy and political ones. The policies and politics of the individual boroughs are not necessarily consonant with those of the GLC. It is not without good reason that the Redcliffe-Maud Commission (majority) stressed the advantages of the all-purpose authority – 'local government in its simplest, most understandable and potentially most efficient form'. But in some areas (a few, according to the majority report; everywhere, according to Senior's 'memorandum of dissent') there are overriding benefits to be obtained from a two-tier structure. Nowhere is this clearer than in London. There has thus to be a 'partnership', or what the GLC inelegantly refer to as an 'iterative process'. But it would be naive to assume that this makes life easy; on the contrary, it underlines the fact that planning has far more to do with politics than with technical issues.

ENGLAND

Prior to reorganisation, English local government was divided first into county boroughs and administrative counties. Administrative counties were further divided into three types of county districts – municipal (or 'non-county') boroughs, urban districts and rural districts. Only county boroughs (of which there were seventy-nine) and administrative counties (of which there were forty-five) were planning authorities, though there were varying degrees of delegation to county districts.

The Redcliffe-Maud Commission recommended fifty-eight all-purpose authorities for the whole of England outside four conurbations. One of these, Greater London, had already been reorganised on a two-tier system in the mid-sixties. For the other three (centred on Birmingham, Manchester and Liverpool) the Commission recommended a two-tier system of metropolitan and metropolitan district authorities.

The Conservative Government rejected the unitary system, and the Local Government Act of 1972 established a two-tier system of counties and districts throughout the country. In six areas there are metropolitan counties (Greater Manchester, Merseyside, South Yorkshire, Tyne & Wear, West Midlands and West Yorkshire) with a total of thirty-five metropolitan districts. Outside these metropolitan areas are thirty-nine counties and 296 districts.

The New English Local Authorities

Metropolitan Counties

Name	Mid-1974 population (thousands)	Number of metropolitan districts
Greater Manchester	2718	10
Merseyside	1603	5
South Yorkshire	1317	4
Tyne & Wear	1190	5
West Midlands	2780	7
West Yorkshire	2082	5

Non-Metropolitan Counties

Name	Mid-1974 population (thousands)	Number of districts
Avon	915	6
Bedfordshire	484	4
Berkshire	653	6
Buckinghamshire	498	5
Cambridgeshire	541	6
Cheshire	902	8
Cleveland	566	4
Cornwall	399	7
Cumbria	476	6
Derbyshire	892	9
Devon	929	10
Dorset	571	8
Durham	611	8
East Sussex	659	7
Essex	1408	14
Gloucestershire	485	6
Hampshire	1435	13
Hereford and Worcester	586	9
Hertfordshire	942	10
Humberside	849	9
Isle of Wight	111	2
Kent	1441	14
Lancashire	1370	14
Leicestershire	830	9
Lincolnshire	520	7
Norfolk	650	7
North Yorkshire	649	8
Northamptonshire	496	7
Northumberland	286	6
Nottinghamshire	981	8
Oxfordshire	535	5
Salop	354	6
Somerset	400	5
Staffordshire	991	9
Suffolk	567	7
Surrey	1006	11
Warwickshire	470	5
West Sussex	615	7
Wiltshire	507	5

Most of the new counties bear the same names as those which they supersede (though the boundaries are not always the same). There are, however, four new names: Avon (centred on Bath and Bristol, and incorporating parts of the former counties of Gloucestershire and Somerset); Cleveland (centred on Hartlepool and Teesside, and incorporating parts of the former counties of Durham and the North Riding of Yorkshire); Cumbria (encompassing the former county boroughs of Barrow-in-Furness and Carlisle, the whole of Cumberland and Westmorland and parts of Lancashire and the West Riding of Yorkshire); and Humberside (incorporating Grimsby, Kingston upon Hull and parts of the counties of the East and West Riding of Yorkshire and of Lincolnshire).

Basically, therefore, there is an entirely new structure of local government in the metropolitan areas while elsewhere reorganisation has been based largely on the old shires. The metropolitan counties bear only a slight resemblance, however, to the concept put forward by the Redcliffe-Maud Commission for the local government of the West Midlands, Merseyside and Greater Manchester conurbations. Instead of having boundaries extending well beyond the built-up areas (to a further distance of some 20–30 miles), they are much more tightly circumscribed. Indeed, their areas extend little beyond the built-up conurbations. Yet the rationale for metropolitan counties (which was accepted and applied also to West Yorkshire, South Yorkshire and Tyne & Wear) was the need for a local government unit of a large size capable of working out 'effective policies for dealing with their massive housing and transportation problems' and planning and undertaking 'redevelopment, with its widespread consequences, on the scale required where so much of the urban fabric is obsolete'.

The debate on this issue has not been settled by the 1972 Act: indeed it is likely to emerge into the forefront of political debate in the context of regional devolution. (See, for example, Derek Senior's paper on 'Regional Devolution and Local Government' in Craven, E. (ed.), *Regional Devolution and Social Policy*.)

In the meantime, however, efforts are rightly being concentrated on making the new system work. So far as planning is concerned, there is no difference between the powers of metropolitan and non-metropolitan counties. They are responsible for structure planning, for agreeing with the district councils a framework for local plan preparation and development control, and for the determination of major development control issues. This is discussed in more detail in the following chapter.

In other fields, the metropolitan districts have a much wider range of functions than the non-metropolitan districts: they are, for instance, the local authority for education, social services and libraries (which elsewhere are the responsibility of the counties).

The overall picture, however, is by no means as neat as this summary suggests. Some services (such as parks, museums and swimming baths) can be provided by either the county (metropolitan and non-metropolitan) or the district. Highway maintenance is divided between counties and districts. Housing is a district function, but counties have reserve powers. Moreover, the legislation provides for the discharge of any local authority function 'by any other authority' (except for police, education and social services): this was mainly to allow districts which were formerly county boroughs to continue to operate, on an agency basis, services which were transferred to the counties. The final result is confusing and, with some services, the division of responsibilities is blurred. Nowhere is this more so than in the case of planning.

Reference also needs to be made to parish councils and meetings (of which there are over 10,000 in England). These were not abolished by the 1972 Act: on the contrary, their powers were extended. Of particular importance is the right of parish councils to be consulted on planning applications affecting their areas. Consideration is currently being given to the establishment of similar local 'neighbourhood councils' in the larger urban areas. (See the Consultation Paper *Neighbourhood Councils in England* issued by the DoE in July 1974.) Unlike the situation in Scotland and Wales, there is no statutory provision for such bodies at the present time.

WALES

Local government reorganisation in Wales has reduced the number of local authorities from 181 to forty-five. In place of 13 counties, 164 districts and 4 county boroughs, there is a complete two-tier system of 8 counties and 37 districts. Three of the counties have been formed by dividing up the former county of Glamorgan. Monmouthshire has remained largely unchanged but is now called Gwent. The other four new counties spread over large areas of the sparsely populated north, central and west Wales.

The New Welsh Local Authorities

Counties	Mid-1974 Population (thousands)	Number of Districts
Clwyd	373	6
Dyfed	320	6
Gwent	441	5
Gwynedd	224	5
Mid Glamorgan	539	6
Powys	100	3
South Glamorgan	391	2
West Glamorgan	371	4

There are no metropolitan counties, and the division of functions between counties and districts is very similar to that between non-metropolitan counties and districts in England. One difference is that the Welsh districts are responsible for refuse disposal as well as refuse collection (which is divided between the English counties and districts).

The Welsh reorganisation abolished parish councils, and provides for statutory community councils which, like the English parish councils, have the right to be consulted on planning applications affecting their areas.

SCOTLAND

The Wheatley Commission recommended that the 4 Counties of Cities, 21 large burghs, 176 small burghs, 33 counties and 196 districts of Scotland should be replaced by a two-tier structure of 7 regional and 37 district authorities. With some modifications, this general structure was accepted by the Government. Following amendments made by Parliament (particularly the addition of Fife as a separate region and the exclusion of several districts around Glasgow from the Glasgow District), the Local Government (Scotland) Act, 1973 provides for a two-tier system except in the three island areas of Orkney, Shetland and the Western Islands (which become 'most-purpose' authorities).

There are 9 regional and 53 district councils. Together with the 3 island authorities there are thus 65 local authorities of which 49 have planning powers.

The fact that, unlike the situation in England, not all local authorities have planning powers is a result of the difficulties of devising a local government structure for those parts of the country which cover a large area but contain few people. By allocating planning powers in these areas of scattered population to the regional authority it was possible to increase the number of districts (and thereby also reduce their enormous geographical size).

There are thus three different types of area:

(i) in the Central, Fife, Grampian, Lothian, Tayside and Strathclyde regions planning is divided between regional and district authorites;

(ii) in the Borders, Dumfries & Galloway and Highland regions, planning is allocated to the regions: the districts have no planning functions. These three regions are termed 'general planning authorities';

(iii) in the three island areas of Orkney, Shetland and the Western Islands there are no districts: there is thus only one local authority who undertake the functions of both a regional planning authority and a district planning authority. These authorities are termed 'islands areas' (not regions) and are designated as 'general planning authorities'.

In effect therefore there is a two-tier planning system in six regions, and a 'general' planning authority system elsewhere. The former include nine-tenths of the population of Scotland. The regions vary greatly in size – Strathclyde (with a population of 2½ million) has nearly half the country's population. Districts range in population from less than 10,000 in Skye & Lochalsh and Badenoch & Strathspey, to nearly half a million in Edinburgh and over 900,000 in Glasgow.

The New Scottish Local Authorities

Regions	Mid-1974 Population (thousands)	Number of Districts
Borders	99,105	4
Central	267,029	3
Dumfries & Galloway	143,711	4
Fife	337,690	3
Grampian	447,935	5
Highland	178,268	8
Lothian	758,383	4
Strathclyde	2,527,129	19
Tayside	401,183	3
Islands Authorities		
Orkney	17,462	
Shetland	18,445	
Western Isles	30,060	

There is a clearer distinction, at least in concept, between the functions of the regions and the districts than is the case south of the Border. The regions were conceived as strategic authorities and are responsible for 'regional planning functions', all highways, public transport, education, social work and water (which in England and Wales has been allocated to *ad hoc* authorities). The districts are responsible for local planning, housing, refuse collection and disposal and a range of other local services. As is explained in the following chapter, the division of planning functions has been made on a much better basis than in England and Wales. Nevertheless, there remains some blurring, particularly in relation to industrial development, tourism, countryside planning, recreation, museums and community centres where the functions are exercised concurrently by regional and district authorities.

Community councils are to be established, as non-statutory bodies, in accordance with schemes to be submitted to the Secretary of State by district and islands authorities. It is not as yet clear what areas these will cover or what their role will be, but 'some alternatives' have been set out in a SDD Memorandum, *Community Councils: Some Alternatives for Community Councils in Scotland*, published by HMSO in 1974.

The New Local Government Structure

London

Greater London Council
|
32 London Boroughs
and the City of London

England Outside London

6 Metropolitan Counties   39 Counties
| |
35 Metropolitan Districts   296 Districts

Wales

8 Counties
|
37 Districts

Scotland

| *Regions* | | *Islands* |

6 Regional   3 General   3 General
Planning   Planning   Planning
Authorities   Authorities   Authorities
| |
37 District   16 District
Planning   (not planning)
Authorities   Authorities

FUNCTIONS REMOVED FROM LOCAL GOVERNMENT

To complete this rapid sketch of the reorganised local government system, it is necessary to point to several services which have been removed from local government. One of the major reasons for the reorganisation was to make local government better able to carry out its functions: it was even hoped that some functions which had been transferred earlier to *ad hoc* bodies could be brought back into local government. With one significant exception, this was not to be; indeed, personal health services and (except in Scotland) water and sewage disposal functions have been removed from local government. This is mainly because these services need areas far larger than those of the new counties. In Scotland, with the establishment of large regional authorities, regional water boards (set up in 1967) were abolished and their functions transferred to the regions. Nevertheless, as in England and Wales, personal health services were moved to a reorganised health services organisation. This is now responsible for a unified health service which also encompasses the hospitals and the general practitioner services (doctors, dentists, opticians and pharmacists). But though 'unified' in this sense, this adhocery has resulted in a split between personal health services and social work services.

Water supply (together with water conservation, sewerage and sewage disposal) was transferred to nine English water authorities and a Welsh National Water Authority. These took the place of 61 local water authorities, 101 joint water boards, 33 statutory water undertakers, 1,300 local sewage disposal authorities and 29 river authorities.

ADMINISTRATIVE ORGANISATION

Previous editions of this book stressed the difficulty of making generalisations about the operation of local planning throughout the country. Indeed, the only generalisation which seemed passable was that, while most counties had separate planning departments, most urban authorities administered planning within an architect's or engineer's department.

It might be thought that, following reorganisation (the term 'reform' has significantly fallen out of use) the possibilities for generalisation would have increased. In fact the opposite is the case (except for the obvious comment that all local authorities are battling with the problems which have followed from the major upheaval caused by reorganisation). There are several reasons for this. One is the point already made: that the division of responsibility between counties and districts (which applies throughout Britain with the notable exception of the 'general planning authority' areas in Scotland) is blurred. It follows (and the evidence is abundant) that it will take some time for the new lines of demarcation to be agreed – if this happy situation ever comes to pass.

Secondly, reorganisation has had the incredible result of increasing the number of planning authorities in England and Wales (outside London) from 141 to 421 – all of which have planning departments. Thirdly, reorganisation has been accompanied by major changes in the internal organisation of local authorities, with a particular emphasis on corporate management – as illustrated (and sometimes slavishly adopted by the new local authorities) in the Bains and Paterson Reports. (Bains Report: *The New Local Authorities – Management and Structure*; Paterson Report: *The New Scottish Local Authorities – Organisation and Management Structures.*)

As a consequence, no examples of administrative organisation can be regarded as typical. What follows are two illustrations based on information kindly provided by the chief planning officers.

LEICESTER CITY DISTRICT PLANNING DEPARTMENT

In devising the structure for the City of Leicester Planning Department, there were two principal objectives in mind. First, it was considered that the new department should strongly reflect the principal functions of a district planning authority, i.e. development control and the preparation of local plans. Second, importance was attached to creating a strong body of support for administrative functions – not only secretarial and clerical; but also other services which could be seen to be common to the other sections of the department, i.e. technical support provided by technicians and trainees, presentation and graphic services. The Information and Policy Section is very small – some five assistants – and is responsible for the preparation of planning policies for the city as a whole (e.g. on housing, industry and recreation), liaison with the county council, providing assistance to them on structure plan matters, and the development of information systems for the department. In this latter connection they work very closely with the Director of Personnel and Management Services who is responsible for computer developments.

The Land Survey Team provide a service for all departments of the city council. They provide a skilled land survey service which is put into operation in any one area at the initial stages of a project. For instance, when a highway scheme or a slum clearance scheme is started, an up-to-date topographical land survey is carried out so that accurate maps and plans are available throughout the city council's project from planning to design and implementation by one department or another.

The Development Control Section manage defined areas which are co-terminous with the local planning areas of the city. The

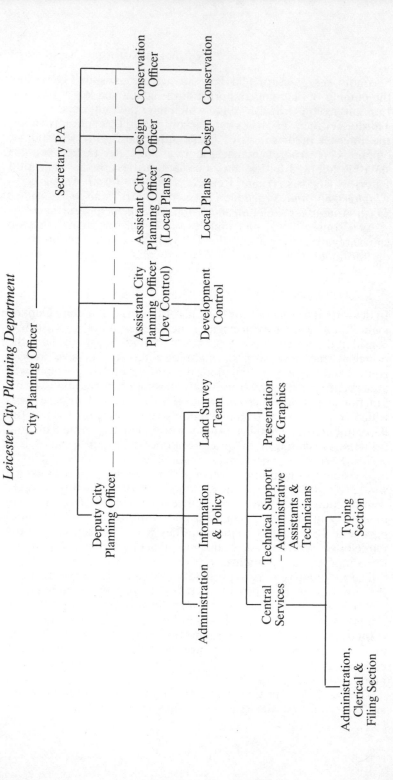

Leicester City Planning Department

intention has been to bring these two activities closer together and it is possible that eventually Development Control will be merged with Local Plans. The section handle some 2,500 applications a year and spend a great deal of effort on public consultation. Where major development proposals arise, public meetings are held, and even on routine matters site notices are posted, and in many other cases there is in addition a system of notifying those affected by postcard.

The Local Plans Section is by far the biggest in the department and has an establishment of some thirty assistants. The section has suffered in recent years from the general shortage of experienced planners, and this has inevitably curtailed their work and necessitated an order of priority in the preparation of local plans. But these teething problems appear likely to be solved fairly quickly. Recent recruitments have enabled the department to expand their local plan activities. One problem which remains to be resolved is the extent to which planning activities arising from the Housing Acts, i.e. General Improvement Areas, should be allocated to the Local Plan teams. Before reorganisation the authority established a separate GIA team and this has continued. It is the intention to integrate Improvement Area work and local planning generally once a much more systematic basis for carrying out GIAs has been established. However, after careful consideration of the provisions of the 1974 Housing Act – introducing, amongst other things, Housing Action Areas – the inclination is towards the establishment of a multi-disciplinary and inter-departmental team to implement the Urban Renewal Policy. This policy is being formulated by the city council in the light of the joint work and advice of the City Planning Officer and the Director of Housing. It is likely that some steering mechanism for any joint team will reflect the extensive collaboration already established.

It has been found necessary to keep two departmental-wide services within separate sections – design and conservation. Design advice is provided for both Development Control and Local Plan purposes by the Design Officer, an architect/planner with some experience who is a third-tier officer. A specialised Conservation Team have been built up since reorganisation under the direction of an architect/planner with an interest in older building methods and traditional designs, one of his assistants being a graduate historian.

LANCASHIRE COUNTY PLANNING DEPARTMENT

The Lancashire County Planning Department is divided into five sections, of which one (concerned with derelict land reclamation) is a joint organisation with the Greater Manchester Metropolitan County.

Structure Plan and Corporate Planning Section (Staff Establishment – 35)
Preparation, monitoring and updating the structure plan; maintenance of the department's information system; provision of planning services to the Corporate Management Team; public participation work; considering strategic significance of important development applications; advising on the planning aspects of public transport co-ordination and assistance policies; preparation of policies for industrial location and the attraction of new industries; liaison with new town development corporations.

Environment Section (Staff Establishment – 26)
Responsible for all matters concerned with recreation, leisure and tourism; giving landscape advice, both generally and concerning development proposals; mineral working policy and proposals; waste disposal; planning aspects of land reclamation; siting of itinerant camps; design and implementation of countryside recreational proposals.

Development Control and Special Plans Section (Staff Establishment – 39)
Provision of advice on matters of architectural design including the conservation of buildings; advising on local plans for central areas, village plans and conservation areas; processing development control cases dealt with at county level; maintaining liaison with district councils.

Administrative Section (Staff Establishment – 21)
Preparation of material for the Planning and Industrial Development Committee, budgetary control and administrative and clerical functions associated with Town and Country Planning Acts and other legislation.

Derelict Land
Prior to local government reorganisation, the former Lancashire County Council had reclaimed 1,192 acres of derelict land to beneficial after-uses (agriculture, education, industry, residential, amenity open space), a further 570 acres of reclamation work was in progress and a rolling programme of future work up to 1976/7 amounted to 2,128 acres. It was at that time (March 1974) estimated that there were 13,055 acres of derelict land in the county which the

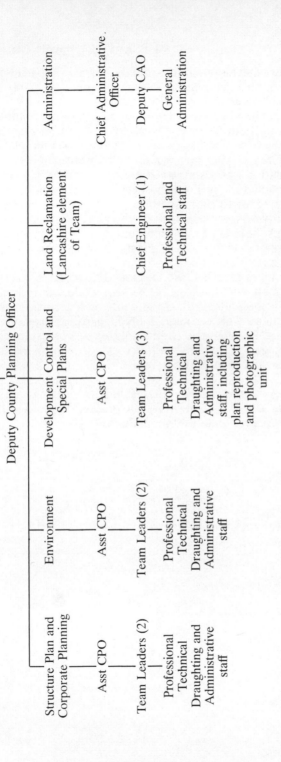

Lancashire County Planning Department

County Planning Officer

Deputy County Planning Officer

Structure Plan and Corporate Planning
Asst CPO
Team Leaders (2)
Professional Technical Draughting and Administrative staff

Environment
Asst CPO
Team Leaders (2)
Professional Technical Draughting and Administrative staff

Development Control and Special Plans
Asst CPO
Team Leaders (3)
Professional Technical Draughting and Administrative staff, including plan reproduction and photographic unit

Land Reclamation (Lancashire element of Team)
Chief Engineer (1)
Professional and Technical staff

Administration
Chief Administrative Officer
Deputy CAO
General Administration

Planning and Development Committee wished to reclaim by 1981. In addition to the reclamation work, approximately 1,700 trees had been planted on a further 1,115 acres.

Agreement had been reached at an early stage to establish a Joint Reclamation Team following local government reorganisation to deal with the reclamation of derelict land in the counties of Lancashire and Greater Manchester and their constituent districts and a joint committee was set up to co-ordinate the arrangements. This decision enabled the well-established Lancashire land reclamation team to be retained almost intact, an example of joint working across county boundaries which has been widely praised and commented on. The team are now based on the Wigan Metropolitan District area, having moved during 1975 from the Lancashire headquarters at Preston.

The Survey of Derelict and Despoiled Land in 1974 allowed the inclusion of sites which were previously excluded and this partly accounts for the Lancashire County Survey identifying 5,849 acres of derelict land. This is considerably higher than previous surveys had indicated and the new county still has one of the most serious dereliction problems in the country. The current programme of reclamation aims to clear this dereliction in about twenty years. The 1974 Survey also identifies 1,587 acres of potential derelict land, mainly arising from old established mineral workings and tipping sites which are not covered by restoration conditions or other arrangements providing for rehabilitation.

Chapter V

THE LEGISLATIVE FRAMEWORK

DEVELOPMENT PLANS

The Town and Country Planning Act of 1968 and the equivalent Scottish Act of 1969 (now consolidated respectively in the Acts of 1971 and 1972) represent a landmark in the evolution of planning policy and administration. This new legislation represents a major attempt to bring the planning system up to date, to shed the cumbersome and inflexible procedures of 'the 1947 system', to redefine the respective roles of central and local government (with far less central concern with detailed planning matters), and to provide the framework for a far greater degree of public participation in the planning process.

It will be some years before the '1947 type' development plans are superseded by the 'new type' development plans (i.e. structure plans and local plans). The '1947 type' development plans are therefore of more than historic interest. It is thus appropriate to outline their main features. But the main emphasis of this chapter is on the new system – and the amendments which have already been made to it. For the sake of clarity the convention has been adopted of referring to the 1947 system in the past tense.

The Scottish system differs in a number of important ways from that which is in operation south of the Border. Major differences are indicated in the main body of the chapter, and a separate section summarises the characteristics of the Scottish legislation.

THE 1947 SYSTEM

Under the pre-war system of planning, an operative planning scheme was in effect a zoning plan. A developer could visit a local town hall and ask to see the planning scheme: he would be shown a written document and a series of coloured maps, each colour representing some particular use. From the published scheme, the developer would find that particular pieces of land were zoned for industry, for open space, for residential development at not more than eight houses to the acre, and so on. The great advantage of this system to the developer was that there were no doubts as to what development would be permitted: it was all written down and had the force of law. But therein lay one of its gravest shortcomings: certainty for the developer meant inflexibility for the local authority. One way of circumventing this was for planning authorities to take advantage of the time-consuming and cumbersome procedure for preparing and obtaining approval to their schemes by remaining at the draft stage for as long as possible. Yet this had the opposite danger: the flexibility thereby attained could easily become mere expediency. The 1947 system attempted to achieve a balance between these two extremes by the introduction of the flexible development plan which was essentially a statement of development proposals. This was intended to show, for example, 'which towns and villages are suitable for expansion and which can best be kept to their present size; the direction in which a city will expand; the area to be preserved as an agricultural Green Belt and the area to be allocated to industry and to housing'.

The 1947 Act, however, defined a development plan as 'a plan indicating the manner in which a local planning authority propose that land in their area should be used, whether by the carrying out thereon of development or otherwise, and the stages by which any such development should be carried out'. Furthermore, it was required that the development plan should 'define the sites of proposed roads, public and other buildings and works, airfields, parks, pleasure grounds, nature reserves and other open spaces, or allocate areas of land for use for agricultural, residential, industrial or other purposes'.

Unlike the pre-war 'operative scheme', the development plan did not of itself imply that permission would be granted for particular developments even if it appeared that they were clearly in harmony with the plan. Development control was achieved by a system of planning permissions. The development plan merely set out the intentions of the local planning authority. Though a developer was able to find out from the plan where particular uses would be likely to be permitted, his specific proposals still needed to be considered by the local planning authority. When considering applications, the authority were expressly directed to 'have regard to the provisions of the development plan', but the plan was not binding in any way, and, indeed, authorities were instructed to have regard not only to the development plan but also to 'any other material considerations'. Furthermore, in granting permission to develop, the authority could impose 'such conditions as they think fit'.

However, though local planning authorities had considerable

latitude in deciding whether to approve applications, they had to be clear on the planning objectives for their areas; otherwise they had no adequate basis on which they could judge the merits and shortcomings of particular applications. This was the essential purpose of the development plan.

The development plan consisted of a series of documents. The *Report of Survey* provided the background to, and the basis of, the plan, but had no statutory effect. The statutory documents were a 'written statement' and a series of maps. The written statement was a short formal (indeed excessively short and formal) summary of the main proposals of the plan. It did not contain any argument substantiating the proposals or any of the factual material on which these were based. The maps were of several types. In counties they included a 'county map' and a related 'programme map' (at a scale of one inch to the mile) covering the whole of the administrative county. For areas requiring more detailed planning there were 'town maps' together with programme maps at the larger scale of six inches to the mile. In the case of a county borough there was, of course, no county map: the principal maps were the town map and its related programme map.

The county and town maps indicated the developments which were expected in the twenty-year period of the plan (and possibly some important developments which were expected somewhat later) and the pattern of land use proposed at the end of the period. (In areas for which no notation was given – which could be extensive in counties – it was intended that the main existing uses should remain undisturbed.) A programme map showed the stages by which the proposed development was to be achieved.

A formidable amount of work was involved in the preparation of development plans. The 1947 Act required local planning authorities to submit plans to the minister for approval within three years (by 1 July 1951), 'or within such extended period as the minister may in any particular case allow' but, not surprisingly, most authorities could not meet the deadline. (Only twenty-two did, in fact, do so.)

The task of the central department was to assess the general provisions of the plan, to weigh all objections to it, to hold a public local inquiry, to consider the report of the inspector on the inquiry and finally to approve the plan (usually with modification). About half the plans had been aproved by 1955 and the bulk had been approved by 1959; but three were not approved until the early sixties: Denbighshire, part of Glamorgan and Manchester.

Development plans, unlike the old 'operative schemes', were not intended to be final statements – even of broad intentions. Local planning authorities were obliged to review them at least every five years, and additionally could propose amendments at any time. The impossibility of coping with the preparation and approval of plans on the original time-scale greatly delayed the review procedure, and many local authorities were still engaged on their first review in the mid-sixties. This was one of the major reasons for introducing the new structure plan system.

The reviews followed the same process as the initial plan: survey, draft written statement and maps, submission to the department, local public inquiry, and approval with or without modification. Alterations or additions to development plans could be made at any time. Often these 'amendments' amounted to more detailed plans for particular areas. In counties, the town maps for the districts were commonly submitted in this way. Another type of detailed planning often submitted as a formal amendment was a 'comprehensive development area' plan (now replaced by the 'action area' procedure discussed later).

THE PLANNING ADVISORY GROUP REPORT

The system of development plans and development control set up under the Town and Country Planning Act of 1947 operated for two decades without significant change. During this time the system proved its value, but it would be surprising if what was appropriate for the mid-forties were equally relevant to the seventies. Furthermore, not only had the tempo of social and economic change increased but also the system has tended to develop its own rigidities. This was particularly the case with development plans. Unlike the 1932 Act 'schemes', they were intended to show only broad land-use allocations. But the definition of 'development plan' in the 1947 Act was a plan 'indicating the manner in which the local planning authority propose that land in their area should be used'. This, together with the way in which plans were mapped, led inexorably towards greater detail and precision. 'The plans have thus acquired the appearance of certainty and stability which is misleading since the primary use zonings may themselves permit a wide variety of use within a particular allocation, and it is impossible to forecast every land requirement over many years ahead.' Above all:

'it has proved extremely difficult to keep these plans not only up to date but forward looking and responsive to the demands of change. The result has been that they have tended to become out of date – in terms of technique in that they deal inadequately with transport and the interrelationship of traffic and land use; in factual terms in that they fail to take account quickly enough of changes in population forecasts, traffic growth and other economic and social trends; and in terms of policy in that they do not reflect more recent developments in the field of regional and urban planning. Over the years the plans have become more and more out of touch with emergent planning problems and policies, and have in many cases become no more than local land-use maps.'

In short, the system became out of tune with contemporary needs and forward thinking, and it was being bogged down in details and cumbersome procedures. The quality of planning suffered, and delays were beginning to bring the system into disrepute. As a result, public acceptability, which is the basic foundation of any planning system, was beginning to crumble.

It was within this context of thinking that the Planning Advisory Group was set up in May 1964 to review the broad structure of the planning system and, in particular, development plans. Their report, *The Future of Development Plans*, published in 1965, proposed a basic change which would distinguish between policy or strategic issues and detailed tactical issues. Only the former would be submitted for ministerial approval: the latter would be for local decisions within the framework of the approved policy.

For urban areas with populations over 50,000 a new type of 'urban plan' was proposed which concentrated on the broad pattern of future development and redevelopment, and dealt with the land-use/transport relationships in an integrated way, but which excluded the detailed land-use allocations of the present town maps. Similarly for the counties a new form of 'county map' was proposed which dealt with the distribution of population and employment, the major communications network, the main policies for recreation and conservation, green belts, and the general development policy for towns and villages.

These were to provide a coherent framework of planning policy and would be submitted for ministerial approval. Each would identify 'action areas' which would require comprehensive planning and on which action would be concentrated over a period of ten years or more.

Local planning authorities would have power to prepare 'local plans', which would not be submitted for approval, but would conform with the policies laid down in the urban plan or county plan. These would serve as a guide to development control and a basis for the more positive aspects of environmental planning. The most significant of local plans would be those for the action areas.

Ministerial approval of the action areas would be limited to the policy proposed, and the local planning authorities would prepare 'action area plans', which would provide the detailed basis for implementation.

These types of plans could not be produced by planning authorities acting in isolation: they needed to form part of a regional strategy and also of what was termed a sub-regional pattern. Here – assuming a continuation of the existing structure of local government – the regional context would be provided by the economic planning councils and boards:

'These are likely to be primarily concerned with creating the conditions for economic growth in some regions and controlling the pace of growth in others, within the framework of national economic planning. As a part of this process, they will have to be concerned with physical planning issues which are of regional significance, with the overall distribution of population and employment, green belt policy and any other limitation on growth in the conurbations. They must also encompass other physical factors of regional significance such as communications, water resources and major industrial projects; the economic implications of major development projects (motorways, docks, airports); and the impact of economic decisions on physical planning. It will consequently be necessary to associate local planning authorities with the regional planning process and to ensure that their development plans give effect to the intentions of the regional plan.'

THE NEW PLANNING SYSTEM

Following a White Paper, *Town and Country Planning*, published in June 1967, legislative effect to the proposals of the Planning Advisory Group was given by the Town and Country Planning Acts of 1968 (for England and Wales) and 1969 (for Scotland). It is essential for an understanding for this legislation – and the difficulties which have arisen in its implementation by the reorganised local authorities – that it be appreciated that it was predicated on the reorganisation of local government into unitary authorities, at least in so far as planning was concerned. In essence the concept was one of a single authority responsible for preparing a broad strategic structure plan, within the framework of which detailed local plans would be elaborated, and development control would be administered. We shall return to this after describing the provisions of the 1968 and 1969 Acts (which have now been consolidated in the Act of 1971 for England and Wales, and the Act of 1972 for Scotland).

STRUCTURE PLANS

A structure plan, which has to be submitted to the Secretary of State for his approval, is primarily a written statement of policy, accompanied by diagrammatic illustrations for counties and major towns. Its range is considerably wider than the old-style development plans. It deals with broad land-use policies (but not with detailed land allocations) and with policies for the management of traffic and the improvement of 'the physical environment'. The legislation provides that the written statement *must*:

(a) formulate the local planning authority's policy and general proposals in respect of the development and other use of land in that area (including measures for the improvement of the physical environment and the management of traffic);
(b) state the relationship of those proposals to general proposals for the development and the other use of land in neighbouring areas which may be expected to affect that area; and
(c) contain such other matters as may be prescribed or as the Secretary of State may in any particular case direct.

The term 'plan' is perhaps misleading, since it might be expected to involve a map; but there is to be no map. Unlike the previous development plans (which required county and town maps, with related programme maps), the structure plan has to be accompanied only by 'diagrams, illustrations, and descriptive matter'.

The plan has to 'have regard to current policies with respect to the economic planning and development of the region as a whole' and 'to the resources likely to be available' for its implementation. High ideals must therefore be tempered by the facts of life.

Of particular note is the character of the survey which is to precede the plan. Differences in the content and scope of the surveys required under the earlier and the new legislation highlight the major change in planning philosophy. The earlier legislation was largely concerned with land use: 'a development plan means a plan indicating the manner in which a local planning authority propose that land in their area should be used'. The 'survey' required as a preliminary to this dealt predominantly with physical matters. Under the new legislation, emphasis is laid on major economic and social forces and on broad policies or 'strategies' for large areas. The 'survey' becomes a major part of the planning process. Unlike the earlier legislation, the Acts spell out the coverage of the survey. In the forefront are 'the principal physical and economic characteristics' of the area and, to the extent that they are relevant, of neighbouring areas as well. In formulating the structure plan, particular attention has to be paid 'to current policies with respect to the economic planning and development of the region as a whole' and to likely availability of resources. It is within this strategic framework that 'local plans' are to be drawn up. The structure plan is essentially a statement of general policy designed to channel major forces in socially and economically desirable directions.

Another major change follows from this. Under the '1947 philosophy', a development plan had to be reviewed 'at least once every five years' and, for this purpose, fresh surveys had to be carried out. This proved totally impracticable for reasons already outlined. Under the new system, the 'survey' is a continuing operation. Though some authorities already adopt this approach, the 1947 concept implied an assembly and interpretation of 'survey material' which was reviewed quinquennially and which led to an amendment of the development plan. The new concept sheds a mass of detail and focuses attention on the major trends: the continual review is designed to ensure that the strategy remains appropriate and adequate. The review relates essentially to the survey; when the continuing review indicates that the structure plan is in need of alteration, the local planning authority will take the initiative of drawing up a new plan. Alternatively, the Secretary of State can direct an authority to submit proposals for an alteration to their structure plan if he regards it as necessary in view of, for instance, major proposals in another area which will have an impact in the authority's areas.

There is another significant difference in the wording of the requirement for a survey in the new Act. Whereas the earlier Acts required a local authority to 'carry out' a survey, the new legislation refers to the duty to *institute* a survey. This change was deliberately designed to facilitate the employment of consultants, particularly by local planning authorities who were short of the necessary skilled staff.

ACTION AREAS

Structure plans 'indicate' action areas where major change, by development, redevelopment or improvement, may be expected. This, ideally, involves more than simply picking out areas where the local authority thinks that action is needed. The intention is that the survey will identify and outline problems which require action; the written statement of the structure plan will discuss these problems, determine priorities and indicate areas where action is required not only on a comprehensive basis, but also at an early date. It will also discuss the nature of the required action, its extent and its feasibility in financial terms.

Action areas, it should be noted, are *indicated*, not *defined*. This deliberate wording was chosen for two reasons. First, if the boundaries of an action area were to be defined precisely and be subject (as part of the structure plan) to ministerial approval, this would involve the very thing which the new system is designed to avoid: detailed consideration by the department and the embodiment of inflexible proposals in a statutory document. Secondly, it was thought likely that it would intensify the problems of planning blight. If boundaries were drawn on a map they would most probably have to be redrawn when more detailed plans were prepared. Thus, some people who thought they would be affected would find that they had been misled, and others who thought they would not be affected would find that they were in fact within an action area. Objections would be made to a structure plan on the basis of individual interests rather than on the basis of the general nature of the proposals.

In short, the definition of an action area would be foreign to the essential concept underlying the structure plan – that it deals with general issues in broad terms; it is a policy document, not a physical design plan. Fundamentally it is a matter of words and diagrams, not of maps.

Once 'adequate publicity' has been given to a structure plan (a matter which is dealt with in Chapter XIV) it is submitted to the Secretary of State (who may approve it in whole or in part and with or without modifications and reservations; or reject it). Objections can be made, as with the old development plans, but instead of a local public inquiry, there is an 'examination in public'. This is concerned, not with the hearing of objections from property owners and others whose interests are affected by the structure plan, but much more broadly with the major policies which are enshrined in the plan. (This is discussed further below.)

LOCAL PLANS

Local plans were initially conceived as detailed elaborations of the broad policies relating to action areas which had been incorporated in a structure plan and which had been approved by the Secretary of State. They consist of a written statement, a map on an ordnance survey base, together with 'diagrams, illustrations and descriptive matter'. The Acts provide for a great deal of flexibility on the form and content of local plans – a matter which, in the debates, ministers pleaded was essential to the underlying conception. It is envisaged that local plans will vary greatly. Where the proposed development is to be undertaken by a local authority, the local plan will be detailed. Thus those affected will know clearly what is proposed. But where the intention is that the development is to be undertaken privately, the local plan will simply provide broad guidelines. To quote a ministerial statement:

'I think we are agreed that one of the defects of the present system is its negative nature and that planning authorities are not able to play the useful and constructive role in positive planning which we would like to see them play. We believe that some of the local plans of the kind that I have been indicating – that would give general broad indications for the developer – would take the form, as it were, of a brief for the developer and his architect. It might, for example, state the general objectives of the plan and the broad outlines of the way in which the planning authority envisaged that they would be achieved. The proper grouping of usages within the area, the density and height of buildings on the site, provision for proper circulation of vehicles and foot passengers – matters of this kind will be indicated in the plan. It does not follow by any means that in such a case the planning authority would need to, or would want to, lay down at the plan-making stage the details of the buildings that it wants to see on the site to achieve the objectives of good design and satisfactory treatment of the environment. I think it will generally be considered advantageous to leave scope within the main framework for the imagination and initiative of private developers.'

There are three types of local plan: district plans, action area plans and subject plans. A district plan is concerned with the detailed planning of an area of substantial size 'where the factors in local planning need to be studied and set out in a comprehensive way'. They typically relate to the whole of a small town or a major sector of a larger one.

An action area plan deals with an area subject to 'intensive change by development, redevelopment or improvement by public authorities or private enterprise, or a combination of these methods and agencies'. Originally it was a requirement that an action area should have been 'indicated' in a structure plan, but, as will be explained shortly, this requirement has been abolished. Action areas replace the comprehensive development areas (CDAs) of the 1947 legislation.

A subject plan, as its name suggests, deals with specific aspects of planning such as conservation, housing or landscaping. They are called by the name of the 'subject' to which they relate.

The most radical feature of a local plan is that at no time does it require to be approved by the Secretary of State (though he has the power to direct that a local plan 'shall not have effect' unless he approves it: this is a reserve power intended to be used only in the exceptional case). The rationale for this (originally) was that a local plan would be prepared within the framework of a structure plan; and since structure plans would be approved by the Secretary of State, local authorities could safely be left to the detailed elaboration of local plans. This went to the very kernel of the philosophy underlying the new legislation – that the department should be concerned only with strategic issues, and that local responsibility in local matters should become a reality.

There were (and remain) two additional safeguards. First, the local authority are required to give 'adequate publicity' to their proposals *before* they are included in a local plan, and to give 'adequate opportunity' for the making of representations on their proposals. In these and similar ways public participation is actually written into the legislation. Second (with one important difference), the normal statutory procedure applies for the deposit of plans, the making of objections and the holding of a hearing or inquiry by an independent inspector and the publication of the inspector's report. The important difference from the traditional procedure is that the inspector will report to the local authority, not to the Secretary of State. This follows, of course, from the principle that the local plan is a local authority, not a central authority, matter. It is clear that public participation is more than a desirable adjunct to the new system – it is an essential feature. If public participation fails, so will the system. (This issue is discussed, within a wider context, in the final chapter of this book.)

These two 'safeguards' remain intact following significant amendments to the first. Indeed, as a result of these amendments, they have become of greater importance. The amendments were consequential on the particular character of local government reorganisation – which was very different from that envisaged when the new planning system was introduced.

There are differences between the position in England and Wales and that in Scotland, and thus Scotland is more easily discussed separately.

LOCAL GOVERNMENT REORGANISATION AND THE NEW PLANNING SYSTEM IN ENGLAND AND WALES

As already noted, the new planning system was devised in advance of local government reorganisation, and was based on the assumption that a single authority would be responsible for both structure planning and local planning. The 1972 Local Government Act, however, established two main types of local authority and divided these functions between them. Thus, while counties are responsible for broad planning strategy (structure planning), districts are independently responsible for local planning (and most matters of planning control). This division has necessitated a series of complex statutory provisions for redefining the respective roles of the two types of authority, particularly since the Government's intention was (to quote the 1971 White Paper, *Local Government in England*), that 'the reorganized system should everywhere be based on two forms of operational authorities: [the Government] do not see the relationship between the two as implying that some authorities are answerable to others'. In short, a system which was originally conceived as a unitary one had to be divided into two parts which would be as clearly differentiated from each other as possible. Before outlining how this has been done, it is relevant to describe more fully the original conception.

Under the 1968 Act, the new-style development plans were conceived as a two-part process: the purpose of a structure plan was to provide a broad strategic framework for the preparation of local plans; and local plans had to 'conform generally' to an approved structure plan. Since the same authority was to be responsible for both plans, there was no need to make legislative provision to ensure that a local plan did in fact 'conform generally', or even to spell out what this meant. Moreover, since this was the case, the Secretary of State, having approved the structure plan, could safely leave the detailed elaboration of its policies at the local level to the (same) local authority *without the necessity of further approval.*

Clearly, once the responsibility for local plans is allocated to a different authority, this concept breaks down, since the districts may have very different ideas from the counties on the way in which the general policies in a structure plan are to be elaborated in their areas. The scope for conflict is very great, particularly since district authorities are independent political entities who are not subservient to the county. Furthermore, given that the districts are responsible for local plans, there is an inevitable temptation for counties to formulate their 'policy and general proposals' in greater detail than would be the case if there were no division of functions. In this way they can keep a tighter rein on the districts. But, of course, this is quite foreign to the original concept, and DoE Circular 98/74 has stressed that counties should 'concentrate on those issues which are of key structural importance to the area concerned, and their inter-relationships'. The Circular advises that, for most authorities, the key issues will include:

(a) the location and scale of employment;
(b) the location and scale of housing (including new development, redevelopment and rehabilitation); and
(c) the transportation system.

Additionally, other issues 'which may be of particular importance' are:

(d) the extent of conservation of the character of the area (whether urban or rural);
(e) the extent of provision for recreation and tourism;
(f) the location and scale of shopping centres; and
(g) the location and scale of land reclamation.

It is noted that counties may decide that 'other structural issues, though of less than key importance', should nevertheless be included in a structure plan. Here, the Circular suggests, it would be adequate for the county 'to safeguard its position [sic] on these matters by describing present policies (which should be compatible with those devised for the key issues) and indicating whether they will be further investigated by the authority at a later stage'.

The very fact that DoE have felt it necessary to issue this advice demonstrates the problem. It has been further compounded by the delays in the preparation of structure plans (itself due in part to the departure from the original concept of 'broad strategies'): these delays – and the necessity of consultations with the districts – have resulted in a complex and difficult web of political relationships. Shortages of staff (for a system which has multiplied the number of planning authorities) have added to the difficulties. Certainly, planning cannot be neatly divided between 'county strategy' and 'district tactics'. To quote DoE Circular 74/73, planning is 'an inter-related process and this will need to be reflected in the arrangements made between authorities'. Statutory provisions requiring counties to consult districts on structure plans, or to certify that a local plan conforms to an approved structure plan, and such like, are legalistic devices which are of far less importance than the working relationships which are established between counties and districts. These working relationships, by their very nature, must be a matter for local authorities to devise. Nevertheless, the Local Government Act provides for a specific procedure 'designed to promote effective co-operation in the planning field and to minimise delay, dispute and duplication'. This is the requirement for the preparation of a 'development plan scheme'. Following consultations between the county and its constituent districts, a document must be prepared (and submitted to the Secretary of State) setting out the allocation of responsibility and the programme for the preparation of local plans.

This has been a matter of considerable controversy. Theoretically, it provides a legal opportunity for a county council to seize the power to undertake responsibility for local plans (though the district could appeal to the Secretary of State). But the objective is precisely the opposite: to secure a constructive and sensible relationship in plan-making between counties and districts which is appropriate to individual circumstances.

It might have been expected that, since local plans are now to be prepared by an authority different from that which is responsible for the structure plan, tighter provisions would have been introduced to ensure that local plans 'conform' with the policies set out in a structure plan. Not so: indeed, the opposite has happened. The original legislative provisions sensibly allowed a local planning authority (envisaged, it must be stressed, as a unitary authority) to prepare a local plan at the same time as a structure plan was being undertaken. But, with the binary system, since it was inconceivable that districts should do no plan-preparation until the county structure plans had been approved, this provision has been carried over to allow districts to prepare local plans while the county is preparing its structure plan.

It is too early to judge how all this is working out, but clearly there are great inherent difficulties and the logical concepts on which the plan-making system was predicated have been jettisoned.

As is explained in the following section, the Scottish system is emerging differently, but before discussing this it is necessary to add a note on development control.

There is no statutory provision for a development control scheme parallel to the development plan scheme. The Secretary of State has, however, advised that 'informal' (i.e. non-statutory) schemes should be drawn up in every area. The legislation clearly allocates responsibility for development control to districts, except in the case of 'county matters'. These include applications concerned with mineral workings, with development in national parks, and with developments which would conflict with county policy. The last (which is spelled out in some detail – if not clarity – in Section 32 of Schedule 16 to the Local Government Act) is obviously the most problematic. On the one hand it could be seen as a sensible way of giving counties reserve powers; on the other hand it could be used as a means of removing large areas of power from districts to a county. There is further discussion of the administration of planning control in the following chapter.

THE NEW SYSTEM IN SCOTLAND

The new system in Scotland differs in several significant ways from that south of the Border. Some may be attributed to the much more thorough-going nature of the Scottish local government reorganisation; others may legitimately be attributed to a canny move to avoid some of the difficulties which can be expected in the English system.

The three major changes in planning legislation are the introduction of 'regional reports', an amendment of the mandatory provisions relating to structure plans, and a provision under which local plans can be prepared in advance of structure plans.

REGIONAL REPORTS

Some of the Scottish regions are far larger than is appropriate for a structure plan. Nevertheless, there is a need for a policy plan to cover the whole of the area. This need is met by the innovation of the 'regional report'. But the opportunity has been taken to make this a flexible feature of the new planning system. Though it may indeed relate to the whole of a region, the legislation enables it to be used to serve a variety of purposes. It may be used to provide a basis of discussion between the Secretary of State and a region about general development policy; it may provide a basis of guidance for the preparation or review of structure plans; and, in the absence of a structure plan, it may serve as a guide to district planning authorities and developers on planning policies. A regional report may cover the whole or only part of a region. Moreover, it may be restricted in its scope to particular issues.

In striking contrast to structure plans, there is no formal procedure for the preparation, submission or approval of a regional report. The only requirements are that a regional report shall be based on a survey, that affected local authorities shall be consulted, that it shall be submitted to the Secretary of State (who shall 'make observations' on it) and that it shall be published (together with the Secretary of State's observations).

Though the Secretary of State will not formally approve or amend a regional report, planning authorities will be required, in their planning practice, to 'take account' of both the report and the Secretary of State's 'observations'.

The Secretary of State can also direct a regional or planning authority to submit a regional report and, in default, prepare a regional report himself.

STRUCTURE PLANS FOR PARTS OF AN AREA

As originally envisaged, structure plans were to be single plans covering the whole area of the authority responsible for their preparation. Though there was provision for a structure plan to be submitted by instalments, the assumption was that these would eventually build up to a single plan which would then be kept up to date as a whole. This concept is radically changed by provisions introduced in the 1973 Local Government (Scotland) Act. Regional and general planning authorities can now prepare structure plans for different parts of their areas. The intention is that the regions should be divided into areas which, by virtue of their geography and cohesion in terms of socio-economic structure and the pattern of communications, form natural structure plan units. Moreover, it is no longer necessary for all parts of a region to be covered by structure plans.

The significance of this change is more striking when it is appreciated that, with the introduction of regional reports, there are three (not two) levels of planning: regional, structure and local. It is unlikely that all three will be necessary in all areas. It is much more likely that regional reports and structure plans will be seen as alternatives. At the least, there will be the possibility of a flexible approach which the English system denies.

Given this loosening-up of the procedures for large-scale planning it is not surprising that changes have also been made in relation to local plans.

MANDATORY LOCAL PLANS

Local plans were conceived as detailed elaborations of proposals sketched out as matters of broad policy in a structure plan. This concept is abandoned in the 1973 Act: 'every general and district planning authority shall, as soon as practicable, prepare local plans for all parts of their district'. Thus local plans are now mandatory and are to be prepared as soon as possible and thus (probably typically) in advance of a structure plan.

The only qualification to this is in cases where a structure plan (or a regional report) is under way and would have a significant impact on the area to be covered by a proposed local plan. Effect is given to this by requiring a district planning authority to obtain the consent of the regional planning authority to the preparation of a local plan. This consent is not to be unreasonably withheld and the district will have the right of appeal to the Secretary of State. (In line with the current emphasis on avoidance of formal proceedings, there would not be a public inquiry: the Secretary of State would decide the matter as simply as possible and his decision would be final.) This procedure, of course, does not apply to general planning authorities since they are responsible for regional, structure and local plans.

Local plans remain the responsibility of the districts (except in the areas of general planning authorities) and therefore are subject to 'approval' only by the authorities who prepare them – unless they are 'called in'. This may be done either by the Secretary of State or by the regional planning authority. Again there is machinery for appeal but no public inquiry.

The 'call-in' power of regional authorities is a new one. The circumstances in which this can be used are set out in the 1973 Act and are:

(i) when a local plan is urgently required to implement the provisions of an approved structure plan, and the district planning authority concerned have failed to adopt an appropriate local plan; *or*
(ii) when the district or more than one district planning authority is likely to be affected by the local plan in question; *or*
(iii) when the local plan does not conform to a structure plan approved by the Secretary of State; *or*
(iv) when the implementation of the local plan will render unlikely the implementation of any other local plan relating to their district.

DEVELOPMENT CONTROL IN SCOTLAND

Development control is a district or general planning authority function but, as in England, certain powers are allocated to the upper-tier authority. The powers of the region are, however, not as far-reaching (or set out in detail) as in the case of the English counties. Moreover, there is no reference to 'county matters'. The Scottish provisions simply supplement the powers previously exercised solely by the Secretary of State by a power of regional planning authorities to call in applications where:

(i) the proposed development does not conform to a structure plan approved by the Secretary of State; *or*
(ii) the proposed development raises a new planning issue of general significance to the district of the regional planning authority.

This power is exercisable only in cases where the application is not called in by the Secretary of State himself.

Planning appeals will continue to be lodged with the Secretary of State, but regional planning authorities will be notified of all appeals and have the right to take part in the appeal proceedings. Regional planning authorities will also be informed of proposals for revocation, modification and discontinuance of use orders and can make representations or objections on them to the Secretary of State. Finally, they will have default powers to make such orders themselves if they think that an order is necessary to prevent 'material prejudice' to an approved structure plan.

These powers of a regional planning authority in relation to development control are essentially rights of intervention to give effect to regional planning policies. They are defined in straightforward terms (avoiding the complexities of the English legislation). In all cases there are simple rights of appeal to the Secretary of State to enable him to resolve any disputes between a district and a region.

THE EXAMINATION IN PUBLIC

As already noted, structure plans are subject, not to a public inquiry, but to an 'examination in public'. The distinction is that, whereas a public inquiry is concerned with the hearing of objections, the examination in public is an investigation of selected matters affecting the Secretary of State's consideration of a structure plan. Though the rights of individuals to object to a structure plan (and the duty of the Secretary of State to consider all objections) are maintained, there is no longer any right for objectors to present their case at an inquiry. The examination deals with only those matters which the Secretary of State considers need examining in public. Moreover, he determines who shall participate in the examination (whether or not they have made objections or representations).

This is a major departure from traditional practice. Its rationale is far more than the negative one of avoiding lengthy, time-consuming and quasi-judicial public inquiries. It is related essentially to the basic purpose and character of a structure plan. A structure plan does not set out detailed proposals and, therefore, does not show how individual properties will be affected. It deals with broad policy issues: the examination in public focuses on these, and on alternatives to those set out in the plan. These include such matters as the future level and distribution of population and employment; transportation policies; and availability of resources for major proposals of the plan.

But the examination does not deal with all the key policy issues. Only those on which the Secretary of State needs to be more fully informed by means of discussion at an examination are selected. In short, the examination is intended to assist the Secretary of State in determining his views on the plan and in arriving at his decision.

The matters needing examination are most likely to arise from clashes between the proposals of a plan and those of a neighbouring area or wider regional and national policies. Additionally, major inconsistencies within the plan or issues on which there is unsettled controversy may be the subject of examination.

The issues selected are published in advance (together with a list of those selected to participate). There is an opportunity for written comments on these to be sent to the department but, although the Secretary of State has power to add to the list of issues or participants, major changes are not envisaged since the selection will have been made on the basis of the contribution which the examination of the selected matters can make to his decision on the plan.

The examination is carried out typically by a panel with an independent chairman. The chairman has the discretion (both before and during an examination) to invite additional participants.

This new procedure clearly gives rise to difficulties, particularly since there is likely to be considerable criticism from any objectors who are excluded from participation in the examination. In this connection it is important to stress that the examination is envisaged as only one part of the process by which the Secretary of State considers the plan, while the plan itself is only part of the total process. Of crucial importance in this process is the extent to which effective citizen-participation has taken place in the preparation of the plan. This is a statutory requirement and, in submitting a structure plan to the Secretary of State, a local planning authority must include a statement on publicity, public participation and consultations. The selection of matters for examination will be closely linked to the effectiveness of the public participation which has been achieved. The hope is that public participation will highlight some of the crucial issues on which alternative policies need to be examined.

The first examinations in public were held in November and December 1973 on the Coventry, Solihull and Warwickshire plans, and at the beginning of 1974 on the Worcestershire plan. The Secretary of State's proposals for these plans were published some eighteen months later in September 1974. In view of the paucity of published information on the outcome of the structure plan process, it is worth quoting at some length from the press release announcing the Secretary of State's proposed modifications:

'Key proposals in all four plans deal with the proposed location of new development. The plans do themselves underline the need for flexibility in response to the changes that have taken place in forecasts of population and employment growth and the Secretary of State has been concerned to reflect these needs in his proposals.

'In Coventry he is asking the authorities to look again at the scope there is for providing additional housing land within the city. In the former Solihull County Borough area, guided by the regional strategy and a recommendation by the panel, he proposes that the plan should provide for an additional 7,000 people and some industry in an area west and south west of Widney Manor station. In addition a further 8,000 people are to be accommodated south west of Solihull outside the former County Borough area. Other additional housing proposed for the plan for the former Warwickshire County Council in areas close to the main sources of jobs in the West Midlands includes proposals for an extra 6,000 people on the eastern edge of the conurbation and 3,000–5,000 people on the eastern periphery of Coventry. In Sutton Coldfield the Secretary of State has said that provision should be made for between 15,000 and 18,500 people, depending on the rate of natural increase of the present population.

'In the case of the Worcestershire plan the panel concluded that too much provision was being proposed in the light of the latest national and regional trends, and the Secretary of State accordingly proposes to reduce by half (4,000 houses) the additional provision at Kidderminster proposed in the plan and to make lesser reductions at Droitwich and around Worcester City.

'In one area, Bromsgrove, the Secretary of State proposes to make some additional provision so that the area can provide housing sufficient for those growing up in the area and make some contribution towards the housing needs of those who have to work in the conurbation. The Secretary of State's proposals would however leave the area of Wythall, on the southern periphery of Birmingham, free from any substantial growth.

'The Secretary of State is concerned about the inadequacies of the transport policies in the plans, particularly those for Warwickshire and Worcestershire, and in these two cases proposes to direct the new local authorities to think again about those sections of the plans now that comprehensive transport programmes are being evolved and to send him proposals for altering the structure plans.

'The green belt policies in the Solihull and Warwickshire plans would broadly be approved, although it will be left to local plans to establish precise boundaries. The Worcestershire plan proposed a general extension of the green belt southwards. The Secretary of

State considers that this would devalue the concept of green belt where it applies at present and proposes to reduce the extension to small areas south of Redditch and between Droitwich and Worcester. The extension of the green belt towards Stratford-upon-Avon proposed by Warwickshire has been accepted.

'In both Worcestershire and Warwickshire, the Secretary of State's proposals would support the intention of the plans to restrict residential development in rural areas, but would leave flexibility in detailed application of the policy.

'In the Coventry plan, the proposals for the Coundon Wedge area were a matter of local controversy. The Secretary of State proposes to delete the proposed golf course from the plan, but to accept policies relating to the expansion of the Jaguar works and the provision of a new road.

'In all four plans the Secretary of State proposes modifications which would remove the policies for development control which are at an inappropriate level of detail for a structure plan and substitute general policies.'

It is not at all clear from this statement (and even less so from the reports of the panels who conducted the examination in public) what *is* the 'appropriate level of detail for a structure plan'. But it is early days yet and no doubt a clearer picture will emerge over the next few years. In this connection, it is interesting to note that, in March 1975, the Secretary of State proposed further modifications to the Worcestershire plan. It was stressed that these did not make any changes of substance to the earlier proposals: they merely 'clarified' them. In particular, it was the objective to make it clear that 'in approving the structure plan, the Secretary of State will not be approving particular sites for development'.

All this is an attempt to ensure that the Secretary of State deals only with strategic issues, leaving detailed proposals for decision by the local planning authorities.

Chapter VI

THE CONTROL OF DEVELOPMENT

With certain exceptions, all development requires the prior approval of the local planning authority. The authority has considerable discretion in this matter. Though it must 'have regard to the provisions of the development plan' it may take 'any other material considerations' into account. Indeed it can approve a proposal which 'does not accord with the provisions of the plan'. If the proposal does not involve a substantial departure from the plan and does not 'injuriously affect the amenity of the adjoining land' its discretion is unlimited. In other cases it requires prior approval of the Secretary of State.

The planning decisions of the authority can be one of three kinds: unconditional permission, permission 'subject to such conditions as they think fit', or refusal. The practical scope of these powers is discussed in a later section. Here it is necessary merely to stress that there is a right of appeal to the Secretary of State against conditional permissions and refusals. If the action of the authority is thought to be *ultra vires* there is also a right of appeal to the courts. Furthermore, planning applications which raise issues which are of major importance, or are of a particular technical nature, can be 'called in' for ministerial decision.

Development control necessarily involves some procedure for enforcement. This is provided by 'enforcement notices' under which an owner who carries out development without permission or in breach of conditions can be compelled to 'undo' the development – even if this involves the demolition of a new building. A 'stop notice' can also be used in conjunction with an enforcement notice to put a rapid stop to the carrying out or continuation of development which is in breach of planning control.

These are very strong powers and clearly it is important to establish the meaning of 'development', particularly since the term has a legal meaning far wider than in ordinary language.

THE DEFINITION OF DEVELOPMENT

In brief, development is 'the carrying out of building, engineering, mining or other operations in, on, over or under land, or the making of any material change in the use of any buildings or other land'. There are some legal niceties attendant upon this definition with which it is fortunately not necessary to deal in the present outline. Some account of the breadth of the definition is, nevertheless, needed. 'Building operations', for instance, include rebuilding operations, structural alterations of or additions to buildings and – somewhat curiously – 'other operations normally undertaken by a person carrying on business as a builder'; but maintenance and improvement works which affect only the interior of the building or which do not materially affect the external appearance of the building are specifically excluded. The demolition of a building does not *of itself* constitute development, though, of course, it may form part of a building operation, or lead to the making of a material change in the use of the land upon which it stood. (There is further discussion on the control of demolition at the end of this chapter.)

The second half of the definition introduces quite a different concept: development here means not a physical operation, but a change in the *use* of a piece of land or a structure. The change has to be 'material', i.e. substantial – a concept which it is clearly difficult to define; and which, indeed, is not defined in the Act. A change in *kind* (for example from a house to a shop) is material, but a change in *degree* is material only if the change is very substantial. For instance, the fact that lodgers are taken privately in a family dwelling-house does not of itself constitute a material change so long as the main use of the house remains that of a private residence. On the other hand, the change from a private residence with lodgers to a declared guest-house, boarding house or private hotel would be material. Difficulties arise with changes of use involving part of a building with secondary uses and with the distinction between a material change of use and a mere interruption. Two changes of use are specifically declared in the legislation to be material. First, if a building previously used as a single dwelling-house is used as two or more dwelling-houses (thereby making decisions under the Rent Restriction Acts on what constitutes a 'separate dwelling' relevant to planning decisions). Second, the deposit of refuse or waste material on land 'notwithstanding that the land is comprised in a site already used for that purpose, if either the superficial area of the deposit is thereby extended, or the height of the deposit is thereby extended and exceeds the level of the land adjoining the site'; in other words the deposit of refuse or waste material always constitutes development unless the deposit is made in a hole – and the shape of the hole is important because though a hole can be filled to the level of the adjoining land the superficial area must not be increased.

This is by no means the end of the matter, but enough has been recorded to show the breadth of the definition of development and the technical complexities to which it can give rise. Reference must, nevertheless, be made to one further issue. Experience has shown that complicated definitions are necessary if adequate development control is to be achieved, but the same tortuous technique can be used to exclude matters over which control is not necessary. Apart from certain matters which are specifically declared not to constitute development (e.g. internal alterations to buildings, works of road maintenance or improvement carried out by a local highway authority within the boundaries of a road), and others which though possibly constituting development are declared not to require planning permission, there is provision for the Secretary of State to make a Development Order specifying classes of 'permitted' development, and a Use Classes Order specifying groups of uses within which interchange is permissible.

The distinction between the Use Classes Order and the General Development Order is that the former lists changes of use which do not constitute development, while the latter lists activities which, though constituting development, do not require *ad hoc* permission. The distinction was of importance during the time when development charges were imposed, since if there was no 'development' then no development charge was payable, whereas development was, by definition, eligible for a charge. (In fact, however, exemption from development charge was specifically made for many of these permitted developments.) These complexities are now mainly of historical interest and are not discussed further in this book.

THE USE CLASSES ORDER

To deal first with the latter: the Use Classes Order prescribes classes of use within which change can take place without constituting development. Thus Class X is 'use as a wholesale warehouse or repository for any purpose', and Class XII is 'use as a residential or boarding school or residential college'. For some classes particular uses which would otherwise fall into a category are specifically excluded: for example, Class I is 'use as a shop for any purpose except as (i) a shop for the sale of hot food; (ii) a tripe shop; (iii) a shop for the sale of pet animals or birds; (iv) a cat's-meat shop; (v) a shop for the sale of motor vehicles'. As a result, to change a sweet shop into a book shop does not constitute development, but to change a shoe shop into a 'noxious trade' such as a tripe shop does. These categories, it should be stressed, refer only to changes of use – not to any building work. Furthermore, the order gives no freedom to change from one class to another; whether such a change constitutes development depends on whether the change is 'material'. It should also be noted that in granting permission for a particular use a local planning authority may impose conditions restricting that use and thus prevent the changes in use allowed by the Order. For instance, a local planning authority may decide that an office of a special character might be allowed in a residential area but at the same time may not wish the premises to be available for any type of office use. Conditions could be imposed on the planning permission which would overrule the general permission given for such a change in use by the Use Classes Order (Class II is 'use as an office for any purpose').

THE GENERAL DEVELOPMENT ORDER

The General Development Order gives the developer a little more freedom by listing classes of 'permitted development'. If a proposed development falls within these classes then no application for planning permission is necessary – the General Development Order itself constitutes the permission. The Order includes certain developments by public authorities and nationalised industries, the erection of agricultural buildings (other than dwelling-houses), and permits the change of use from a shop for the sale of hot food, a tripe shop, etc. (as listed in Class I of the Use Classes Order), to any other type of shop – but not, of course, the other way round.

Permissions given under this Order are not unqualified. Apart from a general limitation relating to development which 'requires or involves the formation, laying out or material widening of a means of access to an existing highway which is a trunk or classified road or creates an obstruction to the view of persons using any highway by vehicular traffic at or near any bend, corner, junction or intersection so as to be likely to cause danger to such persons', particular conditions are laid down for each of the different classes of development listed. Thus, under Class I, the enlargement, improvement or other alteration of a dwelling-house is permitted (including the building of a garage) subject to limitations of size and elevation.

This by no means complete account of 'development' is sufficient for present purposes. The cynic may perhaps be forgiven for commenting that the 'freedom' given by the Use Classes Order and the General Development Order is so hedged by restrictions, and frequently so difficult to comprehend (though he may note with relief that painting is not subject to control – unless it is 'for purpose of advertisement, announcement or direction') that it would be safer to assume that any operation constitutes 'development' and requires planning permission. The framers of the legislation have here been helpful. Application can be made to the local planning authority (either as part of an application for planning permission or as a separate application) for a 'determination' as to whether a proposed operation constitutes 'development' and, if so, as to whether planning permission is required. Should the local planning authority determine that the proposals do constitute or involve development, they have to inform the applicant of grounds on which they have reached this decision and also of his rights of appeal. Most planning decisions are administrative acts against which appeal lies only to the Secretary of State, but in the case of a determination of whether planning permission is required, the question is a mixed one of fact and law: thus not only is there the normal right of appeal against the local authority's decision to the Secretary of State, there is also a right of appeal against his decision to the High Court.

CONDITIONAL PERMISSIONS

A local planning authority can grant a planning permission subject to conditions. This can be a very useful way of permitting development which would otherwise be undesirable. Thus residential development in an area liable to subsidence can be permitted subject to the condition that the foundations are suitably reinforced, or a garage may be approved in a residential area on condition that 'no panel beating or paint spraying is carried out, and the hours of business are kept within reasonable limits'. The local planning authority's power to impose conditions is a very wide one. The legislation allows them to grant permission subject to 'such conditions as they think fit' – but this does not mean 'as they please'. The conditions must be appropriate from a planning point of view: 'the planning authority are not at liberty to use their powers for an ulterior object, however desirable that object may seem to them to be in the public interest. If they mistake or misuse their powers, however *bona fide*, the court can interfere by declaration and injunction.'* Three types of condition are specifically referred to in the legislation:

* *Pyx Granite Co. Ltd v. Ministry of Housing and Local Government*, 1 QB 554, p. 572. This famous case is widely reported in legal texts.

(1) Conditions can be imposed for regulating the development or use of *any* land under the control of the applicant, whether or not it is land to which the application relates, so long as there is a definite relationship between the object of the condition and the development permitted.

(2) A 'time condition' can be imposed on a permission. This is referred to in the legislation as 'permission granted for a limited period only'. Such a condition is particularly appropriate where the proposed development is undesirable on a long-term view, but there is no reason why a temporary permission should not be granted. This would occur where a local authority has definite plans for redevelopment in the near future.

(3) A condition can be imposed requiring operations to commence within a specified time. It should be borne in mind that planning permissions normally run with the land. This particular condition can be imposed where the planning proposals for the area will require substantial revision, but the degree of risk that the proposed development will conflict with these proposals is not sufficient to justify outright refusal.

Until the passing of the 1968 Act, there was no general time-limit within which development had to take place: unless a specific condition was imposed, planning permission development could take place at any time. The 1968 Act, however, made all planning permissions subject to a condition that development is begun within five years. If the work is not begun within this time-limit, the permission lapses. The Secretary of State or the local planning authority can vary the period, and there is no bar to the renewal of permission after the period (whether it be five years or more or less) has elapsed.

The purpose of this new provision is to prevent the accumulation of unused permissions and to discourage the speculative land-hoarder. (For this reason it applies to pre-1968 Act permissions as well as later ones.) Accumulated unused permissions could constitute a difficult problem for some local authorities: they create uncertainty and could make an authority reluctant to grant further permissions, which might result in, for example, too great a strain on public services. The new provision is directed towards the bringing forward of development for which permission has been granted, and thus to enable new allocations of land for development to be made against a reasonably certain background of pending development.

The provision relates, however, only to the beginning of development and this apparently includes 'digging a trench or putting a peg in the ground'. But (if the permission is not a pre-1968 Act one) the trench-digger may be brought up against a further new provision: he may be served with a 'completion notice'. Such a notice states that the planning permission lapses after the expiration of a specified period (of not less than one year). Any work carried out after then becomes liable to enforcement proceedings.

ENFORCEMENT OF PLANNING CONTROL

If the machinery of planning control is to be effective some means of enforcement is essential. Under the pre-war system of interim development control there were no such means. A developer could go ahead without applying for planning permission, or could even ignore a refusal of permission. He took the risk of being compelled to 'undo' his development (e.g. demolish a newly built house) when – and if – the planning scheme was approved, but this was a risk which was often worth taking. And if the development was inexpensive and lucrative (e.g. a petrol station or a greyhound racing track) the risk was virtually no deterrent at all. This flaw in the pre-war system has been remedied. There is now machinery for dealing with development carried out without planning permission or in contravention of conditions laid down in a grant of permission.

Development undertaken without permission is not an offence in itself; but ignoring an enforcement notice is – there is a maximum fine following conviction of £400 and a penalty of £50 for each day during which the requirements of the notice remain unfulfilled.

These are very drastic powers; but there are a number of safeguards. In the first place a local authority can serve an enforcement notice only 'if they consider it expedient to do so having regard to the provisions of the development plan and to any other material considerations'; in short, they must be satisfied that enforcement is necessary in the interests of good planning. Secondly, in the case of building or other operations (but not of material changes of use) the notice must be served within four years of the development being carried out. (Prior to the 1968 Act this 'four-year rule' applied to all development including change of use.) Thirdly – and this meets the case of development carried out in good faith, or ignorance – application can be made for retrospective permission. It is hardly likely that a local authority would grant permission for a development against which they had served an enforcement notice, but they could, of course, attach conditions; and for the owner there is the usual right of appeal. Fourthly, there is a right of appeal against an enforcement notice to the Secretary of State and to the courts.

Appeals can be made on several grounds, e.g. that permission ought to be granted, that permission has been granted, and that no permission is required.

The 1968 Act introduced a further enforcement device: the 'stop notice'. This is an attempt to prevent delays in the other enforcement procedures (and advantage being taken of these delays) resulting in the local authority being faced with a *fait accompli*. Previously, when an appeal was lodged against an enforcement notice there was nothing to stop development continuing while the appeal was being 'determined'. The appeal could take several months, particularly in cases where a local inquiry was held. No liability was involved, since, until the enforcement order was made (if it was), no offence was being committed. The stop notice prohibits the continuation of development which is alleged (in the enforcement notice) to be in breach of planning control. Development carried out in contravention of a stop notice constitutes an offence. Local authorities must, however, use this new power with circumspection, since if the enforcement notice is quashed on appeal they are liable to pay compensation for loss due to the stop notice.

REVOCATION, MODIFICATION AND DISCONTINUANCE

The powers of development control possessed by local authorities go considerably further than the granting or withholding of planning permission. They can interfere with existing uses and revoke a permission already given even if the development has actually been carried out.

A revocation or modification order is made when the development has not been undertaken (or before a change of use has taken place). The local authority must 'have regard to the development plan and to any other material considerations', and an order has to be confirmed by the Secretary of State. Compensation is payable on two grounds: first, for any expenditure or liabilities incurred after the permission has been granted (e.g. expenditure on the preparation of plans); and second (following the 1954 Act), for the loss in the development value of the land. The logic in the latter is based on the curious situation caused by the abolition of development charges. The granting of planning permission increases the value of the land in question, but since no development charge is now levied the development value is thus given to the owner along with the planning permission. The revocation of that permission deprives the owner of a value which had been specifically given to him, hence compensation is payable. (Before the 1954 Act, logic demanded otherwise. The fact that revocation thereby deprived the owner of potential development value did not in itself warrant compensation, since if permission had been given the development value would be transferred to the State through the development charge.)

A revocation or modification order is not very often made. One case which attracted some attention was that of the Eton Fish and Chip Restaurant. This concerned an application for planning permission to use premises in Eton High Street as a fish and chip restaurant. The Eton Urban District Council granted permission (under delegated powers), but after a petition, mainly from local shopkeepers, decided to seek a revocation order on the ground that 'the existence of a fish and chip restaurant in the High Street would be detrimental to the amenities, would cause nuisance, offence and annoyance to occupiers of properties in the vicinity and to users of the public highway, and would adversely affect the general appearance of the High Street'. The order was confirmed by the minister. In this particular case it would seem that planning permission had been given after inadequate consideration of publicity. The revocation was therefore a rectification of a 'mistake'.

Quite distinct from these powers is the much wider power to make a discontinuance order. This power is expressed in extremely wide language: an order can be made 'if it appears to a local planning authority that it is expedient in the interests of the proper planning of their area (including the interests of amenity)'. Again ministerial confirmation is required and compensation is payable – for depreciation, disturbance and expenses incurred in carrying out works in compliance with the order. Under this power, action can be taken against any development (or use) whether it was specifically permitted under the post-war planning Acts or established prior to the Acts. It would appear that an order will be confirmed only if the case is a strong one. In rejecting a discontinuance order on a scrap metal business in an 'attractive residential area', for instance, the minister said: 'the fact that such a business is out of place in an attractive residential area must be weighed in the light of an important distinction between the withdrawal of existing use rights, as sought in the discontinuance order, and the refusal of new rights'. In this particular case the minister did 'not feel justified in overriding the proper interests of the objector as long as his business is maintained on an inoffensive scale'. Other cases have established the principle that a stronger case is needed to justify action to bring about the discontinuance of a use than would be needed to warrant a refusal of permission in the first instance.

It needs to be stressed that British planning legislation does not assume – as does American planning – that existing non-conforming uses must disappear if planning policy is to be made effective. This may often be the avowed policy, but the Planning Acts explicitly permit the continuance of existing uses.

This problem of non-conforming uses is an extremely difficult one. As the Uthwatt Committee pointed out:

'The question whether the right to maintain, replace, extend and use an existing building is to subsist in perpetuity, notwithstanding that the building does not conform to the provisions of the scheme is fundamental in relation to the replanning of built-up areas. On the one hand, it would not be equitable, without compensation, at any time and for any reason to remove, or to prohibit the maintenance, replacement, extension or use of an existing building. On the other hand, an unqualified right, unless compensation is paid, to replace non-conforming buildings and to maintain existing uses permanently is inconsistent with the present conception of planning. The problem is one of finding a proper balance between the two considerations.'

The Committee proposed that a 'life' should be placed on non-conforming uses and that at the expiration of that life the use should be brought to an end without compensation. This recommendation was not accepted, and thus local planning authorities can extinguish a non-conforming use only by paying compensation: this can be a very expensive business.

CONTROL OF DEVELOPMENT UNDERTAKEN BY GOVERNMENT DEPARTMENTS

Development by government departments does not require planning permission, but there have been special arrangements for 'consultations' since 1950 (set out in MTCP Circular 100 of that year). Increased public and professional concern about the inadequacy of these led to new (but still non-statutory) arrangements being made in 1971 (DoE Circular 80/71). These provide that:

(a) proposals for development by government departments are in general given publicity in the same way as proposals for private development;
(b) the extent to which departments undertake development without consultation has been redefined by reference to the kind of development permitted by the General Development Order;
(c) proposals to demolish or materially alter buildings of special architectural or historical interest have been brought formally into the system;

(d) time limits now apply to the start of development by government departments which has been cleared after consultation in the same manner as they apply to private development.

These provisions apply to all bodies entitled to Crown exemption from planning control, including health authorities and the industrial estates corporations. The Crown Estate Commissioners and the Duchies of Cornwall and Lancaster have agreed to consult local authorities about their proposals in the same way.

Consultations take place when the proposed development falls within one of three categories: when it is of a nature for which, if the government department were a private developer, local authority or statutory undertaker, they would require planning permission; when it involves a change of use which is not within any of the classes set out in the current Use Classes Order; and when it is a motorway service area or motorway maintenance compound, a lorry area, picnic site or lavatories proposed in connection with a trunk road.

The formal procedure is for the government department to send to the local authority a 'notice of proposed development'. The local authority can then make 'representations' to the department concerned and, if any differences of view cannot be resolved, the matter is referred to the DoE. The next steps 'depend upon the circumstances', and range from an informal meeting to a non-statutory public inquiry.

CONTROL OF DEVELOPMENT UNDERTAKEN BY LOCAL AUTHORITIES AND STATUTORY UNDERTAKERS

Development undertaken by local authorities and statutory undertakers is also subject to special planning procedures. ('Statutory undertakers' are defined as 'persons authorized by any enactment to carry on any railway, light railway, road transport, water transport, canal, inland navigation, dock, harbour, pier or lighthouse undertaking, or any undertaking for the supply of electricity, gas, hydraulic power or water'.) Where a development requires the authorisation of a government department (as do developments involving compulsory purchase orders, work requiring loan sanction, and developments such as local authority housing on which government grants are paid) the authorisation is usually accompanied by 'deemed planning permission'. Much of the normal development of local authorities and statutory undertakers (e.g. road works, laying of underground mains and cables) is 'permitted development' under the General Development Order. Local planning authorities are also 'deemed' to have permission for any development in their area which accords with the provisions of the development plan. The Secretary of State has power, however, to require them to apply for his permission in any particular case. Other local authorities are normally required to obtain planning permission from the local planning authority. If a local planning authority wish to develop in the area of another planning authority they must apply to that authority for planning permission in the same way as would a private developer.

Statutory undertakers wishing to carry out development which is neither 'permitted development' nor authorised by a government department have to apply for planning permission to the local planning authority in the normal way, but in the case of 'operational land' appeals are considered jointly by the Secretary of State and the 'appropriate Minister'. ('Operational land' is land which, in respect of its nature and situation, is not 'comparable with land in general'. This is a rather imprecise definition, but land used for railway sidings or a gas works is operational land whereas land used for showrooms or offices is not.) Until recently, statutory undertakers could be 'controlled' only on the payment of compensation by the local planning authority.

The privileged position of statutory undertakers has not escaped criticism, and two highly controversial developments proposed in 1967 created a public outcry. The first was the proposal by the Southern Gas Board to erect a 128-feet-high gasholder in the historic centre of Abingdon. The second was the proposal by the Gas Council for a terminal at Bacton in East Anglia to process North Sea Gas.

In the former case the minister withdrew the Gas Board's right of 'permitted development' and planning permission for the gasholder was refused. Compensation of £250,000 was involved and this was met on a fifty-fifty basis between the local authorities concerned and the Gas Board.

In the Bacton case, permission for development was given after two exhaustive public inquiries, but subject to rigorous conditions.

These cases brought matters to a head. The original justification for the special position of statutory undertakers was that they are under an obligation to provide services to the public and cannot, like a private firm in planning difficulties, go elsewhere. If a planning authority wished to restrict their activities, it was held that it was only right for the extra costs to be reimbursed.

In the debates on the 1968 Town and Country Planning Bill, the minister said that the climate of opinion had now changed. It was still necessary for planning to pay sensible attention to the need to provide essential public services economically. But modern industrial undertakings had to be prepared to conduct their businesses in a way which minimised ugliness and to accept any reasonable cost involved in making their buildings, plant and operations acceptable to public opinion.

A working party of officials of statutory undertakers and government departments was set up to consider the planning implications of developments by statutory undertakers and to review the relevant planning legislation. The first fruit of their work was legislation which provided that no land which was not already operational could become so unless certain planning requirements were met, The most important of these is that there shall be a specific planning permission for development for operational purposes. Moreover, a long-standing compensation principle was breached: compensation for refusal of planning permission was abolished in certain types of case.

The privileged position of statutory undertakers was further reduced in 1973 when a 'code of practice' was agreed between departments and 'commended' by the appropriate ministers to statutory undertakers (DoE Circular 12/73, Appendix C). Essentially this 'asks' statutory undertakers 'to ensure that both planning authorities and the public know of proposals for permitted development that are likely to affect them significantly before the proposals are finalised'. Though there is 'difficulty of defining classes of development and sensitive areas in general terms', this in itself 'makes it the more important that there should be local consultation between statutory undertakers and planning authorities'.

In an earlier edition of this book, this section ended with the comment that statutory undertakers (and government departments) were either exempted from planning provisions or were effectively beyond their reach. This statement is no longer true, and it is likely that it will become even less so in the future.

CARAVANS

In view of the controversy (and extensive litigation) on caravan sites which occurred in the fifties, caravan sites were made subject to special control in 1960 (by Part I of the Caravan Sites and Control of Development Act, 1960). This legislation has remained as a separate code and is not consolidated in the Town and Country Planning Act of 1971. (The Caravan Sites Act, which deals mainly with the protection from eviction of caravan dwellers and gypsies is similarly separate: this is touched on later in this section.)

Sir Arton Wilson's report, *Caravans as Homes*, highlighted the problems of residential caravanning. In 1959 about 60,000 caravans in England and Wales were being used as homes by some 150,000 people – mainly young married couples, often with small children. About 80 per cent of caravan dwellers hoped to move into normal dwellings. To quote the report, they live in caravans 'because they could not get other dwellings in the right places or on the right terms; or because caravans meet their needs for cheapness, convenience or mobility'. Some simply like caravan life.

The report estimated that about 38,000 of the 60,000 caravans were on sites for which permission, usually conditional or temporary, had been given; about 12,000 had 'existing use' rights; and about 10,000 were on sites which appeared to contravene planning control. With some notable exceptions, local authorities tended to regard caravans as a sub-standard form of accommodation and (less debatably) difficult to control. (It was the publicity given to a case in Egham which led to the setting up of the Arton Wilson Committee.) The caravan interests, on the other hand, argued the case for recognition of caravanning as an acceptable way of life and pressed for more positive approaches by the local authorities.

The 1960 Act gave local authorities new powers to control caravan sites, including a requirement that all caravan sites had to be licensed before they could start operating (thus closing loopholes in the planning and public health legislation). These controls over caravan sites operate in addition to the normal planning system: thus both planning permission and a licence have to be obtained. Most of the Act dealt with control, but local authorities were given wider powers to provide caravan sites. The *Policy Note* on caravans states:

'Planning policy recognizes the demand for sites. The main objectives of policy are, first, to enable the demand to be met in the right places, while preventing sites from springing up in the wrong places; and, second, to allow caravan sites, where permitted, to be established on a permanent or long-term basis, in order to facilitate the provision of proper services and equipment and to allow the occupants reasonable security of tenure.'

In fact, in 1973, of the 6,930 residential caravan planning applications decided in England and Wales nearly a third were refused and over three-fifths were granted for a limited period only. Only 619 were granted without a time-limit. Local authorities face strong pressure from their ratepayers 'to preserve local amenities and property values', to which caravans are seen as a threat. The DoE may be clear as to what 'planning policy recognizes' but the reality differs considerably from the official statement.

One group of caravanners is particularly unpopular: gypsies, or, to give them their less romantic statutory description, 'persons of nomadic life, whatever their race or origin' (but excluding 'members of an organized group of travelling showmen, or persons engaged in travelling circuses, travelling together as such'). The appalling conditions in which the majority of the 15,000 gypsies live in England and Wales were portrayed in the 1967 report of the DoE's Sociological Research Section, *Gypsies and Other Travellers.** As was stated in the foreword to this report, the basic problem is that no one wants gypsies around: 'all too often the settled community is concerned chiefly to persuade, or even force, the gypsy families to move on'. Under Part II of the Caravan Sites Act, 1968, local authorities in England and Wales (but not Scotland) have a duty to provide adequate sites for gypsies 'residing in or resorting to' their areas.

Holiday caravans are subject to the same planning and licensing controls as residential caravans. To ensure that a site is used only for holidays (and not for 'residential purposes'), planning permission can include a condition limiting the use of a site to the holiday season. Conditions may also be imposed to require the caravans to be removed at the end of each season or to require a number of pitches on a site to be reserved for touring caravans.

A DoE *Policy Note*, published in 1969, states that it is the aim 'to steer holiday caravan development to a limited number of areas, usually those in which caravans are already established, rather than allow them to be scattered more widely'.

In 1973, of the 1,770 planning applications for holiday caravan sites, a half were refused, a third granted for a limited period and 292 granted without a time-limit.

PURCHASE NOTICES

A planning refusal does not of itself confer any right to compensation. On the other hand, revocations of planning permission or interference with existing uses do rank for compensation, since they involve a taking away of an existing right. There are other circumstances in which planning controls so affect the value of the land to the owner that some means of reducing the hardship is clearly desirable. For example, the allocation of land in a development plan for a school will probably reduce the value of houses on this land or even make them completely unsaleable. In such cases the affected owner can serve a notice on the local authority requiring them to purchase the property at an 'unblighted' price. Broadly,

* See also the Scottish report, *Scotland's Travelling People*, HMSO, 1971.

such a purchase notice can be served, if, as a result of a planning action, land becomes 'incapable of reasonably beneficial use'. In all cases ministerial confirmation is required. The cases in which a purchase notice can be served include:

(i) refusal or conditional grant of planning permission;
(ii) revocation or modification of planning permission;
(iii) discontinuance of use;
(iv) 'planning blight'.

Normally, if an owner is refused permission to develop his land (or, if onerous conditions are laid down) there is nothing he can do about it – except, of course, appeal to the Secretary of State. But, if the refusal or the conditions prevent him from obtaining 'reasonably beneficial use' of the land, he can serve a purchase notice. MHLG Circular 33/69 states that 'the question to be considered in every case is whether the land in its existing state and with its existing permissions (including operations and uses for which planning permission is not required) is incapable of reasonably beneficial use. In considering what capacity for use the land has, relevant factors are the physical state of the land, its size, shape and surroundings, and the general pattern of use in the area. A use of relatively low value may be reasonably beneficial if such a use is common for similar land in the neighbourhood.'

A purchase notice is not intended to apply to a case in which an owner is simply prevented from realising the full potential value of his land. This would imply the acceptance in principle of paying compensation for virtually all refusals and conditional permissions. It is only if the existing and permitted uses of the land are so seriously affected as to render the land incapable of reasonably beneficial use that the owner can take advantage of the purchase notice procedure.

BLIGHT NOTICES

Redress by way of a purchase notice provided for owners affected by planning blight was introduced in 1959. It was extended in 1968 (since when it has been termed a 'blight notice') and further extended in 1973. The object is to deal with the problem presented to certain classes of owners by the fact that a development is planned to take place on their land at some future (probably uncertain) date. A development plan may, for instance, show the line of a proposed road, though not necessarily the year in which it is to be constructed. In the meantime, an owner who wishes to move and sell his property has to wrestle with the problem of 'blight'. These purchase notice provisions are restricted to owner-occupiers of houses and small businesses who can show that they have made reasonable attempts to sell their property but have found it impossible to do so except at a substantially depreciated price because of certain defined planning actions. These include land designated for compulsory purchase or allocated or defined by a development plan for any functions of a government department, local authority, statutory undertaker or the National Coal Board; and land on which the Secretary of State has given written notice of his intention to provide a trunk road or a 'special road' (i.e. a motorway).

The introduction of the new type of development plan under the 1968 Act involved new provisions in relation to planning blight. Briefly, the effect of these is that in those areas where a structure plan comes into force, blight caused by either the structure plan or the previous development plan is covered by the planning blight provisions until a local plan allocating land succeeds the old development plan. That local plan then becomes the relevant plan for the blight provisions. Since local plans provide a much more precise indication of the possibility of public acquisition of any land, the structure plan is then no longer relevant.

Structure plans, however, lack this precise indication. Whether they will give rise to more or to less planning blight than the old development plan system remains to be seen. The Planning Advisory Group thought it unlikely that there would be any more and, 'in so far as they show less detail (e.g. town map primary school and minor open space allocations) it may be less'. On the other hand, in the debates on the Bill, it was officially stated that:

'When we are dealing with the structure plan for which there is no local plan in force, we have a new problem which is that, owing to the diagrammatic nature of the plans, no one will be able to say with certainty that this does or does not affect the claimant's property, but that nevertheless, because of that very uncertainty, a wider number of properties may be affected.'

After parliamentary pressure, the Secretary of State advised a wider range of circumstances in which local authorities were urged to use their discretionary powers (DoE Circular 46/70). More recently, the 1973 Land Compensation Act has given statutory effect to these and has made other significant changes to the planning blight provisions and, furthermore, extended them to cover land affected by new town designation orders, slum clearance orders and new street orders.

THE LAND COMPENSATION ACT, 1973

The 1973 Act extends beyond planning blight and takes us into the much broader field of the law relating to compensation. This is an extremely complex field, and only an indication of some of the major features can be attempted here. Further detail is to be found in DoE Circular 73/73, *Land Compensation Act 1973*, HMSO, 1973; DoE Roads Circular 44/73, *Land Compensation Act 1973: A New Approach to the Planning and Design of Roads* (obtainable only from DoE); and, for Scotland, SDD Circular 84/1973, *Land Compensation (Scotland) Act 1973* (obtainable only from SDD).

The provisions of the Act can be rapidly summarised under five headings which relate to the five main parts of the Act.

(i) *Compensation for depreciation caused by use of public works*: this creates a new statutory right to compensation for a fall in the value of property arising from the use of highways, aerodromes and other public works which have immunity from actions for 'nuisance'. The depreciation has to be caused by physical factors such as noise, fumes, dust and vibration and the compensation is payable by the authority responsible for the works. The use of new roads or runways is thought to be the most likely to give rise to such depreciation.

(ii) *Mitigation of injurious effect of public works*: there is a range of new powers under this heading, e.g. in relation to sound insulation; the purchase of owner-occupied property which is severely affected by construction work or by the use of a new or improved highway; the erection of physical barriers (such as walls, screens or mounds of earth) on or alongside roads to reduce the effects of traffic noise on people living nearby; the planting of trees and the grassing of areas; and the development or redevelopment of land for the specific purpose of improving the surroundings of a highway 'in a manner desirable by reason of its construction, improvement, existence or use'.

(iii) *Provision for benefit of persons displaced from land*: of particular significance here is the introduction of Home Loss Payments as a mark of recognition of the special hardship created by compulsory dispossession of one's home. Since these payments are for this purpose they are quite separate from, and are not dependent upon, any right to compensation or the new Disturbance Payment which is described below. Logically they apply to tenants as well as to owner-occupiers and are given for all displacements whether by compulsory purchase, redevelopment or any action under the Housing Acts.

Additionally, there is a general entitlement to a Disturbance

Payment for persons who are not entitled to compensation, and local authorities are given a duty 'to secure the provision of suitable alternative accommodation where this is not otherwise available on reasonable terms, for any person displaced from residential accommodation' by acquisition, redevelopment, demolition and closing orders, etc. This provision goes a long way towards implementing the recommendation on rehousing obligations of the Central Housing Advisory Committee. (See CHAC, *Council Housing: Purposes, Procedures and Priorities*, HMSO, 1969, Chapter 7.)

(iv) *Compulsory purchase*: a number of changes are made in the law relating to the assessment of compensation. These are aimed at improving the provisions and meeting some particular problems. A right is also given to the advance payment of compensation.

(v) *Planning blight*: important changes are made to the planning blight provisions. In particular the classes of land in respect of which blight notices may be served are extended, for example, to land affected by proposals in structure plans or local plans submitted to the Secretary of State, to new town areas covered by a draft or substantive New Town Designation Order, and to dwellings and other buildings within areas declared to be a Clearance Area (in Scotland, a Housing Action Area).

DEVELOPMENT CONTROL IN ENGLAND AND WALES FOLLOWING REORGANISATION

Before reorganisation, development control was the responsibility of county boroughs and counties, though in the counties there was a wide measure of delegation to districts. The amount of delegation depended on the size and staffing of the districts, but there was a clear trend to greater delegation during the sixties. There was, however, much criticism (except on the part of the district councils) on the efficiency of any system of delegation. In their evidence to the Redcliffe-Maud Commission, the Ministry of Housing and Local Government (as it then was) argued that it led neither to an improved speed nor to a better quality of development control: the advantages which flowed from delegating some of the work load to district councils was offset by the shortage of qualified planning staff in most district offices, by the limited range of problems which arose within any one area, the difficulties caused by the natural inclination of district councils to take a 'narrow view', and the extra administrative complications that limited delegation usually entailed. The ministry thought that decentralisation of planning control to area committees of the planning authority produced better results than delegation to another elected body. This view was supported by the report of the *Management Study on Development Control.* The management consultants who undertook this study concluded that, within the context of the two-tier system in administrative counties, area committees provided the best method of reconciling the rights of individuals with speed of decision, low cost and the interests of the wider community.

Delegation was essentially a means of attempting to adjust planning machinery to an out-dated local government system. It was the primary purpose of reorganisation to recast local government in a way which would make such palliatives unnecessary. But this was not to be, and the new structure makes district-county relationships even more crucial to the smooth working of the planning system. As with development plans, counties are responsible for strategic issues while districts are responsible for local issues. But since the districts are not subservient to the counties, the concept of 'delegation' is inappropriate, and thus it is essential that some clear guidelines are given to distinguish county issues from district issues.

This is done in detail in the Local Government Act of 1972 (Section 32 of Schedule 16). Though all planning applications are made, in the first instance, to the district, those which fall within the category of 'county matters' fall to be determined by the county council. These include applications:

(a) that relate to the working of minerals;
(b) that 'would conflict with, or prejudice the implementation of, fundamental provisions of the structure plan';
(c) that 'would be inconsistent with a local plan prepared by the *county council*';
(d) that 'would be inconsistent in any respect with any statement of planning policy adopted by the county planning authority or with any proposals of theirs for development which in either case have been notified by them to the district planning authority'.

DEVELOPMENT CONTROL SCHEMES

It might have been expected that, as in the case of development plan schemes, there would be a statutory requirement for the preparation (and submission to the Secretary of State) of schemes setting out the allocation of responsibilities for development control between counties and districts. This was explicitly rejected on the grounds that relationships between counties and districts should be a matter for mutual agreement, and that the Secretary of State should not be required to act as an arbitrator. Nevertheless, the DoE have advised that 'informal' (i.e. non-statutory) development control schemes should be drawn up in every area. These are to 'set out procedures for co-operation, including agreement between authorities to keep double handling to a minimum, and for the rapid resolution of differences between them about the handling of planning applications in which both have an interest' (DoE Circular 74/73).

There is, as yet, little collated information on the experience of development control in the reorganised local authorities. The Dobry Report (*Review of the Development Control System: Final Report*) sets out in full the development control schemes operated in Leicestershire and West Sussex. (These differ greatly in their detail and length: while the Leicestershire scheme takes up only one and a half pages, the West Sussex schemes takes up twenty.) Dobry notes that 'there is no clear pattern as to division of responsibility between county and district council', and lists eleven illustrations (the italics are as in the Dobry Report):

'(1) In all counties, an application which raises county matters can be *refused* by the district without reference to the county council.

(2) In one county, the county council can give *an approval in principle to* proposed development, and then leave it to the district council to process the application and to settle the details.

(3) Some county councils deal with applications within their jurisdiction after having taken *the opinion* of the district council concerned.

(4) In some counties the Development Control Scheme spells out *in detail the categories* of applications to be dealt with by the county council.

(5) In one area, *district councils are enabled to decide all applications,* including those raising 'county matters', on the advice of a joint team of county and district planning officers.

(6) In another, the district council sends *copies of all applications* to the county council each week, and county and district officers meet to discuss any case which raises county matters. The *county council* then recommends a decision to the district council.

(7) Several other county councils *insist on seeing every* application.

(8) There is an even more circuitous system whereby the *county council check every application* against approved plans and policies, and notify district councils of any potential conflicts.

Major development proposals are checked by the county *plan* staff.

(9) In another case the *county council scrutinises the agenda for each district planning committee meeting*; they are thus aware of the applications coming forward for decision without having to see each one.

(10) One county council have devised an unusual way of keeping themselves informed. They pay 25 per cent of the salary of each district planning officer, who is expected to keep the county planning officer informed, and to act for the county council on applications which raise county matters.

(11) A unique solution found provides for a *county* planning committee made up of twenty county and ten district councillors, on the assumption that each *district* would have a planning committee of fourteen district and seven county councillors. It is, therefore, possible for the district council committee to have full delegated powers, to deal with all applications. In theory, this removes the need for deciding which give rise to county matters or for categorisation of applications, except where a proposal involves more than one district or would substantially and adversely affect county interests. In these circumstances it is referred to the county planning committee. (Theory is not fully translated into practice because not all districts have set up joint committees: unfortunately, only two out of five districts have agreed to implement the arrangements described.)'

In Leicester, the City Planning Officer, Mr John Dean, notes (in a personal communication) that their experience over the first sixteen months of the new system was that the number of county matters was very small. In dealing with some 2,400 planning applications, only 25 were classified as county matters:

(a) Departures from city development plan	10
(b) Matters conflicting with county policy	5
(c) County matters determined as refusals by city council	10
	25

Though it is obviously impossible within the scope of this book to recount the experience of even a selection of local authorities, it is interesting to note the further comments which Mr Dean makes. These nicely illustrate the problems of the binary system:

'There were at one time some differences of view about how a very important planning application – for an extensive city centre redevelopment scheme – should be dealt with. Whilst the application did not conflict with the Structure Plan and did not represent a substantial departure from the existing Development Plan, the scale and impact of the proposals were such that the City Council took the view that the County authority should be brought into the deliberations, although firmly of the view that the City itself should determine the application. Despite initial disagreements about which Authority should determine the application, it finally came before the City Council together with the County Council's observations. In fact, at an earlier stage the City Planning Committee had met the prospective developers together with elected representatives and officers of the County Council. In other words, I think it could be accepted, at least in the case of Leicester and Leicestershire that there is ample scope within the flexible development control system established in this County for problems to be dealt with on a joint basis in a spirit of goodwill. At the same time it must be said that this particular application was undoubtedly extremely difficult to determine because of the interests of the City Council as local planning authority on the one hand, and the policies of the County Council as transportation authority on the other.'

STREAMLINING THE PLANNING MACHINE – THE DOBRY REPORTS

Between 1968 and 1972, the number of planning decisions by local authorities in England and Wales increased from 425,000 to 615,000, while the number of appeals rose even more dramatically. At the end of November 1973, 16,354 were outstanding, and the average period from receipt to decisions ranged up to sixty-five weeks (for cases decided by the Secretary of State after a local inquiry).

This unforeseen situation developed at the very time when local authorities were also facing the problems of reorganisation and of the introduction of structure planning. Pressure therefore mounted for 'streamlining the planning machine'. The DoE issued advice (in Circular 142/73 bearing this title) on a wide range of administrative matters related to planning applications, increased their inspectorate to deal with appeals, and appointed Mr G. Dobry, QC to undertake a rapid review of the development control system. His terms of reference were:

(i) 'To consider whether the development control system under the Town and Country Planning Acts adequately meets current needs and to advise on the lines along which it might be improved, bearing in mind the forthcoming redistribution of planning functions between local authorities, and the new system of structure and local plans.'

(ii) 'To review the arrangements for appeals to the Secretary of State under the Planning Acts, including the right of appeal and the handling of appeals in the Department of the Environment, and to make recommendations.'

Dorby issued three reports: an interim and a final report on *The Development Control System* (HMSO, 1974 and 1975) and a report on *The Control of Demolition* (HMSO, 1974).

The two reports on development control are lengthy, detailed, and very difficult to summarise (partly because of the almost staccato style in which the main analysis and recommendations are presented). Dobry's detailed recommendations (which total 161) are aimed, in his words, at giving greater freedom to harness development but also at guarding against harmful development by retaining the current scope of planning control; at separating from the main stream of applications all those which might cause harm and disposing of 'main stream applications' by rapid and routine procedures; and applying the same approach to appeals. Among the more important features of the proposed system are:

(i) a single standard application form;

(ii) a leaflet explaining how to fill it in;

(iii) information centres and (later) advice centres to help applicants and interested parties;

(iv) full publicity, to nationally laid down standards, for all planning applications;

(v) the division of the planning applications into two classes:
(A) minor and uncontroversial and
(B) major and/or controversial;

(vi) a simpler and speedier treatment for Class A applications, and a realistic but strict timetable for Class B applications;

(vii) a firm timetable for the principal steps for processing applications (which is set out in the Dobry Report);

(viii) separate public consultation codes for each of these classes;

(ix) the device of deemed permissions for Class A applications, so that in default of a decision they are automatically approved;

(x) a clearer, stricter definition of responsibility for handling planning applications as between district and county councils;

(xi) complete revision of the General Development Order to make it clearer and more comprehensible to the public.

Two Classes of Applications
The most important issue here is clearly that of dividing applications into two classes. Dobry's argument on this is worth setting out in full:

'It is tempting to assume that minor developments are automatically simple, and that planning authorities, therefore, always need less information and less time to reach sound decisions on them. That is clearly not so. As amenity societies and professional bodies were quick to point out, in commenting on the tentative distinction made in my Interim Report between house-holder applications and others, some quite "small" proposals raise major questions of principle. It should not be necessary for a small and relatively simple proposal, unlikely to arouse much objection, to run the gamut of the same stringent procedures as a major or controversial proposal. Nor ought it to wait as long for a decision. Some cases, however, including otherwise minor ones which give rise to issues of principle or could arouse controversy, will always demand a lengthier, more stringent appraisal. And so long as we have only one procedure applying to all applications, there is little hope of achieving simplicity and speed for the majority of applications. They will tend to move at the pace of the complex or the controversial few.'

Dobry concludes that, therefore, the solution is to have two categories of applications: those that are minor and uncontroversial (Class A), and those that are major or controversial or both (Class B). Applications should be streamed accordingly.

Initially, an applicant could choose in which category to place his application. An explanatory leaflet would help him to decide whether A or B better fitted his needs. He would make his application on a standard form. A wrongly categorised application would be re-streamed as a matter of course by the local authority and the applicant notified.

Any attempt to lay down rigid rules for classifying applications 'is doomed to failure', but guidance should be given in a 'national code of practice'. This would ensure that at least the following are treated as Class A:

(i) all simple cases;
(ii) all applications conforming with an approved development plan (this may have to be subject to specified limits for an experimental period);
(iii) development which only just exceeds that permitted by the

General Development Order, including Class I (development within the curtilage of a dwelling-house), Class VI (agricultural) and Class VIII (industrial) developments;

(iv) the approval of reserved matters relating to cases classed as 'A' when outline permission was sought.

Standard consultation procedures are proposed together with strict compliance with time-limits (twenty-one days for Class A, and forty-two days for Class B). Class B applications require more extensive publicity than Class A, but both classes should be subject to both compulsory and discretionary publicity:

Compulsory and Discretionary Publicity

Compulsory	Discretionary
Class A 1. Site notices or neighbour notification 2. Notification of parish council	1. Notification to local societies 2. Other compulsory items under Class B
Class B 1. Site notice *or* neighbour notification 2. Notification of parish council 3. Publication of lists of applications in local newspapers *or* on public notice boards (perhaps specially allocated for that purpose) and to registered local societies	1. Notification to local societies 2. Advertisements for individual applications in local newspapers or on notice boards (perhaps specially allocated for that purpose)

A notable innovation is the proposal that Class A applications should be deemed granted if not decided upon in forty-two days. No similar proposal is made in relation to Class B applications, but it is recommended that there should be a three-month time-limit which should be strictly adhered to. However, in cases of specially significant development, local authorities should be able to require an 'impact study', and in these cases the time-limit should be six months.

An impact study would describe the proposed development in detail and explain its likely effects on its surroundings. It would comprise a written report and whatever plans, maps, photographs, diagrams, etc. would be needed to assist understanding. In particular, it should deal with the proposed development's effect on traffic, roads and public transport; foul and surface water drainage; publicly provided services, such as schools; the appearance of the neighbourhood; employment; and noise and air pollution. Other aspects to be considered in the statement might include whether the development or its location constitute a hazard (e.g. fire risk); whether it is likely to trigger off other development; and investigation of alternative sites.

Dobry lays great emphasis on consultations and meetings between applicants and the local planning authority, particularly in relation to Class B applications. There are a number of recommendations on this, e.g. that the planning committee should interview applicants 'in suitable cases' (undefined), particularly where there is a difference of view within the committee.

Outline and Detailed Applications
Dobry maintains that the borderline between 'outline' and 'detailed' applications is at present unclear and the distinction is too inflexible. He recommends that there should be four types of application:

Outline: these should be accompanied only by a site plan.
Illustrative: these should be accompanied by a site plan and illustrative plans which would determine the character of the development.
Detailed: these should be accompanied by all building plans.
Guideline: these should include the general likely land use within an area. It is suggested that there should be a Future Development Certificate for such cases, setting out the future use likely to be permitted.

Other Recommendations
Other recommendations include the introduction of a stamp duty or similar standard charge for planning applications; the retention of detailed design control ('in spite of its subjective nature'); the use of 'design guides' for 'homogeneous areas' and of 'design briefs' for particular sites; greater delegation to officers; speedy production of structure and local plans (in accordance with a national timetable); stronger control procedures in 'special environmental areas' (e.g. national parks, conservation areas, and other areas identified in development plans or policies); the establishment of local authority information centres and independent planning advice centres (on which details of current pioneering examples are given in an Appendix to the Report).

Comment

The starting point for the Dobry inquiry was the lengthening delay in the processing of planning applications, but Dobry was quick to point out that 'not all delay is unacceptable: it is the price we must pay for the democratic planning of the environment'. Moreover, his review took into account factors which were very different from those relevant to 'streamlining the planning machine': the increasing pressure for public consultation and participation in the planning process; and the 'dissatisfaction on the part of applicants because they often do not understand why particular decisions have been made, or why it is necessary for what may seem small matters to be the concern of the planning machinery at all'. Additionally, he noted that 'many people feel that the system has not done enough to protect what is good in an environment or to ensure that new development is of a sufficiently high quality'.

Dobry therefore had a difficult task of reconciling apparently irreconcilable objectives: to expedite planning procedures while at the same time facilitating greater public participation and devising a system which would produce better environmental results. His solutions attempt to provide more speed for developers, more participation for the public *and* better quality development and conservation.

This is effected by the division of applications into 'minor' and 'major'. Despite the inherent difficulties of determining this in advance (at least to the satisfaction of the public and the local amenity societies) it is nevertheless a fact that some 80 per cent of all applications are granted, and that many of these *are* 'simple and straightforward'. Dobry's proposal, in essence, is that the 'simple' should be distinguished and treated expeditiously – though with the opportunity for some participation and with a safety channel to allow them to be transferred to the 'major' category if this should prove appropriate. These Class A applications would be dealt with by officials acting under powers delegated to them by planning committees (or, if this is unacceptable, by small sub-committees of two or three members). Publicity would be restricted in time to twenty-one days and decisions would be reached within forty-two days – failing which an application would be deemed to be approved.

This would, so Dobry believes, relieve the overloaded planning machine to deal more thoroughly with the major and/or controversial applications (which he suggests would constitute less than a half and, hopefully, only a third of the total). These would receive greater scrutiny than hitherto, and the period for decision would be increased from the present statutory (but – when applied to all applications – impracticable) two months to three months. They would receive greater public advertisement, and more important applications would need to be accompanied by an 'impact study'.

Dobry's scheme is an heroic attempt to improve the planning control system to everyone's satisfaction. It must thus inevitably disappoint everybody. For example, though he makes a number of proposals to increase effective public participation, his overriding concern for expediting procedures forces him to compress these into an impracticable time-scale. This is particularly so with his Class A applications, where twenty-one days is far too short a period for effective publicity let alone considered public reaction. Moreover, it is open to question whether the Class A procedure would relieve planning administration or, in fact, overload it still further. In practice the result might well be either a collapse of the new procedure of a perfunctory and rapid processing which would deny the public participation which Dobry wishes to increase.

In his *Interim Report*, Dobry explored some possibilities of reducing controls over aesthetic aspects of design (as distinct from 'massing or bulk') and over 'householder applications' ('applications by residential occupiers for their own better use of the property, in accordance with local authority plans or policies and giving rise to no substantial public interest'). Here the rationale was that 'the degree of control must depend upon what is practicable':

'However ideal a control system may be in theory, it will not succeed unless there are the resources (and this really means the people) to operate it. In practice it may be vital to exercise priorities, perhaps involving some lessening of control in certain respects or over certain kinds of development, in order to ensure that control is successfully achieved where it matters most. The danger, otherwise, is that work may have to be skimped so that the environment is not adequately protected anywhere, or unacceptable delays may build up. Such consequences are as unacceptable, in economic or social terms, as the environmental ills which control aims to prevent.'

He was, however, led away from this line of thought (which warrants much wider examination than Dobry gave it), and the main gist of his final conclusions is in favour of tightening control – including the control of demolition.

But the biggest shortcoming of the Dobry Report is that he never really comes to grips with the major weakness of the development control system: its general isolation from the remainder of the planning process. In Eddison's words (*Town and Country Planning,* April 1975):

'Although Dobry's terms of reference specifically refer to the "new system of structure and local plans" the essential relationships are barely mentioned, and certainly not explored, in the Review. Yet these relationships (or lack of them) are really at the heart of the weakness of the development control system . . . Development control is not, in practice, an integral part of policy making and implementation. . . .'

Similarly Jowell (*Political Quarterly*, July–August 1975) has commented that 'the major omission of the report is its failure to see development control's place in a planning system whose scope has expanded radically since 1968 . . . somehow development control has not kept pace with this change'. Nevertheless, Dobry has started a debate which may well prove to be much wider, and of greater long-term significance, than was envisaged when he was commissioned to assist in 'streamlining the planning machine'.

THE CONTROL OF DEMOLITION

It has been generally accepted that demolition of itself does not constitute 'development' and, though there is some legal uncertainty on the matter, local authorities have typically assumed that demolition is outside the ambit of development control. Nevertheless, there are extensive powers (outlined in Chapter IX) to prevent the demolition of buildings of historic or architectural quality – of which the most recent is the Town and Country Amenities Act of 1974 which brings the demolition of all buildings in conservation areas under control.

Nevertheless, there has been increasing disquiet in recent years about the lack of clear and 'blanket' control of demolition, particularly on the part of amenity societies, but also on the part of local authorities who have been concerned at some of the effects of commercial enterprise. Following the resulting parliamentary pressure, Dobry was asked to report specifically on this issue. This he did in a terse report, *Control of Demolition*, published in 1974.

He concluded that there were several 'persuasive' arguments in favour of subjecting demolition to control. These were, firstly, that 'there is a good deal of concern that the planning system should permit town centre and residential development that is sometimes strikingly out of scale or sympathy with the area affected'. Secondly, there is some uncertainty as to the law. Thirdly, there is some 'inconsistency': here the argument, curiously, is that though there are powers for the control over the demolition of certain buildings, there is no 'overall system'. Fourthly, 'and most importantly', there are four practical reasons for the general extension of control over demolition:

'(1) *The aftermath of demolition.* Barren sites, inadequately fenced, often become a dumping ground causing general deterioration of the neighbourhood. This is bad everywhere, but I am told is at its worst in twilight and other poorer areas of our cities. Vacant sites are despoiled with random deposits of furniture, broken bottles, dumped cars and other paraphernalia of vandalism and disorder.

(2) *Demolition as a 'fait accompli'* can be used by developers to force the grant of planning permission.

(3) *Premature demolition of houses.* Premature demolition and vacancy of residential accommodation in anticipation of development causes public disquiet.

(4) *Need to preserve commercial and community use.* Premature demolition of shops in a redevelopment area is clearly harmful. Many think that to prevent the demolition of useful residential buildings, theatres and cinemas is equally important.'

APPENDIX: GOVERNMENT REJECTION OF THE DOBRY REPORTS

The Dobry inquiry was instigated by a Conservative Government at a time when the property market was booming. On its completion the boom had collapsed and a Labour Government had published their outline proposals for the community land legislation. In short, the planning scene had changed fundamentally. In purely administrative terms (to quote from the January 1976 issue of the *Journal of Planning and Environment Law*), 'authorities concerned with distinguishing between applications for exempt development, excepted development, designated relevant development and non-designated relevant development could not also be expected to distinguish between Class A and Class B applications, and between outline, illustrative, detailed and guideline applications'.

The Government's decisions on the Dobry Reports are set out in detail in DoE Circular 113/75. Most of Dobry's recommendations have been rejected, though it is stressed that their objectives can typically be achieved if local authorities adopt 'the most efficient working methods'. Dobry's view that 'it is not so much the system which is wrong but the way in which it is used' is endorsed, and his *Final Report* is commended 'to students of our planning system as an invaluable compendium of information about the working of the existing development control process, and to local authorities and developers as a source of advice on the best way to operating within it'.

Chapter VII

PLANNING AND LAND VALUES

THE UTHWATT REPORT

'It is clear that under a system of well-conceived planning the resolution of competing claims and the allocation of land for the various requirements must proceed on the basis of selecting the most suitable land for the particular purpose, irrespective of the existing values which may attach to the individual parcels of land.' It was the task of the Uthwatt Committee, from whose report this quotation is taken, to devise a scheme which would make this possible. Effective planning necessarily controls, limits or even completely destroys, the market value of particular pieces of land. Is the owner therefore to be compensated for this loss in value? If so, how is the compensation to be calculated? And is any 'balancing' payment to be extracted from owners whose land appreciates in value as a result of planning measures?

This problem of compensation and 'betterment' arises fundamentally 'from the existing legal position with regard to the use of land, which attempts largely to preserve, in a highly developed economy, the purely individualistic approach to land ownership'. This 'individualistic approach', however, has been increasingly modified during the past hundred years. The rights of ownership were restricted in the interests of public health: owners had (by law) to ensure, for example, that their properties were in good sanitary condition, that new buildings conformed to certain building standards, that streets were of a minimum width, and so on. It was accepted that these restrictions were necessary in the interests of the community – *salus populi est suprema lex* – and that private owners should be compelled to comply with them even at cost to themselves.

'All these restrictions, whether carrying a right to compensation or not, are imposed in the public interest, and the essence of the compensation problem as regards the imposition of restrictions appears to be this – at what point does the public interest become such that a private individual ought to be called on to comply, at his own cost, with a restriction or requirement designed to secure that public interest? The history of the imposition of obligations without compensation has been to push that point progressively further on and to add to the list of requirements considered to be essential to the well-being of the community.'

But clearly there is a point beyond which restrictions cannot reasonably be imposed on the grounds of 'good neighbourliness' without payment of compensation – and 'general consideration of regional or national policy require so great a restriction on the landowner's use of his land as to amount to a taking away from him of a proprietary interest in the land'.

This, however, is not the end of the matter. Planning sets out to achieve a selection of the most suitable pieces of land for particular uses. Some land will therefore be zoned for a use which is profitable for the owner, whereas other land will be zoned for a use having a low – or even nil – private value. It is this difficulty of 'development value' which raises the compensation problem in its most acute form. The development which may legitimately – or hopefully – be expected by owners is in fact spread over a far larger area than is likely to be developed. This *potential* development value is therefore speculative, but until the individual owners are proved to be wrong in their assessments (and how can this be done?) all owners of land having a potential value can make a case for compensation on the assumption that their particular pieces of land would in fact be chosen for development if planning restrictions were not imposed. Yet this 'floating value' might never have settled on their land, and obviously the aggregate of the values claimed by the individual owners is likely to be greatly in excess of a total valuation of all the pieces of land. As Haar has nicely put it (in *Land Planning Law in a Free Society*), the situation is akin to that of a sweepstake: a single ticket fetches much more than its mathematically calculated value, for the simple reason that the grand prize may fall on any one holder.

Furthermore, the public control of land use necessarily involves the shifting of land values from certain pieces of land to other pieces: the value of some land is decreased, while that of other land is increased. Planning controls do not destroy land values: in the words of the Uthwatt Committee, 'neither the total demand for development nor its average annual rate is materially affected, if at all, by planning ordinances'. Nevertheless, the owner of the land on which development is prohibited will claim compensation for the full potential development of his land, irrespective of the fact that that value may shift to another site.

In theory, it is logical to balance the compensation paid to aggrieved owners by collecting a betterment charge on owners who benefit from planning controls. But previous experience with the collection of betterment had not been encouraging. The principle had been first established in an Act of 1662 which authorised the levying of a capital sum or an annual rent in respect of the 'melioration' of properties following street widenings in London. There were similar provisions in Acts providing for the rebuilding of London after the Great Fire. The principle was revived and extended in the Planning Acts of 1909 and 1932. These allowed a local authority to claim, first 50 per cent, and then (in the late Act) 75 per cent, of the amount by which any property increased in value as the result of the operation of a planning scheme. In fact, these provisions were largely ineffective since it proved extremely difficult to determine with any certainty which properties had increased in value as a result of a scheme (or of works carried out under a scheme) or, where there was a reasonable degree of certainty, how much of the increase in value was directly attributable to the scheme and how much to other factors. The Uthwatt Committee noted that there were only three cases in which betterment had actually been paid under the Planning Acts, and all these were before the 1932 Act introduced a provision for the deferment of payment until the increased value had actually been realised either by sale or lease or by change of use. In short, it had not proved possible to devise an equitable and workable system.

The Uthwatt Committee concluded that the solution to these problems lay in changing the system of land ownership under which land had a development value dependent upon the prospects of its profitable use. They maintained that no new code for the assessment of compensation or the collection of betterment would be adequate if this individualistic system remained. The system itself had inherent 'contradictions provoking a conflict between private and public interest and hindering the proper operation of the planning machinery'. A new system was needed which would avoid these contradictions and which so unified existing rights in land as to 'enable shifts of value to operate within the same ownership'. The logic of this line of reasoning led to a consideration of land nationalisation. But this the Committee rejected on the grounds that it would arouse keen political controversy, would involve insuperable financial problems, and would necessitate the establishment of a complicated national administrative machinery. In their view the solution to the problem lay in the nationalisation not of the land itself but of all development rights in undeveloped land.

THE 1947 ACT

Essentially, this is precisely what the 1947 Town and Country Planning Act did. Effectively, development rights and their associated values were nationalised. No development was to take place without permission from the local planning authority. If permission were refused, no compensation would be paid (except in a limited range of special cases). If permission were granted, any resulting increase in land value was to be subject to a development charge. The view was taken that 'owners who lose development value as a result of the passing of the Bill are not on that account entitled to compensation'. This cut through the insoluble problem posed in previous attempts to collect betterment values created by public action. Betterment had been conceived as 'any increase in the value of land (including the buildings thereon) arising from central or local government action, whether positive, for example by the execution of public works or improvements, or negative, for example by the imposition of restrictions on the other land'. The 1947 Act went further: all betterment was created by the community, and it was unreal and undesirable (as well as virtually impossible) to distinguish between values created, e.g. by particular planning schemes, and those due to other factors such as the general activities of the community or the general level of prosperity.

If rigorous logic had been followed, no payment at all would have been made for the transfer of development value to the State, but this – as the Uthwatt Committee had pointed out – would have resulted in considerable hardship in individual cases. A £300 million fund was therefore established for making 'payments' to owners who could successfully claim that their land had some development value on the 'appointed day' – the day on which the provisions of the Bill which prevented landowners from realising development values came into force. Considerable discussion took place during the passage of the Bill through Parliament on the sum fixed for compensation and it was strongly opposed on the ground that it was too small. The truth of the matter was that in the absence of relevant reliable information any global sum had to be determined in a somewhat arbitrary way; but in any case it was not intended that everybody should be paid the full value of their claims. Landowners would submit claims to a centralised agency – the Central Land Board – for 'loss of development value', i.e. the difference between the 'unrestricted value' (the market value without the restrictions introduced by the Act) and the 'existing use value' (the value subject to these restrictions). When all the claims had been received

and examined, the £300 million would be divided between claimants at whatever proportion of their 1948 value that total would
allow. (In the event the estimate of £300 million was not as far out as
critics feared. The total of all claims eventually amounted to £380
million.)

The original intention was to have a flexible rate of development
charge. In some cases 100 per cent would be levied, but in others a
lower rate would be more appropriate in order to encourage
development 'on account of economic conditions in the country
generally, or in particular areas where unemployment is above the
average', or where it was important to secure 'a particular piece of
development now, instead of in, say twenty years'. However, when
the regulations came to be made, the Government maintained that
the policy which had been set out during the passage of the Bill
through the House was unworkable. The only explanation given for
this was that 'the whole conception is that the value of land is
divided into two parts – the value restricted to its existing use and
the development value. The market value is the sum of the two. If,
by the action of the State, the Development value is no longer in the
possession of the owner of the land, then all he has left is the existing
use value. Moreover, the fund of £300 million is being provided for
the purposes of compensating the owner of land for this reduced
value . . . therefore the owner of land can have no possible claim to
any part of the development value and it is logical and right that the
State should, where development takes place, make a charge which
represents the amount of the development value.'

The whole idea of variable development charges (particularly for
the depressed areas) was rejected, and a flat-rate 100 per cent levy
introduced.

These provisions – of which only the barest summary has been
given here – were very complex, and, together with the inevitable
uncertainty as to when compensation would be paid and how much
it should be, resulted in a general feeling of uncertainty and
discontent which did not augur well for the scheme. The principles,
however, were clear. To recapitulate, all development rights and
values were vested in the State: no development could take place
without permission from the local planning authority and then only
on payment of a betterment charge to the Central Land Board. The
nationalisation of development rights was effected by the 'promised' payment of compensation. As a result landowners only
'owned' the existing use rights of their land and it thus followed,
first, that if permission to develop was refused no compensation was
payable, and, secondly, that the price paid by public authorities for
the compulsory acquisition of land would be equal to the existing

use value, i.e. its value excluding any allowance for future development.

THE 1947 SCHEME IN OPERATION

The scheme did not work as smoothly as was expected. In their first annual report the Central Land Board 'noted with concern some weeks after the Act came into operation that despite the liability for development charge land was still being widely offered and, still worse, taken at prices including the full development value'. This remained a problem throughout the lifetime of the scheme – though the magnitude of the problem still remains a matter of some controversy. It is certainly true that conditions were such that developers were prepared to pay more than existing use prices for land; but the conditions were rather extraordinary. As the Board pointed out in their second report:

'The evidence available to the Board of prices paid for land for development suggests that sales at or near existing use value are more the exception than the rule. To a large extent this is due to the severe restriction on building. Building licences are difficult to get and the developer who has been fortunate enough to obtain one is often willing to pay a much inflated price for a piece of land upon which to build. In other words, a "scarcity value" attaches at present to the possession of a licence. The theory that the development charge would leave the developer unwilling or unable to pay more than existing use value for his land is not at present working out in practice, especially since a would-be house-owner who pays building value to the seller of the land, as well as a development charge to the Board, is still paying less in the total cost of his house than he would have to pay for an existing house with vacant possession.'

It was to prevent such problems that the Central Land Board had been given powers of compulsory purchase at the 'correct' price. These powers were used – not as a general means of facilitating the supply of land at existing use prices, but selectively, 'as a warning to owners of land in general'. Furthermore, they were used only where an owner had actually offered his land for sale at a price above existing use value. Thus, purchase by the Board would have done nothing to facilitate an increase in the total supply of land for development even if they had been much more numerous. But, in fact, their very rarity served only to make the procedure arbitrary in the extreme and indeed, may have added to the reluctance of owners to offer land for development at all.

The Conservative Government which took office in 1951 were intent on raising the level of construction activity and particularly the rate of private house-building. Though, within the limits of building activity set by the Labour Government, it is unlikely that the development charge procedure seriously affected the supply of land, it is probable that the Conservative Government's plans for private building would have been jeopardised by it. This was one factor which led the new Government to consider repealing development charges.

The basic difficulty was that purchasers of land were compelled to pay a premium above the existing use value in order to persuade an owner to sell: a development charge of 100 per cent therefore constituted a permanent addition to the cost of development.

Further problems began to loom ahead as the final date for payments from the £300 million fund (1 July 1953) drew near. First, the payment of this sum of money over a short period would have a considerable inflationary effect. Secondly, all claimants on the fund would receive payment whether or not they had actually suffered any loss as a result of the 1947 Act. (Some would have already recovered the development value of the land by selling at a high price; others may never have wished to develop their land, and, indeed, might even have bought it for the express purpose of preventing its development.) But the main difficulty was that if compensation were paid out on this 'once for all' basis, 'it would be exceedingly difficult for any future Government ever to make radical changes in the financial provisions, however badly they were working. For all the holders of claims on the fund would have been compensated for loss of development value – those who will be allowed to develop their land as well as those who will not.'

Some amendment of the 1947 Act scheme was clearly desirable, but though there might have been agreement on this, there was no equal agreement on what the amendments should be. There was a real fear that an 'amendment' which satisfied developers would seriously weaken or even wreck the planning machine: the scheme was part of a complex of planning controls which might easily be upset and result in a return to the very problems which the 1947 Act was designed to solve. Various proposals were currently being canvassed, but the most popular was a reduction in the rate of development charge. The intention was to provide an incentive to owners to sell their land at a price which took account of the developer's liability to pay the (reduced) charge. The Government took the view that this was not possible: 'vendors of land, like vendors of any other commodity, will always get the best price that they can, and the development charge, however small, would in effect be passed on, in whole or in part, to the ultimate user of the land'. Furthermore, the Government's objective was not merely one of easing the market in land: they were particularly concerned to encourage more private development, and even a low rate of development charge would act as a brake. On the (implicit) assumption that market prices for land would rise, the time would inevitably come when the charge would begin to greatly exceed the corresponding claim on the £300 million fund. Finally, it was felt that once the rate of development charge was reduced there would be no clear principle as to the level at which it should continue to be levied – 'the process of reduction, once begun, would be difficult to stop'. In short, the Government held that the financial provisions of the 1947 Act were inherently unsatisfactory and could not be sufficiently improved by a mere modification: what was needed was a complete abolition of development charges.

THE 1954 SCHEME

The abolition of development charges was made on the ground that they had proved 'too unreliable an instrument to act as the lynch-pin of a permanent settlement'. But, at the same time, if the main part of the planning system was to remain, some limit to the liability to compensation for planning restrictions was essential. Otherwise effective planning controls would be prohibitively expensive: the cost of compensation for restrictions, if paid at the market value, would be crippling. The solution arrived at was to compensate only 'for loss of development value which accrued in the past up to the point where the 1947 axe fell – but not for loss of development value accruing in the future'.

There were some clear advantages in this scheme: not only was the State's liability for compensation limited, but it was to be paid only if and when the owner of land suffered from planning restrictions. The compensation would be the 'admitted claim' on the £300 million fund (plus one-seventh for accrued interest on the amount of the claim). But not all admitted claims were to be met, even where loss of development value was caused by refusal of planning permission or by conditions attached to a permission. The 1932 Act had clearly established the principle that compensation should not be paid for restrictions imposed in the interest of 'good neighbour-liness' and this principle was extended. No compensation was payable for refusal to allow a change in the use of a building; or for restrictions regarding density, layout, construction, design and so on; or for refusal to permit development which would place an undue burden on the community (e.g. in the provision of services).

Some of these matters clearly fall within the 'good neighbour' concept,* while others are based on the principle that compensation is not to be paid merely because maximum exploitation has been prevented so long as development of a reasonably remunerative character is allowed.

The 1954 scheme† did not put anything in place of the development charge: the collection of betterment was now left to the blunt instruments of general taxation. Hence the attempt to 'hold the scales evenly between those who were allowed to develop their land and those who were not' was abandoned, but the use of 1947 development values as a 'permanent basis for compensation' safeguarded the public purse. On the other hand this meted out only a very rough justice to owners. The official view – at this date – was that this was not so; to quote the 1952 White Paper:

'It may be suggested that to limit compensation in the way proposed will work unfairly in certain cases. Land which in 1947 had little development value, and therefore no claim or only a small claim on the fund, may at some future date acquire considerable development value. Values will tend to follow the development plans, and land which acquires a high development value will normally be land on which development will be permitted; but there will be exceptions and it may be thought that to limit compensation in these cases will inflict hardship on owners who are refused permission to develop or whose land is bought compulsorily. It is important, however, to remember that all transactions in land since 1947 have taken place in the full knowledge that the 1947 development value was the most that anyone would hope to receive by way of compensation from the £300 million fund. Purchasers in future will be able to safeguard themselves by ensuring that permission to develop is forthcoming before they pay more than current existing-use value or, where a claim on the fund passes with the land, current existing-use value plus 1947 development value.'

But this ignored the fact that the new scheme established a dual market in land. Compensation both for planning restrictions (in

---

* The Act did, however, extend this principle drastically: a matter which evoked some opposition. For a fuller discussion see, for example, Corfield, F. V., *Compensation and the Town and Country Planning Act, 1959*, p. 53 *et seq.*

† There were two Acts. The Town and Country Planning Act, 1953, abolished development charges, while the Town and Country Planning Act, 1954, limited compensation for the loss of development values to those sites for which a claim had been approved, and then only under defined circumstances when an application to develop was actually refused.

cases where a claim had been admitted) and for compulsory purchase by public authorities was to be paid on the basis of existing use
plus any admitted 1947 development value, but private sales would
be at current market prices. The difference between these two
values might be very substantial, particularly where development of
a far more valuable character than had been anticipated in 1947
took place. Furthermore, with the passage of time land values
generally would increase, especially if inflation continued. Whatever theoretical justification there might be for a dual market it
would appear increasingly unjust. Again, there is a real distinction
between the hardships inflicted by a refusal of planning permission
(i.e. the loss of the development value of land) and that caused by
the loss of the land itself (i.e. compulsory purchase). In the first case
the owner retains the existing use value of his land and is worse off
only in comparison with owners who have been fortunate in owning
land on which development is permitted and who can therefore
realise a capital gain. But in the second case compulsory acquisition
at less than market price involves an actual loss since the owner is
not only deprived of his property, he is also compensated at a price
which might be less than he paid for it and would almost certainly be
insufficient to purchase a similar parcel of land in the open market.

Finally, though it must be generally accepted that individuals
cannot be protected from foolish actions based on an inadequate
knowledge of the law, the situation following the 1954 Act was so
complex and – because of the inevitable unpredictability of the
necessity for compulsory purchase – so risky that it appeared likely
(in retrospect at least) that public opinion would demand a further
change. There was an omen of this even while the legislation was
passing through Parliament. A certain Mr Pilgrim had bought, in
1950, a vacant plot of land adjoining his house. To pay for this he
raised a mortgage of £500 on his house. Some years later the
Romford Borough Council compulsorily acquired the land at the
existing use value of £65. (No claim had ever been made on the £300
million fund for loss of development value.) Mr Pilgrim committed
suicide. Naturally the case attracted a lot of attention and as a result
a new provision was introduced in the 1954 Bill to alleviate the
position of persons, usually small owners, who suffered loss on
compulsory acquisition because there was no established claim on
the £300 million fund. This provision permitted the payment of an
ex gratia supplement in cases of this kind.

To recapitulate, the effect of the complicated network of legislation which was now (1954) in force was basically to create two values
for land according to whether it was sold in the open market or
acquired by a public authority. In the former case there were no

restrictions and thus land changed hands at the full market price. But in the latter case the public authority would pay only the existing (1947) use value plus any agreed claim for loss of 1947 development value. This was a most unsatisfactory outcome. As land prices increased, due partly to planning controls, the gap between existing use and market values widened – particularly in suburban areas near green belt land. The greater the amount of planning control, the greater did the gap become. Thus, owners who were forced to sell their land to public authorities considered themselves to be very badly treated in comparison with those who were able to sell at the enhanced prices resulting in part from planning restrictions on other sites. The inherent uncertainties of future public acquisitions – no plan can be so definite and inflexible as to determine which sites will (or might) be needed in the future for public purposes – made this distinction appear arbitrary and unjust. The abolition of the development charge served to increase the inequity.

The contradictions and anomalies in the 1954 scheme were obvious. It was only a matter of time before public opinion demanded further amending legislation.

THE 1959 ACT: THE RETURN TO MARKET VALUE

Opposition to this state of affairs increased with the growth of private pressures for development following the abolition of building licences. Eventually the Government were forced to take action. The resulting legislation (the Town and Country Planning Act, 1959) restored 'fair market price' as the basis of compensation for compulsory acquisition. This, in the Government's view, was the only practicable way of rectifying the injustices of the dual market for land. An owner now obtained (in theory at least) the same price for his land irrespective of whether he sold it to a private individual or to a public authority.

These provisions thus removed a source of grievance, but they did nothing towards solving the fundamental problems of compensation and betterment, and the result proved extremely costly to public authorities. If this had been a reflection of basic principles of justice there could have been little cause for complaint, but in fact an examination of the position shows clearly that this was not the case.

In the first place, the 1959 Act (like previous legislation) accepted the principle that development rights should be vested in the State. This followed from the fact that no compensation was payable for the loss of development value in cases where planning permission was refused. But if development rights belong to the State, surely so should the associated development values? Consider, for example, the case of two owners of agricultural land on the periphery of a town, both of whom applied for planning permission to develop for housing purposes – the first being given permission and the second refused on the ground that the site in question was to form part of a green belt. The former benefited from the full market value of his site in residential use, whereas the latter could benefit only from its existing value. No question of compensation arose since the development rights already belonged to the State, but the first owner had these given back to him without payment. There was an obvious injustice here which could have eventually led to a demand that the 'penalised' owner should be compensated.

Secondly, as has already been stressed, the comprehensive nature of our present system of planning control has had a marked effect on values. The use for which planning permission has been, or will be, given is a very important factor in the determination of value. Furthermore, the value of a given site is increased not only by the development permitted on that site, but also by the development not permitted on other sites. In the example given above, for instance, the value of the site for which planning permission for housing development was given might be increased by virtue of the fact that it was refused on the second site.

THE LAND COMMISSION, 1967–1971

Mounting criticism of the inadequacy of the 1959 Act led to a number of proposals for a tax on betterment, by way either of a capital gains tax or of a betterment levy. The Labour Government which was returned to power in 1964 introduced both. The 1967 Finance Act introduced a capital gains tax, and the 1967 Land Commission Act introduced a new betterment levy. Broadly, the distinguishing principle was that capital gains tax was charged on increases in the current use value of land only, while betterment levy was charged on increases in development value. The Land Commission was abolished by the Conservative Government in 1971, but a summary account of its powers and operations is appropriate.

The rationale underlying the Land Commission Act was set out in a 1965 White Paper:

'In the Government's view it is wrong that planning decisions about land use should so often result in the realizing of unearned increments by the owners of the land to which they apply, and that desirable development should be frustrated by owners withholding

their land in the hope of higher prices. The two main objectives of the Government's land policy are, therefore:
(i) to secure that the right land is available at the right time for the implementation of national, regional and local plans;
(ii) to secure that a substantial part of the development value created by the community returns to the community and that the burden of the cost of land for essential purposes is reduced.'

To enable these two objectives to be achieved a Land Commission was established (with headquarters located at Newcastle upon Tyne – in line with the dispersal of offices policy). The Commission could buy land either by agreement or compulsorily, and they were given very wide powers for this purpose. The second objective was met by the introduction of a betterment levy on development value. This was necessary not only to secure that a substantial part of the development 'returned to the community', but also to prevent a two-price system as existed under the 1954 Act. The levy was deducted from the price paid by the Commission on their own purchases and was paid by owners when they sold land privately. A landowner thus theoretically received the same net amount for his land whether he sold it privately, to the Land Commission or to another public authority.

Though the Commission could buy by agreement they had to have effective powers of compulsory purchase if they were 'to ensure that the right land is made available at the right time'. There were two reasons for this. First, though the levy was at a rate (initially 40 per cent) thought to be adequate to leave enough of the development value to provide 'a reasonable incentive', some owners of land might still be unwilling to sell. Secondly, though the net price obtained by the owner of land should have been the same irrespective of whether the body to whom he sold it was private or public, some owners might have been unwilling to sell to the Land Commission.

The Act provided two sets of compulsory powers. One was the normal powers available to local authorities, with the usual machinery for appeals and a public inquiry. Under these powers the Commission had to disclose the purpose for which they required the land. These powers could be used for purchasing land scheduled for development in a development plan, or for land permitted for development.

The second set of compulsory powers were not to become operative until the 'second appointed day' and were to be brought into effect only if it appeared 'that it is necessary in the public interest to enable the Commission to obtain authority for the compulsory acquisition of land by a simplified procedure'. They were intended to provide a rapid procedure under which objectors would have no right to state their case at a public inquiry, and the Commission were not required to disclose the purpose for which the land was needed. The purpose here was to deal quickly and effectively with landowners who were holding up development. In fact they did not become operative during the lifetime of the Land Commission.

It was intended that the Commission would often be acquiring land in advance of need. They were, therefore, given wide powers of managing and disposing of land; but they could also develop land themselves. Land could be sold or leased to public or private bodies for any purpose – even if the purpose was different from the one for which the land was purchased. Land which was sold could be made subject to restrictions and future development value could be reserved to the Commission. Such land disposals were known as 'crownhold'.

Normally, the Commission had to dispose of land at the best price they could obtain, but there was one important exception. This was the 'concessionary crownhold disposition' which could be made for land which was to be developed *for housing purposes*. Here the Commission could dispose of land at less than the market price. All such housing land was subject to crownhold restrictions or covenants. In the case of owner-occupiers the Commission had the right of pre-emption on terms which ensured that the amount of the concession (and future increases in development value) accrued to them. Concessionary crownholds were also applicable to 'bodies which can effectively supervise the assignment of such houses', such as housing associations.

The Betterment Levy

The levy differed from the development charge of the 1947 Act in two important ways. First, it did not take all the development value. The Act did not specify what the rate was to be, but it was made clear that the initial rate of 40 per cent would be increased to 45 per cent and then to 50 per cent 'at reasonably short intervals'. (In fact, it never was.)

The second difference from the development charge was that though the levy would normally be paid by the seller, if 'when the land comes to be developed, it still has some development value on which levy has not been taken in previous sales, that residual value will be subject to levy at the time of development'. Thus (ignoring a few complications and qualifications), if a piece of land was worth £500 in its existing use but was sold for £3,500 with planning permission, the levy was applied to the difference, i.e. £3,000 – the levy, at the initial rate was £1,200. If, however, the land were sold (at existing use value plus a 'hope' value that planning permission might be obtained) at £1,000, while the full development value was £3,500, the levy would be paid by both seller and purchaser: £200 by the former and £1,000 by the latter.

Certain bodies were exempt from the levy – for instance, local authorities, new town development corporations, the Housing Corporation and housing societies.

The proceeds of the levy were expected to amount to £80 million in a full year. In fact, however, the amount levied did not approach this figure. In 1968–9 it amounted to £15 million and in 1969–70 £31 million.

Land for Development

The Land Commission's first task was to assess the availability of, and demand for, land for house-building, particularly in the areas of greatest pressure. In their first annual report, they pointed to the difficulties in some areas particularly in the south-east and the west midlands where the available land was limited to only a few years' supply. Most of this land could not, in fact, be made available for early development. Much of it was in small parcels; some was not suitable for development at all because of physical difficulties; and, of the remainder, a great deal was already in the hands of builders. Thus there was little that could be acquired and developed immediately by those other builders who had an urgent need for land. All this highlighted the need for more land to be allocated by planning authorities for development.

The Land Commission had to work within the framework of the planning system. Though a Crown body, they did not operate as such and thus were subject to the same planning control as private developers. The intention was that the Commission would work harmoniously with local planning authorities and form an important addition to the planning machinery. As the Commission pointed out, though Britain has perhaps the most sophisticated planning system of any country, it is one designed to control land use rather than to promote the development of land. The Commission's role was to ensure that land allocated for development was in fact developed – by channelling it to those who would develop it. They could use their powers of compulsory acquisition to amalgamate land which was in separate ownerships and acquire land whose owners could not be traced. They could purchase land from owners who refused to sell for development or from builders who wished to retain it for future development.

In their first report, the Land Commission gently referred to the importance of their role in acting 'as a spur to those local planning authorities whose plans have not kept up with the demand for various kinds of development'. Though they stated their hope that planning authorities would allocate sufficient land, they warned that in some cases they might have to take the initiative and, if local authorities refused planning permission, go to appeal. In their second report their line was much stronger. They pointed out that, in the pressure areas, they had had only modest success in achieving a steady flow of land on to the market. This was largely because these are areas in which planning policies are aimed at containing urban growth and preserving open country.

In 1969–70 the Land Commission purchased 1,000 acres by agreement and a further 240 acres by the use of its compulsory powers. But the use of these compulsory powers was on the increase, and a further 2,500 acres were subject to compulsory purchase at March 1970.

It is not easy to appraise what success the Land Commission achieved. They were only beginning to get into their stride in 1970 when a new Government was returned which was pledged to the abolition of the Commission on the grounds that they 'had no place in a free society'. This pledge was fulfilled in 1971 and thus the Land Commission went the same way as their predecessor, the Central Land Board.

THE COMMUNITY LAND ACT, 1975

The early seventies experienced a major property boom and virtual panic about the shortage of available land for development. But before the Government could come to grips with the problem they were replaced by a Labour Government committed to establishing 'a permanent means to enable the community to control the development of land in accordance with its needs and priorities: and to restore to the community the increase in value of land arising from its efforts' (1974 White Paper on *Land*). At the time of writing (December 1975) the first legislative instalment had been passed (with considerable amendments to the original Bill) as the Community Land Act. This gives local authorities in England and Scotland (and a new agency for Wales – the Land Authority) wider powers to acquire land for development. It is to be followed by a Development Land Tax Bill, the proposed provisions of which have been published in the White Paper *Development Land Tax*.

The Community Land Act is a complex piece of legislation – and will become more so as its attendant regulations, ministerial directions and circulars emerge. All that can be attempted here is a summary of its main provisions and an interim comment on the likelihood of its representing a case of 'third time lucky'.

The provisions of the Act are to come into force by phases. The first phase starts on the 'first appointed day' (6 April 1976). In this first phase, authorities will have a general duty to have regard to the desirability of bringing development land into public ownership. In doing so, they will have 'to pay particular regard to the location and nature of development necessary to meet the planning needs of their areas'. To assist them in carrying out this role, they have new and wider powers to buy land to make it available for development. When the development land tax is introduced, all land acquisitions by authorities will be made at a price *net* of any tax payable by the sellers of development land.

The second phase is to be introduced gradually. As authorities build up resources and expertise, and become able to take on the responsibility for making available all land needed for particular types of development, the Secretary of State may make orders providing that land for development of the kind designated in the order and in the area specified by the order must have passed through public ownership before development takes place. These 'duty orders' will be brought in to match the varying rates at which authorities become ready to take on such responsibilities.

When duty orders have been made covering the whole of Great Britain, the 'second appointed day' (or SAD Day as critics have dubbed it) can be brought in. This will have the effect of changing the basis of compensation for land publicly acquired from a market value (net of tax) basis to a current use value basis, i.e. its value in its existing use, taking no account of any increase in value actually or potentially conferred by the grant of a planning permission for new development.

This phasing of the implementation of the Act is intended, according to government statements, to enable the build-up of the acquisitions and disposals 'to be matched to available resources and expertise'; and also 'to enable authorities to work in co-ordination with private interests during the transition to the full scheme, allowing both to develop good working relationships and adapt to their new long-term role as partners and co-operators in the development process'. However, it also provides for a great deal of flexibility as experience is gained – particularly since so much of the detailed operation of the Act is to be determined by delegated legislation. For instance, regulations are to be made for 'excepted development' (in addition to 'exempt development' which is specified in the Act). Currently it is envisaged that this will be development which 'is not large enough to be brought normally within the scope of the Act'; but the Act goes even wider and refers to 'development of such class or classes as may be prescribed'. Clearly this gives great scope for restricting the operation of the Act to major developments (or, alternatively, to extending it to cover most developments).

But perhaps the most striking factor in the current scene is the relative absence of real opposition to the major principles of the new scheme. As the first report of the Pilcher Committee on *Commercial Property Development* has put it:

'It might perhaps have been expected that we should hear voices raised against the basic principle of recouping a substantial measure of development value. None has been heard . . . The wide acceptance of the principle of recoupment of development value, which has never been present at previous attempts, therefore offers a real opportunity to find a lasting solution.'

It could be, of course, that this is in part a result of the current slump in development. Only time will tell, but it is significant that increasing concern is being expressed in the property industry at the Opposition's declared intention to repeal the Act if they are returned to power. As one spokesman is reported as saying, 'it was high time to stop playing politics and to try to reach some sort of common agreement'.

It is precisely this lack of 'common agreement' which led to the failure of the 1947 Act and Land Commission schemes. The 1975 Act is essentially an enabling Act and it therefore offers the opportunity for a more pragmatic approach than was possible in the earlier schemes. At the least, it is encouraging that there are some grounds for ending this chapter on an unaccustomed note of optimism.

Chapter VIII

PLANNING FOR TRAFFIC

Major changes in transport policy have emerged since the last edition of this book was prepared. These reflect revised population and car ownership forecasts, the work energy situation and the increased cost of private motoring, a lower rate of economic growth, the need to restrain public expenditure, and changing public attitudes to road developments (particularly in urban areas). All these have led to a reduction in planned investment in roads. At the same time they have given added force to the trends towards greater priority for public transport and comprehensive transport planning.

THE GROWTH OF TRAFFIC

Between 1950 and 1960 the number of vehicles on the roads of Great Britain doubled, to 9½ million. By 1970 the number had increased to 15 million. The proportion of households with a car rose from less than a third in 1961 to over a half in 1970. This upward trend continued in the early seventies, with a total number of vehicles increasing to 16·1 million in 1972 and 17·0 million in 1973. More recent (and hence more relevant) figures were not available at the time of writing, but forecasts up to the year 2010 have been drastically reduced. The Buchanan Report referred to a prospect of 27 million vehicles by 1980 and perhaps 40 million by 2010. A forecast made by the Transport and Road Research Laboratory in 1973 reduced the estimates to 22 million in 1980 and 33 million in 2010 – most of the reduction being due to a major downward revision in population projections. A later forecast by the Laboratory, made in 1974, took account of further downward revisions in population projections, a lower rate of economic growth and substantial fuel price increases. In view of the increased uncertainty about the future (in terms both of such factors as energy supplies and economic growth, and of the role and impact of governmental policies), a number of alternative forecasts were made. These ranged from 19·2 to 22·0 million in 1980, and from 29·2 to 31·1 in 2010. Given even further reductions in population forecasts since then and current indications about fuel costs and economic growth, it is likely that new forecasts will be still lower.

INTER-URBAN TRAFFIC

Nevertheless, all estimates continued to show a significant growth in the number of vehicles, and even if this were not so, the present traffic situation obviously demands action. So far as inter-urban traffic is concerned, the long term policy was formulated in 1970, following the publication of the 1969 'green paper', *Roads for the Future: A New Inter-Urban Plan*. The policy (set out succinctly in *Roads in England 1971*) has the following main objectives:

   (i) to achieve environmental improvements by diverting long-distance traffic, and particularly heavy goods vehicles, from a large number of towns and villages, so as to relieve them of the noise, dirt and danger which they suffer at present;
  (ii) to complete by the early 1980s a comprehensive network of strategic trunk routes to promote economic growth;
 (iii) to link the more remote and less prosperous regions with this new national network;
  (iv) to ensure that every major city and town with a population of more than 250,000 will be directly connected to the strategic network and that all with a population of more than 80,000 will be within ten miles of it;
   (v) to design the network so that it serves all major ports and airports; and
  (vi) to relieve as many historic towns as possible of through trunk road traffic.

Cuts in public expenditure for 1973/4 and 1974/5 have involved a reduction in the road-building programme, and priority is currently given to a national network of roads planned particularly for the needs of heavy lorry traffic. Details of the proposed network are given in the DoE Consultation Paper of July 1974, *Routes for Heavy Lorries*.

TRAFFIC IN TOWNS

Traffic between towns gives rise to few problems which cannot be solved in time by expenditure on road building and landscaping.

Traffic in towns presents problems of a very different character. It is these which forcibly demonstrate that the motor car is a 'mixed blessing' (to borrow the title of an earlier book by Buchanan). As a highly convenient means of personal transport it cannot (at present) be bettered. But its mass use restricts its benefits to car users, imposes severe penalties (in congestion, pollution and reduction of public transport) on non-motorists, involves huge expenditure on roads, and at worst plays havoc with the urban environment.

THE BUCHANAN REPORT

A major landmark in the development of thought in this field was the Buchanan Report. This is a masterly survey which surmounts the administrative separatism which has until recently prevented the comprehensive co-ordination of the planning and location of buildings on the one hand and the planning and management of traffic on the other. With due acknowledgement of the necessarily crude nature of the methods and assumptions used, the Report proposes as a basic principle the canalisation of larger traffic movements on to properly designed networks servicing areas within which environments suitable for a civilised urban life can be developed. The two main ideas here are for 'primary road networks' and 'environmental areas'.

'There must be areas of good environment – urban rooms – where people can live, work, shop, look about and move around on foot in reasonable freedom from the hazards of motor traffic, and there must be a complementary network of roads – urban corridors – for affecting the primary distribution of traffic to the environmental areas.'

This simple concept is not, of course, new, but the urgency of the need for its application on the scale required presents enormous problems. A striking result of the case studies included in the Report is the great scale of the networks and interchanges that are needed. The capital cost of the new primary distribution roads in the Newbury Scheme, for example, would be about £4½ million. But, as the accompanying report of the Steering Committee (the Crowther Report) points out: 'This would be once-for-all expenditure. It is estimated that the motor vehicles registered in the Newbury area will pay in 1963 about £770,000 in licence duty and fuel duty. By 1983 it is estimated that the vehicles registered will be paying (assuming unchanged rates) at the rate of £1,560,000. This admittedly crude calculation serves to show "what a fund of future revenue there is available to finance a programme of urban rede-velopment".'

But what of the alternatives? Buchanan stressed that the general lesson is unavoidable: 'If the scale of road works and reconstruction seems frightening, then a lesser scale will suffice *provided there is less traffic.*' Crowther argues that the scope for deliberate limitations on the use of vehicles in towns would be almost impossible to enforce, even if a car-owning electorate were prepared to accept such limitations in principle. Not all would agree and, as traffic grows, the practical possibilities of the various forms of pricing assume an increased significance. Indeed, it is striking how far opinion on this has changed over the last few years. The White Paper, *Transport in London*, published in 1968, could say quite blandly (as could not have been said a decade earlier):

'The control of traffic must be regarded as a deliberate part of highway and transport planning. In many cases regulation is ap-propriate. But the price mechanism is often more flexible and more sensitive. It may in time prove possible and worthwhile to reflect in charging systems the costs which journeys on overcrowded roads impose on other road users. Meanwhile, parking charges and time-limits can provide effective control. There will have to be control of all street parking in inner London – with preference being given to short-term callers for whom the use of public transport may well be less convenient than for the regular commuter, and to residents. And there will also have to be control over the amount of privately available off-street parking space in new developments which attract a significant number of workers. (In the past, such space has often encouraged additional car commuting.) The GLC has recently announced new policies along these lines. Finally, there is need to control the ways in which publicly available off-street car parks can be used.'

To return to Buchanan, the great danger in his view lies in the temptation to seek a middle course between a massive investment in replanning and a curtailing of the use of vehicles 'by trying to cope with a steadily increasing volume of traffic by means of minor alterations resulting in the end in the worst of both worlds – poor traffic access and a grievously eroded environment'.

An improvement of public transport is no answer to these prob-lems, though it must be an essential part of an overall plan; indeed, the case studies show that it is quite impossible to dispense with public transport. The implication is that there must be a planned co-ordination between transport systems, particularly with regard to the work journeys in concentrated centres. On this, the Report recommended that 'transportation plans' should be included as part of the statutory development plans. This was accepted and passed into legislation by the 1968 Town and Country Planning Act (though its implementation will take many years). But of equal importance is the momentous Transport Act passed in the same year. Many of the provisions of this lie outside the scope of the present book, though they are by no means irrelevant to the issues selected for discussion. Attention here is focused on the new machinery for traffic planning, the report of the Urban Motorways Committee, and the introduction of Transport Policies and Programmes.

TRAFFIC PLANNING MACHINERY

The 1967 White Paper *Public Transport and Traffic* opened on a lyrical note: 'one of the most precious achievements of modern civilization is mobility. It enriches social life and widens experience.' It continued by stressing the implications for planning and transport policy:

'To build mobility into the urban and rural life of this crowded island without destroying the other elements of good living must be one of the major purposes of transport policy. To achieve this, far-reaching changes in attitudes and administration will be necessary. The provision of transport – whether public or private – can no longer be considered in isolation from other developments. It must be built into the whole planning of our community life so that no factory is sited, no housing estate or "overspill" developed, no town re-planned without the implications for the movement of people and goods having been studied and incorporated from the outset.'

This, of course, is the rationale for the new-style development plans which will treat basic transport planning as a part of the general planning of the structure of each locality. But the important point is that 'basic transport planning' means far more than 'road planning', particularly since no conceivable road investment programme could support city structures designed on the basis that nearly all journeys were to be made by private car. (And it must not be forgotten that there will always be a significant proportion of households without cars. Even in the United States this is a fifth.) In short, 'our major towns and cities can only be made to work effectively and to provide a decent environment for living by giving a new dynamic role to public transport as well as expanding facilities for private cars'.

Five 'principles of organisation' flow from this:

1. Since local authorities are responsible for 'planning' they must be the authorities responsible for public transport.
2. All transport matters for which local authorities are to be responsible – the improvement of the local road network, investment in public transport, traffic management measures, the balance between public and private transport – must be focused in an integrated transport plan, which in its turn is related to the general planning for each area.
3. Investment in local public transport must be grant-aided by central government just as investment in the principal road network receives 75 per cent Exchequer grants.
4. The main network of public transport must be publicly owned.
5. The planning and operation of public transport can only be done intelligently over areas which make sense in transport terms. In some of the major urban areas, the traffic situation is so bad and is deteriorating so rapidly that reorganisation cannot await general legislation on local government.

It was for this last reason that Passenger Transport Authorities were established (under powers provided by the 1968 Transport Act) in South East Lancashire/North East Cheshire (SELNEC – now Greater Manchester), Merseyside, West Midlands, Tyneside and Greater Glasgow. Local government reorganisation made all the English metropolitan county councils Passenger Transport Authorities (thus adding South Yorkshire and West Yorkshire to the list). The Greater Glasgow PTA were transferred to the Strathclyde Regional Council.

It is the duty of a PTA to promote the provision of a co-ordinated and efficient system of public transport in their area. Each PTA appoint a professional management body – the Passenger Transport Executive. The PTEs are responsible for the management and operations of the former municipal passenger transport undertakings and for reaching agreement with the British Railways Board concerning the operation of local rail services.

In non-metropolitan counties, the county council now has (under the Local Government Act 1972) a parallel duty to that of a PTA in relation to 'a co-ordinated and efficient system of public transport' in its area. There is corresponding provision in the Scottish Local Government Act for the regional and islands authorities.

In London, the London Transport Executive is the equivalent to the provincial and Scottish PTEs. The Greater London Council is the transport planning authority.

Thus there is now a network of local transport authorities covering the whole country. This massive reorganisation has been accompanied by a radical change in the system for the preparation and financing of transport plans. Grants are paid by the central government by way of the Rate Support Grant, and a Transport Supplementary Grant which is determined on the basis of approved Transport Policies and Programmes (TPPs).

THE URBAN MOTORWAYS COMMITTEE

In July 1972, the report of the Urban Motorways Committee was published (DoE, *New Roads in Towns*, HMSO). This Committee was established, under the chairmanship of Sir James Jones, with the following terms of reference:

1. to examine present policies used in fitting major roads into urban areas;
2. to consider what changes would enable urban roads to be related better to their surroundings, physically, visually and socially;
3. to examine the consequences of such changes, particularly from the point of view of:
   (a) limitations on resources, both public and private;
   (b) changes in statutory powers and administrative procedures;
   (c) any issue of public policy that the changes would raise;
4. to recommend what changes, if any, should be made.

The Committee were supported by a full-time team of officials who had the responsibility for a series of research studies and for the preparation of material on problems and procedures. Their report was published separately (*Report of the Urban Motorways Project Team to the Urban Motorways Committee*, HMSO, 1973).

The Committee's main recommendation was that 'the planning of new urban roads should form an integral part of planning the urban area as a whole; and that indirect costs and benefits of building urban roads should be looked at with the same care as the direct cost and movement benefits'.

The first part of this recommendation led (in conjunction with an unpublished review of compensation law) to the White Paper *Development and Compensation – Putting People First* (Cmnd 5124, 1972) and the Land Compensation Act 1973, which applies to Scotland as well as to England and Wales. (The Scottish provisions were re-enacted in the Land Compensation (Scotland) Act 1973.)

The second led to a new system of transport grants and the introduction of Transport Plans and Programmes.

The major emphasis in the first of these changes is on giving a greater priority to the social and human implications of road and other types of public development. As the White Paper put it:

'The Government believe the time has come when all concerned with development must aim to achieve a better balance between provision for the community as a whole and the mitigation of harmful effects on the individual citizen. In recent years this balance in too many cases has been tipped against the interests of the individual. A better deal is now required for those who suffer from desirable community developments. . . . The answer is not to stop community developments that would make life more comfortable, convenient and pleasant. To do that would simply deprive many people of the opportunity of a better environment. The answer must be to plan new development so as to minimise the disturbance and disruption they can cause and to improve the compensation code to alleviate any remaining distress.'

But to talk of 'desirable community developments' begs the issue, and the very pressures which led to the review of road planning procedures and compensation have also led to a more searching attitude to development proposals. Thus the question is no longer how best to develop a road, but whether a road is needed at all, and whether it is not better to allocate the resources to public transport. This was a main theme of the Expenditure Committee's Report on *Urban Transport Planning* (HC Paper 57, 3 vols, HMSO, 1972), and arose not only from an appreciation of the physical consequences of major urban highways and their effects on the communities through which they pass, but also from a growing awareness of the wider distributional consequences of current transport policies and the social significance of personal mobility. (See the Report, paragraphs 25 and 59–61; and the evidence of Meyer Hillman, pages 235–50; also Hillman, M., *et al.*, *Personal Mobility and Transport Policy*, PEP, 1973.) The Committee went so far as to recommend that policy should be directed towards promoting public transport and discouraging the use of cars for the journey to work in city areas. Government policy is moving in this direction, but the current emphasis is on comprehensive planning through the *Transport Policies and Programmes* – the TPPs which will cover the whole transport field: roads, public transport, parking, traffic management and the movement of goods. (See *Government Observations on the Second Report of the Expenditure Committee; Urban Trans-*

port Planning, Cmnd 5366, HMSO, 1973; and DoE Circular 104/73, *Local Transport Grants,* HMSO, 1973.)

TRANSPORT POLICIES AND PROGRAMMES

TPPs are intended to be comprehensive statements of the objectives and policies which local transport authorities plan to pursue in their areas, together with an expenditure programme. Though initially they can be little more than statements of existing commitments, they are expected (in the words of DoE Circular 104/73) 'to be based increasingly on a proper evaluation of alternative options against explicit objectives within a realistic resource constraint'. The Circular continues:

'Eventually, therefore, the TPP will consist of a series of interrelated proposals covering both capital and current expenditure over the whole transport field – public transport, roads, parking, traffic management, pedestrians. It would need to contain some overall assessment of policy county-wide, including the allocation of expenditure between different parts of the county as well as between different types of expenditure. Within this framework the TPP would be broken down as appropriate into sections dealing with each of the major urban areas in the county (which probably pose the most difficult transport problems); with each new town; and with the inter-urban network and the smaller towns. It would identify the most important factors influencing the transport needs of the area in question; the problems arising from them; the council's objectives and its proposals:
 (i) for investment (in public transport, roads and parking);
 (ii) for pricing and operation of parking and public transport;
 (iii) for the management of the road network (i.e. maintenance, traffic management and environmental and road safety measures).'

Unlike development plans, TPPs are not statutory documents; nor are they subject to any formal inquiry procedures. Nevertheless, they must obviously be closely related to structure and local plans. Indeed, once the new system is bedded down, it is envisaged that there will be 'a single process which expresses itself on the one hand in TPPs (for the purpose of grant and resource decisions) and, on the other, in structure and local plans'. It will be the structure and local plans (with their statutory framework for publicity and participation) which will provide the wider context for TPPs.
The multiplicity of transport grants (at different rates, some

payable to operators, others to local authorities) is not suited to the comprehensive approach which characterises TPPs, and they have therefore been replaced by a new system. Under this, the majority of specific grants are replaced by a unified grant for all transport services which is distributed to local authorities on the basis of estimated expenditure. The major support, however, continues to be the Rate Support Grant which provides Exchequer aid towards all local services, including transport. Some specific grants have been absorbed into this: the remainder are now paid through a new Transport Supplementary Grant. (In Scotland, with minor exceptions *all* transport grants are paid through the Rate Support Grant – see SDD Circular 13/1975.)

This system (which will take several years to come into full operation) represents a major shift in transport policy. Two particularly interesting features are, first, that grant will be based not on the actual cost of individual schemes (the traditional procedure), but on county programmes of estimated expenditure backed by a comprehensive statement of transport policies for the area. (This also allows a major reduction in detailed central government controls.) Secondly, financial support for public transport will be largely channelled through local authorities instead of being paid direct to the operators.

It is in this financial context that TPPs assume an important operational status. They are annual statements of policy which will form the basis for grant-aid and for loan sanctions. They contain not only financial estimates for the year but also (1) a statement of the county's transport objectives and strategy over a 10–15 year period; (2) a 5–year rolling programme for the implementation of the strategy; and (3) a statement of past expenditure and physical progress, and the extent to which objectives and policies are being met.

Chapter IX

PLANNING THE ENVIRONMENT

AMENITY

'Amenity' is one of the key concepts in British town and country planning: yet nowhere in the legislation is it defined. The Act merely states that 'if it appears to a local planning authority that it is expedient in the interests of amenity', they may take certain action – in relation, for example, to unsightly neglected waste land or to the preservation of trees. It is also one of the factors that may need to be taken into account in controlling advertisements and in determining whether a discontinuance order should be made. It is a term widely used in planning refusals and appeals: indeed the phrase 'injurious to the interests of amenity' has become part of the stock-in-trade jargon of the planning world. But like the proverbial elephant, amenity is easier to recognise than to define – with the important difference that, though all would be agreed that an elephant is such, there is considerable scope for disagreement on the degree and importance of amenities: which amenities should be preserved, in what way they should be preserved, and how much expense (public or private) is justified. The problem is relatively straightforward in so far as trees are concerned, as is apparent from the excellent book *Trees in Town and City* produced by the department in 1958. It is much more acute in connection with electricity pylons – yet the Central Electricity Generating Board is specifically charged not only with maintaining an efficient and co-ordinated supply of electricity but also with the preservation of amenity. Here the question is not merely one of sensitivity but also of the enormous additional cost of preserving amenities by placing cables underground.

Apart from the problems of cost, there is the problem of determining how much control the public will accept. Poor architecture, ill-conceived schemes, 'mock-Tudor' frontages may upset the planning officer, but how much regulation of this type of 'amenity-injury' will be publicly acceptable? And how far can negative controls succeed in raising public standards? Here emphasis has been laid on design bulletins, design awards and such ventures as those of the Civic Trust – a body whose object is 'to promote beauty and fight ugliness in town, village and countryside'. Nevertheless, local authorities have power not only to prevent developments which would clash with amenity (e.g. the siting of a repair garage in a residential area) but also to reject badly designed developments which are not intrinsically harmful. Indeed 'outline planning permission' for a proposal is often given on the condition that detailed plans and appearance meet the approval of the authority.

In recent years, there has been a marked sharpening of interest in amenity, caused partly by the rapid rate of development, and an awareness of the inadequacy of the planning system automatically to preserve and enhance amenity. The Transport Act of 1968, for instance, enables the use of a road by vehicles to be prohibited on amenity grounds for certain periods of the day. Perhaps the most striking provision is to be found in the Countryside (Scotland) Act 1967 and the Countryside Act 1968 which requires every minister, government department and public body to have regard to the desirability of conserving the natural beauty and amenity of the countryside in all their functions relating to land. Lawyers may rightly point out that this does not constitute, of itself, an effective restriction on any statutory power or discretion, but it is an important statement of policy and one which the statutory and voluntary guardians of amenity will seize upon whenever it is infringed. There is more to planning than law.

The preservation and development of amenity thus form a basic objective of planning policy. From this point of view, amenity can hardly be discussed separately. Nevertheless, there are certain matters where planning controls are specifically, and almost exclusively, concerned with amenity. The control of advertisements is a prime example of this.

CONTROL OF ADVERTISEMENTS

The need to control advertisements has long been recognised. Indeed, the first Advertisements Regulation Act of 1907 antedated by two years the first Town Planning Act. But even when amended and extended (in 1925 and 1932) the control was quite inadequate. Not only were the powers permissive, they were also limited. For instance, under the 1932 Act, the right of appeal (on the ground that an advertisement did not injure the amenities of the area) was to the magistrates court – hardly an appropriate body for such a purpose. The 1947 Act set out to remedy the deficiencies. There are, however, particular difficulties in establishing a legal code for the control of advertisements. Advertisements may range in size from a small window-notice to a massive hoarding; they vary in purpose from a bus-stop sign to a demand to buy a certain make of detergent; they could be situated alongside a cathedral, in a busy shopping street or in a particularly beautiful rural setting; they might be pleasant or obnoxious to look at; they might be temporary or permanent; and so on. The task of devising a code which would take all the relevant factors into account and, at the same time, achieve a balance between the conflicting interests of legitimate advertising or notification and 'amenity' presents real problems. Advertisers themselves frequently complain that decisions in apparently similar cases have not been consistent with each other. The official departmental view is that no case is exactly like another, and hard and fast rules cannot be applied: each case has to be considered on its individual merits in the light of the tests of amenity and – the other factor to be taken into account – public safety.

The control of advertisements is exercised by regulations. The Secretary of State has very wide powers of making regulations 'for restricting or regulating the display of advertisements so far as appears to the Secretary of State to be expedient in the interests of amenity or public safety'. The question of 'public safety' is rather simpler than that of amenity – though there is still ample scope for disagreement: the relevant issue is whether an advertisement is likely to cause danger to road users (and also to 'persons who may use any railway, waterway – including any coastal waters – dock, harbour or airfield'). Examples are advertisements which obstruct the line of sight at a corner or bend, or obstruct the view of a traffic sign or signal, and illuminated advertisements which are likely to dazzle or confuse road users or are likely to be mistaken for traffic lights.

The definition of an advertisement is not quite as complicated as that of 'development', but it is very wide: 'advertisement means any word, letter, model, sign, placard, board, notice, device or representation, whether illuminated or not, in the nature of, and employed wholly or partly for the purpose of, advertisement, announcement or direction . . .'. Five classes of advertisement are 'excepted' from all control – those on enclosed land, within a building, on or in a vehicle, incorporated in and forming part of the fabric of a building, and displayed on an article for sale. As one might expect, there are some interesting refinements of these categories, which can be ignored for the present purposes (though we might note, in passing, that a vehicle must be kept moving, or to use the more exact legal language, must be normally employed as a moving vehicle on any highway or railway – and the same applies to vessels). With these exceptions, no advertisement may be displayed without 'consent'. However, certain categories of advertisement can be displayed without 'express consent'; so long as the local authority takes no action, they are 'deemed' to have received consent. These include bus-stop signs and timetables, hotel and inn signs, profession or trade plates, 'To Let' signs, election notices, statutory advertisements and traffic signs.

Except in relation to advertisements to which the 'deemed consent' procedure applies, a local authority can serve a discontinuance order when they are satisfied that removal is necessary 'to remedy a substantial injury to the amenity of the locality or a danger to members of the public'. There is the normal right of appeal to the Secretary of State.

This is not, however, all there is to advertisement control. In some areas, e.g. national parks or near a cathedral, it may be desirable virtually to prohibit all advertisements of the poster type and seriously to restrict other advertisements including those normally displayed by the ordinary trader. Accordingly, local planning authorities have power to define 'areas of special control' where 'special protection on grounds of amenity' is thought desirable. (Over a third of England and Wales is now subject to this 'special control'.) Within an area of special control the general rule is that no advertisement may be displayed; such advertisements as are given express consent are considered as exceptions to this general rule.

This has proved a very difficult field in which to obtain unanimity, but the effectiveness of the controls and agreements is very apparent to the European (and, still more, the American) visitor.

CONSERVATION

Britain has a remarkable wealth of historic buildings, but changing economic and social conditions often turn this legacy into a liability. The cost of maintenance, the financial attraction of redevelopment, the need for urban renewal, the roads programme and similar factors often threaten buildings which are of architectural or historic interest. This is a field in which voluntary organisations have been particularly active – as witness the work of the National Trust, the Ancient Monuments Society, the Society for the Protection of Ancient Buildings, the Victorian Society and others. As is so often the case, voluntary effort preceded State action. The Society for the Protection of Ancient Buildings was founded in 1877. The National Trust (or to use its full name, the National Trust for Places of Historic Interest or Natural Beauty) was founded in 1895. Though the first State action came in 1882 with the Ancient Monuments Act, this was important chiefly because it acknowledged the interest of the State in the preservation of ancient monuments. Such preservation as was achieved under this Act (and under similar Acts passed in the following thirty years) resulted from the goodwill and co-operation of private owners. It was not until 1913 that powers were provided to compulsorily prevent the damage or destruction of monuments. Strictly speaking, the Ancient Monuments Acts are outside the legal realm of town and country planning, but their objectives and scope demand that they be considered within the same context. The term 'ancient monument' is defined very widely and could include almost any building or structure made or occupied by man at any time: the DoE are responsible for the care and preservation of pre-historic settlements, Roman walls, Norman castles and Gothic abbeys. The department are advised by three Ancient Monuments Boards for England, Scotland and Wales, who recommend monuments whose preservation is of national importance. Such monuments are 'scheduled': obligations are thereby imposed on owners and occupiers. The owner of a scheduled monument must give the department three months' notice if he wishes to repair, alter, demolish or, indeed, do any work affecting it.

There are over 12,000 protected monuments in Britain. In cases where a monument is in danger of destruction or damage, an 'interim preservation notice' (lasting for a maximum period of twenty-one months) or a more permanent 'preservation order' can be made, which prohibits any work without the written consent of the Secretary of State. The department can become the 'guardian' of a monument whereby they become permanently responsible for preservation, maintenance and management, or they can acquire monuments. In total, nearly 800 monuments are in the charge of the department.

Under the Historic Buildings and Ancient Monuments Act, 1953, the DoE have power to make grants for the preservation of 'buildings of outstanding historic or architectural interest' – and of their contents and adjoining land. They can also purchase such buildings or accept them as gifts. Three Historic Buildings Councils (for England, Scotland and Wales) were set up as advisory bodies. The 1953 Act was passed primarily to deal with the problem of preserving houses or buildings which were inhabited or 'capable of occupation' – these were not covered by the earlier legislation.

LISTED BUILDINGS

Under planning legislation, the central departments maintain lists of buildings of 'special architectural or historic interest'. There are two objectives here. First, 'listing' is intended to provide guidance to local planning authorities in carrying out their planning functions. For example, in planning redevelopment, local authorities will take into account listed buildings in the area. Buildings in a slum clearance area may be preserved with the aid not only of grants from the Historic Building Council but also with house improvement grants available under the Housing Acts. Secondly, and more directly effective, when a building is listed no demolition or alteration which would materially alter it can be undertaken by the owner without the approval of the local authority. This is technically termed 'listed building consent'.

Applications for listed building consent have to be advertised and any representation must be taken into account by the local authority before they reach their decision. Where demolition is involved, the local authority have to notify the appropriate local amenity society, and a number of other bodies, namely, the Ancient Monuments Society, the Council for British Archaeology, the Georgian Group, the Society for the Protection of Ancient Buildings, the Victorian Society, as well as the Royal Commission on Historical Monuments. Again, any representations have to be taken into account when the application is being considered.

If, after all this, the local authority are 'disposed to grant consent' for the demolition (and, in certain cases, the alteration) of a listed building, they have to refer the application to the Secretary of State so that he can decide whether to 'call in' the proposal and deal with it himself.

All these provisions apply to listed buildings (of which there were, in 1974, some 230,000), but the Secretary of State has power to list a building at any time, and local authorities can serve a 'building preservation notice' on an unlisted building; this has the effect of protecting the building for six months, thus giving time for considering whether or not it should be listed.

With a listed building the presumption is in favour of preservation. Indeed 'listing' is in essence a collective preservation order. It is an offence to demolish or to alter a listed building unless listed building consent has been obtained. This is different from the general position in relation to planning permission where an offence arises only after the enforcement procedure has been invoked. Fines for illegal works to listed buildings are related to the financial benefit expected by the offender.

The legislation also provides a deterrent against deliberate neglect of historic buildings. This was one way in which astute owners could circumvent the earlier statutory provisions: a building could be neglected to such an extent that demolition was unavoidable, thus giving the owner the possibility of reaping the development value of the site. In such cases the local authority can now compulsorily acquire the building at a low price, technically known as 'minimum compensation'. If the Secretary of State approves, the compensation is assessed on the assumption that neither planning permission nor listed building consent would be given for any works to the building except those for restoring it to, and maintaining it in, a proper state of repair; in short, all development value is excluded.

The strength of these powers (and others not detailed here) reflect the concern which is felt at the loss of historic buildings. They are not, however, all of this penal nature. Indeed, ministerial guidance has emphasised the need for a positive and comprehensive approach. Grants are available under the Local Authorities (Historic Buildings) Act, 1962, the Historic Buildings and Ancient Monuments Act, 1953, and under the Housing Acts. Local authorities can also purchase properties by agreement, possibly with Exchequer aid under the 1953 Act. Furthermore, an owner of a building who is refused 'listed building consent' can, in certain circumstances, serve a notice on the local authority requiring them to purchase the property. This is known as a 'listed building purchase notice'. The issue to be decided here is whether the land has become 'incapable of reasonably beneficial use'. It is not sufficient to show that it is of less use to the owner in its present state than if developed.

More important is the emphasis on areas, as distinct from individual buildings, of architectural or historic interest. This was introduced by the Civic Amenities Act, 1967 (promoted as a Private Member's Bill by Duncan Sandys, President of the Civic Trust, and passed with government backing). This gave statutory recognition for the first time to the area concept, and made it a duty of local planning authorities 'to determine which parts of their areas are areas of special architectural or historic interest, the character of which it is desirable to preserve or enhance' and to designate such areas as 'conservation areas'. When a conservation area has been designated, the Act requires special attention to be paid in all planning decisions to the preservation or enhancement of its character and appearance.

The 1974 Town and Country Amenities Act extended the powers of local authorities in dealing with conservation areas and the preservation of historic buildings. In particular, it has brought the demolition of most buildings in conservation areas under control.

In mid-1974 there were over 3,000 conservation areas in Great Britain – ranging from the whole of the centres of such historic sites as Chester to small rural villages.

PRESERVATION OF TREES AND WOODLANDS

Trees are clearly – so far as town and country planning is concerned – a matter of amenity. Indeed, the powers which local authorities have with regard to trees can be exercised only if it is 'expedient in the interests of amenity'. Where the local authority are satisfied that it is 'expedient', they can make a tree preservation order – applicable to trees, groups of trees or woodlands. Such an order can prohibit the cutting down, topping or lopping of trees except with the consent of the local planning authority. Mere preservation, however, leads eventually to decay and thus defeats its object. To prevent this, a local authority can make replanting obligatory when they give permission for trees to be felled. The aim is to avoid any clash between good forestry and the claims of amenity. But the timber of woodlands always has a claim to be treated as a commercial crop, and though the making of a tree preservation order does not necessarily involve the owner in any financial loss (isolated trees or groups of trees are usually planted expressly as an amenity), there are occasions when it does. Yet though woodlands are primarily a timber crop from which the owner is entitled to benefit, two principles have been laid down which qualify this. First, 'the national interest demands that woodlands should be managed in accordance with the principles of good forestry', and secondly, where they are of amenity value, the owner has 'a public duty to act with reasonable regard for amenity aspects'. It follows that a refusal to permit felling or the imposition of conditions on operations which are either contrary to the principles of good forestry or destructive of amenity ought not to carry any compensation rights. But where there is a clash between these two principles compensation is payable. Thus in a case where the 'principles of good forestry' dictate that felling should take place, but this would result in too great a sacrifice of amenity, the owner can claim compensation for the loss which he suffers. Normally a compromise is reached whereby the felling is deferred or phased. The commercial felling of timber is subject to licence from the Forestry Commission and special arrangements exist for consultation between the Commission, the central department and the local planning authority.

Planning powers go considerably further than simply enabling local authorities to preserve trees. The National Parks and Access to the Countryside Act, 1949, enabled planning approvals to be given subject to the condition that trees are planted, and local authorities themselves have power to plant trees on any land in their area. With the increasing vulnerability of trees and woodlands to urban development and the needs of modern farming, wider powers and more Exchequer aid have been provided by successive statutes. Local planning authorities are now *required* to ensure that conditions (preferably reinforced by tree preservation orders) are imposed for the protection of existing trees and for the planting of new ones. This, together with the department's continuous emphasis on the importance of trees, has led to a substantial increase in the number of tree preservation orders being made. At the end of 1973, some 17,000 orders were in force.

PLANNING AND GOOD DESIGN

Good design is an elusive quality which cannot easily be defined. As Sir William Holford said (in *Design in Town and Village*), 'design cannot be taught by correspondence; words are inadequate, and being inadequate may then become misleading, or even dangerous. For the competent designer a handbook on design is unnecessary, and for the incompetent it is almost useless as a medium of instruction.' Yet local authorities have to pass judgement on the design merits of thousands of planning proposals each year, and pressure is mounting from governmental, official and professional bodies for higher design standards to be imposed. The principles of good design and their execution lie outside the scope of this book; here reference can be made only to the powers and practices of local authorities, and some of the particular problems which arise. It needs to be stressed, however, that good design is not basically a matter of cost, but of the combined skills and sensitivity of the architect, the client and the builder.

Planning authorities have a clear legal power to grant planning permission subject to conditions relating to design and appearance. Planning permission is frequently given for a proposed development on the basis of an 'outline application', and subject to the condition that the detailed plans meet with their approval: if the detailed plans are unsatisfactory they can be rejected. There is a difficult problem here which basically stems from the fact that it is not the function of the planning authority to provide developers with good designs, and the amendment of a poor design may produce a compromise result almost as unsatisfactory as the original. Furthermore, the impossibility of laying down generally applicable principles (except that of employing a 'good' architect!) makes the task of the local planning authority a difficult one. A well-staffed and organised authority will spend considerable time with developers discussing sketch-plans – but not all authorities are well staffed or organised, and the importance which is placed on this aspect of planning control varies greatly between authorities. Some have prepared notes for the guidance of developers, and there are various publications of the DoE and of voluntary bodies which have the same objective. Major developments are often referred to the Royal Fine Art Commissions for their opinion.

THE CONTROL OF POLLUTION

Concern about pollution is not new: it was as early as 1273 that action in Britain was taken to protect the environment from polluted air: a royal proclamation of that year prohibited the use of coal in London. (It was not effective, despite the dire penalties: it is recorded that a man was sent to the scaffold in 1306 for burning coal instead of charcoal.)

What is new (apart from the abolition of capital punishment) is, first, the huge scale of the pollution problem and, secondly, the increasing determination to tackle it; 1970 – European Conservation Year – saw the publication of the White Paper on *The Protection of the Environment*, and the establishment of a Royal Commission on Environmental Pollution. Previously there had been numerous inquiries on specific problems of pollution – from the Beaver Committee on air pollution, to the Pippard Committee on 'the effects of heated and other effluents and discharges on the condition of the tidal reaches of the River Thames'; from the Browne Committee on refuse storage and collection, to the Wilson Committee on the problem of noise; from the Key Committee on 'the experimental disposal of house refuse in wet and dry pits', to the Jeger Committee on sewage disposal. By contrast the remit of the Royal Commission is boundless: 'to advise on matters, both national and international, concerning the pollution of the environment; on the adequacy of research in this field; and the future possibilities of danger to the environment'.

Also of particular note is the Protection of the Environment Bill, introduced by the Conservative Government in 1973, but passed as the Control of Pollution Act, 1974, by a Labour Government. In its first guise, there was an interesting debate (in the House of Lords) on a proposal to introduce a 'general standard' for environmental protection: this would have required all public bodies to have regard to the impact of any major development (whether public or private) on the environment. This was explicitly based on American legislation (the National Environment Protection Act), with its requirement that any federal project has to be preceded by an 'environmental impact statement'. This proposal made no progress, and the new title of the Act is more accurate than that of the initial

Bill: it deals with four main issues: the deposit and disposal of waste on land; water pollution; noise, and atmospheric pollution.

It is impossible to deal with all these and other relevant issues within the confines of this chapter; and the selection of issues must be arbitrary. As with 'town and country planning' and 'amenity', 'environmental pollution' admits of no simple delimitation. The issues selected are derelict land, minerals, air pollution and noise.

DERELICT LAND

Though there is no statutory definition, derelict land is generally regarded as 'land so damaged by industrial or other development that it is incapable of beneficial use without treatment'. (This is the definition used in connection with the payment of government grants for reclamation.) Derelict land is commonly thought of as a legacy of the Industrial Revolution but this is only part of the picture: of the 43,000 hectares of 'inherited dereliction' in England recorded in 1974, some 10,000 hectares represented as *increase* since the end of 1971. Making allowance for land which had been reclaimed, the net increase in derelict land over the period was around 4,000 hectares. Detailed figures are given in the DoE statistical reports on the *Survey of Derelict and Despoiled Land in England 1974* (DoE, 1975).

Much derelict land (particularly waste tips and abandoned industrial land) is concentrated in relatively small parts of the older industrial areas of the north, the midlands and South Wales. It is this 'random incidence' (to use a phrase from the Hunt Committee Report on *Intermediate Areas*) which hinders a more rapid rate of reclamation. Quite small authorities with small resources of money, staff or expertise may find themselves faced with large problems. Even larger authorities may be faced with a formidable problem. The Hunt Committee called for a national programme and the establishment of a derelict land reclamation agency. (Specialist land reclamation units have now been established within the DoE, the Welsh Office and the SDD.)

Great advances in reclamation techniques have been made since the thirties. Slow and costly 'pick and shovel' methods have now given way to modern earth-moving machines which can move mountains of material at relatively low cost. Techniques of 'making soil' have been refined, and it is now possible to make grass and trees grow in the most uncongenial conditions. Furthermore, rising land values and the need for sites for open space, playing fields and all types of urban development have added an impetus to reclamation, particularly in or near urban areas. But local authorities have no statutory duty to reclaim derelict land or to improve its appearance. Their powers are purely permissive and, as is so often the case, much depends on the energy of individual local authorities.

There are various powers available to local authorities quite apart from their normal powers to provide housing, open space and schools under which they can acquire derelict land and reclaim it during the normal course of development. Derelict land can also be acquired under the wider powers provided by the Planning Acts; these enable local authorities to undertake any work for which powers are not already available. Finally, the National Parks and Access to the Countryside Act gives specific powers for the acquisition of derelict land and the restoration and improvement of such land whether or not it is owned by the local authority. There is, thus, no shortage of powers.

Government grants towards the cost of acquisition and reclamation of derelict land are available under several Acts. Under the Industrial Development Act, 1966, the rate is 85 per cent in development areas, provided that the clearance of the land 'is expedient with a view to contributing to the development of industry'. The local Government Act of the same year provided a 50 per cent grant for other areas. Following the report of the Hunt Committee, the Local Employment Act, 1970, provided for 75 per cent grants in intermediate areas and also in 'derelict land clearance areas'. The latter are areas where 'the economic situation in the locality is such' that it is 'particularly appropriate with a view to contributing to the development of industry in the locality' that grants should be paid.

This complicated system is a result of an attempt to give differential assistance according to the local employment needs of different areas. The underlying rationale is (in the words of the Hunt Committee) that an unfavourable environment depresses economic opportunity: dereliction 'deters the modern industry which is needed for the revitalization of these areas and helps to stimulate outward migration'. There is, thus, a clear ulterior motive. The same is not the case with the grants (this time at the rate of 75 per cent) in national parks and areas of outstanding natural beauty. Here the objective is the 'enhancement of natural beauty', or at least the restoration of beauty.

Additional to these two specific grant schemes, there is Exchequer assistance through the resources element of the Rate Support Grant. Here the object is straightforward assistance to local government finance. (The resources element is payable to any authority with rate resources lower than the national average in proportion to their population.) In 1973/4, local authority expenditure on land restoration and improvement throughout Great Britain exceeded £15 million, while Exchequer grants totalled some £9 million.

Much of the problem is, as already indicated, that of keeping pace with new dereliction. In England 94,000 hectares of land has permission for mineral working (of which a third is for sand and gravel). Such operations are, of course, subject to control but, as is explained in the following section, safeguarding environmental quality is only one of the several relevant considerations.

CONTROL OF MINERAL WORKING

The reconciliation between economic and amenity interests in mineral working is an obvious matter for planning authorities. It would, however, be misleading to give the impression that the function of planning authorities is simply to fight a continual battle for the preservation of amenity. Planning is concerned with competing pressures on land and with the resolution of conflicting demands. Amenity is only one of the factors to be taken into account. Thus it is a general policy to ensure that mineral working is carried on 'with proper regard for the appearance and other amenities of the area', and that when the working is finished the land should (wherever practicable) not be left derelict but 'restored or otherwise treated with a view of bringing it back to some form of beneficial use'. At the extreme – where mineral working would involve 'too great injury to the comfort and living conditions of the people in the area or to amenities generally' – mineral working can be limited or even prevented. Here a balance has to be struck between the economic need for minerals and the interests of amenity, and it is relevant (and indeed essential) to consider whether economic needs can be satisfactorily met from other sources with less damage to amenity.

There is, however, the equally important matter of safeguarding mineral deposits. Planning authorities have the positive function of ensuring that mineral deposits are not unnecessarily sterilised by surface development but are kept available for exploitation.

These are the broad policy matters with which planning authorities are concerned. The necessary powers are provided in the Planning Acts. Briefly these are for the making of the essential survey of resources and potentialities, the allocation of land in development plans, and the control (by means of planning permission) of mineral workings.

The survey required for the development plan is not, of course, simply a geological one. The planning authority have to assess the amount of land required for mineral working, and this requires an assessment of the future demand likely to be made on production in their area.

Mineral undertakers have long-standing powers to obtain rights over land containing mineral deposits. These were extended by regulations made under the Planning Acts (the latest were issued in 1971, as SI 1971, No. 756). With the range of powers available, mineral workings cannot, without good cause, be prevented by private landowners.

Powers to control mineral workings stem from the definition of 'development', which includes 'the carrying out of . . . mining . . . operations in, on, over or under land'. Further, the tipping of waste constitutes development (i.e. a material change of use) if, generally speaking, the area or height is extended. Special provisions apply to the National Coal Board's operations, which can be ignored for the moment. Apart from this, all mineral workings, ancillary buildings, depositing of waste and the construction of means of access to sites require planning permission. Because of the national need for minerals, planning authorities have been strongly advised by the DoE to pay attention to economic considerations: 'A fundamental concern of planning policy must be to ensure a free flow of mineral products at economic cost.' The long-term planning that is required for mineral exploitation means that planning permissions have generally been given for a working with a long life – commonly not less than fifteen years, and on occasion, up to sixty years. Before reaching a decision on an application, it is often necessary for the planning authority to consult a number of interested parties: the Ministry of Agriculture, the Forestry Commission, the statutory water undertakers, a river or conservancy board, and perhaps the Countryside Commission, the Nature Conservancy and the Inspector of Ancient Monuments. The representations of these bodies can lead to the making of conditions or the reinforcement of conditions which the planning authority wishes to impose in the interests of amenity. Conditions can be imposed, for example, requiring a phased programme of work in order to minimise the disturbance to agriculture, or a planned programme of working and restoration can be required. Conditions relating to restoration are among the most important. A mineral undertaker cannot, however, be required to put the land to any specific use after extraction has been completed, but *where practicable*, he can be required to leave it in a condition comparable to that in which he found it. Unfortunately, restoration is not always practicable. To quote from *The Control of Mineral Working*:

'The extent to which reclamation is possible will depend first on the physical nature of the quarry. About one-third of the land used for quarrying represents the wet working of gravel; about one-third deep quarries working into a hillside or deep holes in the ground or a combination of both; one-sixth shallow quarries; and the remaining sixth, workings in which a thin seam is extracted from beneath thick overburden. Wet gravel pits and other excavations which became waterlogged can be reclaimed only when suitable extraneous material is available at an economic cost; they sometimes have value for fishing, yachting or other recreational purposes, possibly after some landscape treatment has been carried out. Other deep holes can generally be put to use only when filling material is available. Waste material – including any overburden – can sometimes be used to reclaim part of the quarry or to raise the general level sufficiently for use to be made of the whole. (But the cost of such operations can often make this impracticable.) Shallow quarries and some hillside quarries where the floor is not much below the level of the adjoining land can often be brought back to use readily without the necessity of filling. Quarries working thin seams beneath thick overburden can also be readily reclaimed, the most numerous of this class being ironstone quarries.'

The Ironstone Restoration Fund

Of particular interest in this connection is the Ironstone Restoration Fund, which was established under the Mineral Working Act, 1951, to assist in the financing of reclamation in the midlands ironstone field where working was by opencast methods. Generally, ironstone operators and landowners make a contribution to the fund for each ton of ironstone extracted by opencast working. The Exchequer makes a further contribution. Payments are made from the fund for old derelict workings and for new workings where the cost of restoration exceeds a certain sum per acre.

The principle underlying this scheme – that land exploitation carries with it a duty to shoulder at least part of the costs of restoration – would at first sight seem incapable of extension. A similar principle – that exploitation involves costs to others which should be borne at least in part by the exploiters – is accepted in the Cheshire brine pumping subsidence scheme. The Brine Pumping (Compensation for Subsidence) Act, 1891, provided for payments to certain owners of property damaged by subsidence, from the proceeds of a levy on each ton of white salt produced within the Northwich area. The Cheshire Brine Pumping (Compensation for Subsidence) Act, 1952, brought the scheme in line with modern operating conditions and considerably extended the area over which it operated. The procedure is, thus, basically the same as with ironstone restoration – a levy on all operators related to their production. For a nationalised industry, the principle can be extended further, as in the Coal Mining (Subsidence) Acts of 1950 and 1957. These place on the National Coal Board the responsibility for making good any damage caused by subsidence resulting from coal mining – or the working of coal and other minerals simultaneously. Under the 1950 Act, grants were paid by the Treasury to the Board in respect of additional expenditure which the Act imposed on them, but this arrangement was not repeated in the 1957 Act. Thus, the Board carries the whole financial responsibility for subsidence damage.

Restoration can be a difficult and expensive operation. It follows that (as with subsidence) there is a case for 'pooling' in order that, for example, the costs of achieving some socially desirable restoration does not involve prohibitive expense for a particular operator. Some costs can, however, legitimately be placed squarely on individual operators. This is the case with improving the appearance of mineral workings by tree and shrub planting. Planning permission for mineral operations can be made conditional on adequate screening being provided.

Coal
Planning control over the operations of the National Coal Board is subject to special provisions. Briefly, the continued working of mines begun before 1 July 1948, is 'permitted development', and, therefore, does not require specific planning approval. The same applies to the continuance of waste tipping. Furthermore, there is a general permission for any development in connection with coal industry activities (as defined in section 63 of the Coal Industry Nationalization Act, 1946) and carried out in the immediate vicinity of a pithead. However, certain restrictions can be imposed (on the erection of buildings) in the interest of amenity. Mining operations on new sites require planning permission in the ordinary way.

Only 4 per cent of coal output in Britain comes from opencast workings – a very much lower proportion than in other countries. One of the reasons for the low proportion is that, despite its profitability, opencast working arouses considerable opposition – from farmers, local authorities, local inhabitants, amenity organisations and even miners. Clearly the visual impact of opencast working is far greater than that of deep mining, yet the loss of amenity is temporary and full restoration is practicable and usual; indeed, there can be a resultant improvement in amenity.

Opencast coal working began during the war under emergency

legislation. It continued under this legislation until 1958 and, though usually constituting 'development', was therefore outside the scope of planning control. The Opencast Coal Act, 1958, laid down a special method of control operated by the then Minister of Power (now the Secretary of State for Energy). Notices must be served on the local authorities concerned and, if they raise objections, a public inquiry must be held. The Secretary of State for Energy can direct that planning permission for the operations concerned 'be deemed to be granted'. His direction may include conditions of the sort commonly applied to planning permissions, and must include conditions to secure the restoration of the site. Where the land is in agricultural use, it is normally obligatory for the conditions to provide for the restoration of the land so that it is fit for agricultural use.

CLEAN AIR

Those who pollute the air are no longer sent to the gallows, but, though gentler methods are now preferred, it was not until the disastrous London smog of 1952 (resulting in 4,000 deaths) that really effective action was taken. The Beaver Report of 1954 described the effects of air pollution on health and made comprehensive recommendations on the prevention of pollution by smoke from industry and domestic chimneys, grit and dust, sulphur dioxide, motor vehicle exhausts and smoke from railway locomotives. Particularly telling was the Committee's estimate of the economic cost of pollution: £50 million a year through inefficiently burning fuel; £150 million in lost efficiency in agriculture, industry and transport caused by reduced plant growth and hours of daylight and increased illness; and £150 million from corrosion (due largely to sulphur dioxide) – a total of £250 million a year. (More recent estimates suggest that the cost of corrosion amounts to £600 million a year.)

There has been a growing emphasis on reducing air pollution as a part of a more general policy of environmental improvement. The Hunt Committee for instance, in discussing problems of economic growth, argued that 'tackling air pollution, like clearing derelict land, is a necessary part of the environmental rehabilitation which the older industrial areas need'.

Domestic Smoke
The Clean Air Acts of 1956 and 1968 prohibit the emission of dark smoke, provide for the control of the emission of grit and dust from furnaces and establish a system for the approval by local authorities

of chimney heights. However, the principal source of air pollution is domestic smoke and it is here that powers are the most extensive. Local authorities are empowered to establish 'smoke control areas' (subject to approval by the Secretary of State) in which the emission of smoke from chimneys constitutes an offence. This involves the conversion of grates to enable smokeless fuels to be burned. Grants are given (normally) equal to seven-tenths of the approved expenditure on the cost of installing smokeless appliances. (Central government reimburse local authorities four-sevenths of their expenditure except where a local authority house is concerned, in which case the proportion is 40 per cent.) The provisions here are flexible. Grant can be made not only on coversion of open grates but also as an alternative an equivalent amount can be given towards the cost of installing central heating or electric space heaters.

A departmental *Memorandum on Smoke Control Areas* stressed the need for detailed surveys of proposed smoke control areas, and the importance of consultation with local fuel producers and distributors, before orders were made defining the areas. Caution was urged:

'The establishment of smoke control areas will necessarily be gradual; it will need to be undertaken in stages, over a period of years in the larger towns. Progress will be governed by the supply of smokeless fuels, the rate at which appliances can be converted or replaced, and the rate at which local authorities are able to formulate and carry through their smoke control plans. Above all, progress – and indeed the whole success of the operation – will depend upon public support; upon people's understanding of the problems involved, and their readiness to co-operate in smoke control measures.'

Industrial Emissions

There are two systems of control of industrial emissions to the atmosphere in Britain. Most industrial processes are controlled by local authorities under the Clean Air and Public Health Acts. There are, however, certain processes which, because of their nature or the specialised and complex methods necessary to minimise emissions, are controlled by an expert and centralised inspectorate responsible directly to the Secretary of State for the Environment. This Alkali Inspectorate, as it is termed, originally came into being under the Alkali Act of 1863, now replaced by the Alkali Etc. Works Regulation Act of 1906, and the Alkali Etc. Works Order of 1966. A new Order, introduced in 1971, considerably extends the DoE's control over manufacturing operations which were previously regulated by local authorities. These new measures affect grit and dust emissions from mineral industry processes, discharges from processes used in the petro-chemical industry and emissions from the smelting of aluminium.

For several years, because of complaints about dust, the Inspectorate had been called in by local authorities to advise on the control of grit and dust emissions from processes involving the crushing, grinding, drying, heating and handling of metallurgical slags, pulverised fuel ash, limestone, chalk, igneous rocks, gypsum, china clay, ball clay and china stone. These processes have now been 'scheduled' and brought under the direct control of the Alkali Inspectorate.

The 1971 Order also covers petroleum works and the primary smelting of aluminium. Until recently, primary aluminium smelters have operated only in Scotland (and were scheduled under the Scottish Alkali Acts). With the development of smelters in England and Wales, the Alkali Inspectorate have been involved from the outset in specifying the best practicable means of controlling emissions from these.

The 1971 Order also brings under the control of the Inspectorate processes involving the use of di-isocynates and the manufacture and purification of acrylates. (Di- isocynates are used, for example, in the manufacture of expanded plastics; acrylates are used, *inter alia*, for surface coatings for plastic production fibres and textiles.)

As is apparent, this is a highly technical field which involves specialist knowledge not to be expected among local authority staffs: hence the centralisation of responsibility in the Alkali Inspectorate.

Pollution by Vehicles
More in the public eye is air pollution by motor vehicle exhausts. The United States Government are requiring stringent standards – despite strong opposition from manufacturers. The 1970 White Paper *The Protection of the Environment: The Fight Against Pollution*, however, states that 'in Europe, due to the differences in climatic conditions, air pollution from petrol-engined vehicles presents a different and less acute problem, and the development of a completely pollution-free car might not be the most sensible use of resources'. The matter is being 'kept under review'; and the Royal Commission on Environmental Pollution, in their first report, have warned against complacency. This is a field in which more research is called for: even though diesel fumes 'can be very offensive . . . there is no firm evidence that the present level of these pollutants is a hazard to health'. But the same can be said about slum housing. It

is to be expected that levels of public tolerability will rise, though the cost will have to be borne by a car-owning electorate.

NOISE

'Quiet costs money . . . a machine manufacturer will try to make a quieter product only if he is forced to, either by legislation or because customers want quiet machines and will choose a rival product for its lower noise level.' So stated the Final Report of the Wilson Committee in 1963. This, in one sense, is the crux of the problem of noise. More – and more powerful – cars, aircraft, transistor radios and the like must receive strong public opprobium before manufacturers – and users – will be concerned with their noise level. Similarly, legislative measures and their implementation require public support before effective action can be taken.

There is abundant evidence that this is growing: from the figures collected by the Association of Public Health Inspectors showing that the number of complaints of noise nuisance received by local authorities is increasing at the rate of about 10 per cent a year, to the Cabinet decision to locate the (now abandoned) third London airport at Foulness.

Transport is the main noise menace. The Road Research Laboratory have estimated that between 25 and 45 per cent of the urban population live in roads with traffic noise levels likely to be judged undesirable for residential areas; if noise levels are not reduced, the projected increase in vehicles will raise the proportion by 1980 to between one-third and two-thirds. The White Paper on *The Protection of the Environment* maintained that new regulations which came into effect in April 1970 had halted the trend towards increasing noise. It cannot be said that this is apparent: in any case (in the words of the Royal Commission), this will not do much to satisfy the public demand for *less* noise.

Aircraft noise is particularly obnoxious, and a battery of new powers have been introduced in recent legislation, such as the Airports Authority Act, 1965, and the Civil Aviation Act, 1968. This is a field in which international co-operation is particularly important, and the first fruits of the International Conference on Aircraft Noise (convened by the British Government) came with the 1970 Air Navigation (Noise Certification) Order. Subsonic jet aircraft will no longer be allowed to land or take off in the United Kingdom unless they have a certificate from the government of the country of registration that they comply with certain defined noise standards. This anticipates an international noise certification scheme in the formulation of which Britain is playing a leading part.

So far as commercial supersonic flights are concerned, the White Paper states that it is the Government's view that those which could cause a boom to be heard on the ground should be banned. This has a somewhat hollow ring following recent decisions on Concorde.

As is evident from the tone of the previous paragraph (based on government announcements) this is an area in which government is prone to make impressive proclamations which suggest that significant progress is being made. It is here that bodies such as the Royal Commission on Environmental Pollution and the Noise Advisory Council have an important role to play. On aircraft noise, the former ends a review of aircraft noise abatement by noting that 'if the volume of air transport continues to expand at a rate of 15 per cent per annum, the nuisance from aircraft will not easily be remedied, particularly if supersonic is added to subsonic flights'. Similarly, stimulating comments may be expected from the Secretary of State's Noise Advisory Council which has as its terms of reference, 'to keep under review the progress made generally in preventing and abating the generation of noise, to make recommendations to Ministers with responsibility in this field and to advise on such matters as they may refer to the Council'.

This is a field in which legislative provision is very scattered: relevant Acts include those dealing with Road Traffic, Civil Aviation and, most recently, Part III of the Control of Pollution Act (which provides for the introduction of 'noise abatement zones'). Reference should also be made to the important Circular on *Planning and Noise*, issued by the DoE in 1973 (Circular 10/73).

OTHER ENVIRONMENTAL POLLUTANTS

Many other pollutants and aspects of pollution would need to be discussed in a comprehensive account, including domestic and industrial waste, pesticides and fertilisers, water resources, litter, car cemeteries, pollution of the sea and radioactive waste disposal. A brief discussion is to be found in the White Paper *The Protection of the Environment* and in the *First Report of the Royal Commission on Environmental Pollution*. Further references are given in the Appendix.

Chapter X

PLANNING FOR LEISURE

The subject – and the problem – of planning for leisure is a large one. It encompasses national parks, access to the countryside, nature reserves, camping, caravanning, rambling and youth hostelling, waterways, parks and many other aspects of recreation. It involves difficult questions of amenity – if only because too many people can easily destroy the amenities they seek. Some aspects of preservation have been discussed in Chapter IX; here we are concerned with some of the major issues not merely of preserving and safeguarding amenities but of catering in a positive way for the increasing demand for leisure.

NATIONAL PARKS AND ACCESS TO THE COUNTRYSIDE

The demand for public access to the countryside has a long history, stretching from the early nineteenth-century fight against enclosures, James Bryce's abortive 1884 Access to Mountains Bill, and the attenuated Access to Mountains Act of 1939, to the promise offered by the National Parks and Access to the Countryside Act of 1949 – an Act which, among other things, poetically provides powers for 'preserving and enhancing natural beauty'. Many battles have been fought by voluntary bodies such as the Commons, Open Spaces and Footpaths Preservation Society and the Council for the Protection of Rural England (whose annual reports clearly indicate that their continued activity is still all too necessary), but they worked largely in a legislative vacuum until the Second World War. By the end of the twenties the campaign for public access to the countryside became concentrated on the need for national parks such as had been established in Europe and North America, but though an official National Park Committee – the Addison Committee – reported (in 1931) in favour of a national policy, no government action was taken. The mood engendered by the Second World War augured a better reception for the Scott Committee's emphatic statement that 'the establishment of national parks is long overdue'. The Scott Committee had very wide terms of reference, and for the first time an overall view was taken of questions of public rights of way and rights of access to the open country, and the establishment of national parks and nature reserves within the context of a national policy for the preservation and planning of the countryside. Government acceptance of the necessity for establishing national parks was announced in the series of debates on post-war reconstruction which took place during 1941 and 1943, and the White Paper on *The Control of Land Use* referred to the establishment of national parks as part of a comprehensive programme of post-war reconstruction and land-use planning. Not only was the principle accepted but, probably of equal importance, there was now a central government department with clear responsibility for such matters as national parks. There followed a series of reports on national parks, nature conservation, footpaths and access to the countryside.

THE DOWER AND HOBHOUSE REPORTS

The Dower Report was a personal report to the Minister of Town and Country Planning by John Dower, published 'for information and as a basis for discussion'. A national park was defined as 'an extensive area of beautiful and relatively wild country, in which, for the nation's benefit and by appropriate national decision and action:

(a) the characteristic landscape beauty is strictly preserved;
(b) access and facilities for public open-air enjoyment are amply provided;
(c) wild life and buildings and places of architectural and historic interest arc suitably protected; while
(d) established farming is effectively maintained'.

This conception of a national park was accepted by the Hobhouse Committee which also agreed with Dower's proposal for a special National Parks Commission – 'a body of high standing, expert qualification, substantial independence and permanent constitution, which will uphold, and be regarded by the public as upholding, the landscape, agricultural and recreational values whose dominance is the essential purpose of National Parks'. This Commission would select the areas for national parks and would employ in each park administrative and technical staff, headed by an assistant commissioner. These local executive bodies would act on behalf of the Commission and the local planning authority for each park. Management was to be under the control of an *ad hoc* park committee consisting of a chairman and fourteen members appointed by the Commission, together with fourteen members appointed by the local authorities in whose areas the park was situated. The whole cost of administering the parks was to be borne by the Exchequer.

This administrative organisation was devised in accordance with the conception of *national* parks as envisaged in both the Dower and Hobhouse Reports. Since the legislation departed substantially from these recommendations, it is worth outlining the reasoning to be found in these Reports. National parks were to be administered for the benefit of the nation: this apparent tautology had the implication that planning in park areas should not be carried out by the ordinary local government bodies with the Commission acting as an adviser and supplier of grants. Such a system would 'tend to separate and oppose, rather than to unite and fuse, the national and local points of view and requirements; it would multiply delays by inserting an additional rung in the planning ladder; and by dividing responsibility, it would encourage inefficient administration and patchy compromise plans. . . . If national parks are provided *for* the nation they should clearly be provided by the nation. . . . Their distinct costs should be met from national funds'.

THE NATIONAL PARKS AND ACCESS TO THE COUNTRYSIDE ACT, 1949

The Government, however, took the view that the newly constituted planning authorities (under the 1947 Act) should be given the responsibility for national parks: these authorities were only just beginning to function, and it was considered to be unreasonable at this stage to suggest that they were incapable of meeting this responsibility. A National Parks Commission was to be established but its functions were to be mainly advisory. As might be expected, criticism was centred on this issue, and it was argued that county councils would be concerend primarily with local interests and would not be keen to incur expenditure for the benefit of visitors.

The Government, however, were not to be shaken. Probably they felt that they had already taken sufficient powers away from local government and that it was politically inadvisable to create another *ad hoc* executive body. Be that as it may, the new functions were laid on the shoulders of local authorities. The National Parks Commission had a predominantly advisory role. (The past tense is used since the National Parks Commission was replaced by the

Countryside Commission in 1968.) They had a general duty to advise the minister on matters affecting the natural beauty of the countryside – primarily but not exclusively in national parks and other areas of outstanding natural beauty. Their main executive function was to select, after consultation with the local authorities concerned, the areas where they considered that national parks should be established. They also had a general responsibility for considering what action was required in the parks in order that these objects might be fulfilled, but could only make recommendations to planning authorities and 'representations' to the Government.

Having decided that executive functions should be the responsibility of local authorities, the problem immediately arose as to what should be done in cases where a park lay in the area of more than one local authority. The Act provided that in such cases a joint planning board was to be the normal organisation, though exceptionally a joint advisory committee might be established as an alternative. In fact, due to the strenuous opposition of local authorities (who were particularly anxious about the financial implications) only two joint boards were set up – for the Peak District and the Lake District parks. Four parks had joint advisory committees as well as separate park planning committees in each of the constituent local authorities. The remaining four parks lay wholly within the area of one local authority and were administered by a single local authority committee. (The position following local government reorganisation is outlined later in this chapter.)

A problem which has particularly exercised the attention of the Commission and the park authorities is that of development by government departments and statutory undertakers. Fears that this would prove a major problem were voiced during the debates on the Bill. Indeed, it was pointed out that 'the demands of these bodies would be more difficult to resist than those of private developers since the Government would in effect be not only the judge but also the defendant'. The catalogue of what Lord Strang, former chairman of the Commission, has called 'alien intrusions' is a formidable one, and includes defence installations in the North Yorkshire moors and on the Pembrokeshire coast; masts for the GPO, the Air Ministry, the Ministry of Aviation, for defence or for communications or for air navigation: masts for the police and other services and for transport undertakings; a nuclear electricity generating station and a pumped storage installation in Snowdonia with the accompanying network of transmission lines on pylons for the supergrid; overhead distribution lines in every part of the country; two oil refineries and an oil terminal on Milford Haven astride the eastern boundary of the Pembrokeshire coast park; recurrent and

increasing demands for water in almost every national park, cul-
minating in the great controversy aroused by the claims of the
Manchester Corporation upon Ullswater and Bannisdale. The
problem is an intractable one. By their very nature national parks
are ideally suitable for military training; they contain valuable
mineral deposits; some of them can provide unrivalled water resources; the development programme of the Central Electricity
Generating Board (to meet a demand for electricity which is
doubling every ten years) involves a wide and high-powered transmission network and thus more and bigger pylons which cannot be
hidden in the landscape and which cannot be obviated – except at
enormous cost – by placing cables underground. These are all
symptoms of the enormous pressures on land exerted by an increasingly affluent society in a densely populated country.

It would, however, be misleading to give the impression that the
Commission have had no success. Much more effort is now being
expended to make 'inevitable' developments as unharmful as possible. Statutory undertakers such as the Central Electricity
Generating Board are now legally required to plan their operations
with regard to amenity and to employ landscape architects; and
public companies can be obliged or persuaded to do likewise. The
nuclear power station in Snowdonia and the development by petroleum companies at Milford Haven can be instanced.

This conflict between utility and beauty arises in a less spectacular
but more intense form in connection with the livelihood and living
conditions of the people who inhabit the parks. National parks in
this country are not vast reserves of the kind found in Africa or
America. They are areas of designated land in which ordinary rural
life, rural industry and afforestation continue normally. The people
living in these areas rightly demand modern amenities such as
electricity and telephones, good-quality housing and – obviously –
employment. These 'amenities' may clash with those sought by
visitors, but the inhabitants cannot be expected to forgo these 'alien
intrusions'. Nor should they be expected to shoulder the financial
burdens involved in placing cables underground, in using expensive
materials in new buildings for the sake of pleasant appearance, or in
repairing damage caused by visitors.

The biggest conflict, however, is that between the twin purposes
of the Act: to preserve amenities and to promote the enjoyment of
the public. This has increased as the amount and character of
recreational demands on the national parks has grown. The implicit
assumption in the 1949 Act (which gave equal weight to the
twin objectives) that conflicts could be readily resolved has proved
to be false (as the Sandford Committee demonstrate). The only

solution lies in much greater positive provision for recreational needs.

NATIONAL PARKS IN SCOTLAND

Though a Scottish Committee (the Ramsay Committee) recommended, in 1945, the establishment of five national parks in Scotland, no action was taken along the lines of the English National Parks Act. Nevertheless, the Secretary of State used the powers of the 1947 Planning Act to issue National Parks Direction Area Orders. These require the relevant local planning authorities to submit to the Secretary of State all planning applications in these areas. In effect therefore (in an almost Gilbertian manner) while Scotland does not have national parks, it has an administrative system which enables controls to be operated as if it did! But of course this approach was inherently negative, and it was not until the Countryside (Scotland) Act 1967 that positive measures could be taken (apart from the establishment of nature reserves and of national forest parks – both the responsibility of all-Britain authorities).

The 1967 Act set up the Countryside Commission for Scotland which (apart from national parks) has operated in a similar manner to the National Parks Commission and its successor, the Countryside Commission. In 1974, the Countryside Commission for Scotland published a report on *A Park System for Scotland*. This rejected the concept of national parks and, instead, proposed a park system (with special park authorities) which seems essentially the same as that which operates under the name of 'national parks' south of the Border.

At the time of writing the Secretary of State is 'actively considering' the proposals in the light of the reactions of local authorities and other bodies concerned with the countryside.

AREAS OF OUTSTANDING NATURAL BEAUTY

Both the Dower and the Hobhouse Reports proposed that, in addition to national parks, certain areas of outstanding landscape beauty should be subject to special protection. These areas did not (at that time) require the positive management which it was assumed would characterise national parks, but 'their contribution to the wider enjoyment of the countryside is so important that special measures should be taken to preserve their natural beauty and interest'. The Hobhouse Committee proposed that these 'conservation areas' should be the responsibility of local planning authorities, but would receive expert assistance and financial aid from the National Parks Commission. Advisory committees (with a majority of local authority members) would be set up to ensure that they would be comprehensively treated as a single unit. A total of fifty-two conservation areas, covering 9,835 acres was recommended – including, for example, the Breckland and much of central Wales, long stretches of the coast, the Cotswolds, most of the Downland, the Chilterns and Bodmin Moor.

The 1949 Act did not contain any special provisions for the care of conservation areas, the power under the Planning Acts being considered adequate for the purpose. It did, however, give the National Parks Commission power to designate 'areas of outstanding natural beauty' and provided for Exchequer grants on the same basis as for national parks. So far, thirty-two areas have been designated covering 5,583 square miles.

Areas of outstanding natural beauty are generally smaller than national parks. They are the responsibility of local planning authorities who have powers for the 'preservation and enhancement of natural beauty' similar to those of park planning authorities. Unfortunately, despite the Exchequer grant-aid which is available for 'improvement' schemes, local planning authorities are often reluctant to make use of their powers. This is partly due to their unwillingness to incur the necessary expenditure and partly due to the fact that they simply do not think in terms of catering for the holiday-maker. Some authorities, however, have followed more enlightened policies. Recent examples quoted in the annual reports of the National Parks Commission and the Countryside Commission include reclamation of a former RAF camp in Cannock Chase, a discontinuance order on a scrap-dump near Old Sodbury, the purchase of land for public access at Durlston Head, Swanage (which is on the route of the South-West Peninsula Coastal Footpath), and increased public access in the Surrey Hills. Nevertheless, there is a good reason to lament with the Commission that progress has been very slow.

THE COASTLINE

About a third of the coastline of England and Wales is included in national parks and areas of outstanding natural beauty. Additionally, development plans indicate 'areas of high landscape value' and 'areas of scientific interest' – national nature reserves or sites of special scientific interest notified to local planning authorities by the Nature Conservancy. Then there are coastal areas owned or protected by the National Trust. Nevertheless, the pressures on the coastline are proving increasingly difficult to cope with. Growing numbers of people are attracted to the coast for holidays, for recreation and for retirement. Furthermore, there are economic pressures for major industrial development in certain parts, particularly on some of the estuaries: Milford Haven and Southampton Water are cases in point.

The problem is a difficult one which cannot be satisfactorily met simply by restrictive measures: it requires a positive policy of planning for leisure. A welcome move in the right direction was started in 1963 with MHLG Circular 56/63, *Coastal Preservation and Development*, to local planning authorities with coastal boundaries. This argued that, because the coast is of exceptional value and subject to heavy pressures for development, it merits special study and control. Authorities with coastal boundaries were, therefore, asked to make a study of their coastal areas in consultation with the National Parks Commission and, for scientific advice, the Nature Conservancy. The Circular was followed in 1965 by a letter expressing the deep concern of the planning ministers about the worsening situation and the inadequacy of the measures being taken to prevent the spread of development on the coast. Meanwhile, local planning authorities were exhorted to speed up plans and policies. MHLG Circular 7/66, *The Coast*, asked for clear statements 'of each planning authority's policy for their coastal area in standard cartographic form'. Nine regional conferences on coastal preservation and development were held in 1966 and 1967 and resulted in a series of detailed reports.

These formed the base of a major coastal study on which a number of major reports have been published by the Countryside Commission. Their final reports *The Planning of the Coastline* and *The Coastal Heritage* were published in 1970. The former attempted to clarify the problems and to identify the principles which should guide planning action. The latter amplified the arguments for stringent protection of the finest coastal scenery. It proposed that these should be designated as 'heritage coasts', for each of which there would be a delegation of planning and management functions from the local planning authority to a special committee whose members would include nationally supported representatives.

This formal designation and special machinery was rejected by the central government, and local authorities were advised (in DoE Circular 12/72) that policies in relation to heritage coasts should be incorporated in the new structure and local plans.

By the end of 1974, eighteen heritage coasts had been defined, extending over 400 miles. Discussions are under way between the

Countryside Commission and the local authorities for defining a further 400 miles. (A map is to be found in the Commission's 1973–4 annual report.)

PUBLIC RIGHTS OF WAY

The origin of a large number of footpaths is obscure. As a result, innumerable disputes have arisen over public rights of way. Before the 1949 Act, these disputes could be settled only by a case-by-case procedure, often with the evidence of 'oldest inhabitants' playing a leading role. The unsatisfactory nature of the situation was underlined by the Scott, Dower and Hobhouse Reports, as well as by the Special Committee on Footpaths and Access to the Countryside. All were agreed that a complete survey of rights of way was essential, together with the introduction of a simple procedure for resolving the legal status of rights of way which were in dispute. The National Parks Act provided for both.

Responsibility for making the survey of paths rests with county councils. Maps are prepared in three stages: draft, provisional and definitive. A 'draft map' shows the paths over which the council, as a result of its survey, decides that there are reasonable grounds for believing that a public right of way exists. When this is published, 'representations' can be made for certain paths to be excluded or new ones added. There is a right of appeal to the minister. This procedure provides an opportunity not only for objections from landowners, but also for organisations and individuals concerned with the preservation of rights of way to present their case for paths which are not included in the map. After all objections and appeals have been settled, a 'provisional map' is published incorporating all the changes which have been decided. At this stage landowners can contest a path by appealing to Quarter Sessions for a declaration as to the existence or non-existence of rights of way. Subject to certain rights of appeal to the High Court, these declarations are final. When all the disputed cases have been dealt with by Quarter Sessions, a 'definitive map' is published: this provides conclusive evidence of the existence of all rights of way shown on it – though there is provision for revision.

The preparation of this 'Domesday Book' of the 103,000 miles of footpaths in England and Wales has proved a laborious and lengthy process. Under the Act, the normal completion date for the preparation of draft maps was to be December 1952; in fact, it was not until June 1960 that all draft maps had been published. By the end of 1971 there still remained eleven counties in England and Wales which had not completed definitive maps.

A Footpaths Committee, under the chairmanship of Sir Arthur Gosling, was appointed in 1967 'to consider how far the present system of footpaths, bridleways and other comparable rights of way in England and Wales and the arrangements for the recording, closure, diversion, creation and maintenance of such routes are suitable for present and potential needs in the countryside and to make recommendations'. Their report was published in 1968, and the majority of the recommendations were implemented in the Countryside Act 1968, and the Town and Country Planning Act 1968. These include placing a duty on landowners to maintain stiles and gates, and requiring highway authorities to make a contribution towards the cost, providing for pedal cyclists to use bridleways, and placing a duty on highway authorities to signpost footpaths and bridleways where they leave a metalled road. A special review must be made of roads used as public paths so that public rights over them will be clear.

The Report of the Select Committee of the House of Lords on *Sport and Leisure* made a number of recommendations in relation to footpaths, following their conclusion that 'local authorities should now show much more energy in enforcing a law which is too often ignored with impunity'.

LONG-DISTANCE FOOTPATHS

Though work on the footpaths survey has been disappointingly slow, considerable progress has been made with what are officially termed 'long-distance routes'. These hikers' highways now extend over some 1,500 miles and include the 250-mile long Pennine Way and the 168-mile Offa's Dyke Path. The designation of these routes has been equally laborious, but they have had the attention and backing of the Commission – who have official responsibility for their establishment. The Commission are the initiating body: they make the proposals, discuss them with the local authorities concerned and presents a report to the Secretary of State. This shows the route together with existing public rights of way, and may contain proposals for the improvement of paths and the provision of new ones; ferries; and accommodation, meals and refreshments. However, though eligible for Exchequer grant, the implementation of approved proposals rests with district councils. The Commission can negotiate, persuade and offer assistance, but they can go no further. Furthermore, since the completion of the statutory survey of rights of way by local authorities has (in the words of the Commission) been so woefully slow, the legal status of footpaths is often uncertain. This – and particularly the slow progress made with the creation of new rights of way – had held back the completion of approved long-distance routes.

FORESTRY

Forestry is relevant in several ways to the subject matter of this book. In the first place it makes major claims on land: the forest area of Great Britain amounts to 4·6 million acres, or 8 per cent of the land surface. Forestry Commission land totals nearly 3 million acres, of which 1·8 million acres are under plantation. The Commission plant over fifty thousand acres each year. However, an adequate discussion of the land needs for forestry and of forestry policy would take us too far afield. (See the *Annual Reports* of the Forestry Commissioners and the Report by them on *Post-War Forest Policy*, Cmd 6447, 1943; also the review of *Forestry Policy*, published in June 1972.) Here attention is briefly focused on the Forestry Commission's recreational policies.

'It is almost a truism that in these small islands it is necessary to reconcile the claims of amenity and economic utilization; if they are kept in watertight compartments there will not be enough land to go round.' So stated the Forestry Commissioners in their 1943 Report on *Post-War Forest Policy*. It is in recognition of this fact that the Forestry Commissioners have evolved a positive policy for providing access facilities in State forests. The policy was first worked out in the New Forest and the Forest of Dean, the only two of the many royal forests which have survived substantially intact from Norman times. Today there are seven forest parks of which two are in England and Wales. Additionally there is the New Forest, in Hampshire, which though not a forest park, can be regarded as such, since it provides equivalent access and recreational facilities.

A statement of 'recreation policy' was published in the Forestry Commission's *Annual Report* for 1971 (and reproduced in the Report of the Select Committee of the House of Lords on *Sport and Leisure*):

'The Commission's policy is to develop the unique recreational features and potential of its forests, particularly where they are readily accessible to large numbers of visitors from the major cities and holiday centres. This will be done in conformity with the Commission's statutory powers and obligations, within the financial resources available and subject to the primary objective of timber production. The Commission will ensure that its recreational development will neither injure the forest environment nor conflict with its conservation.'

Public recreational facilities provided by the Commission are increasing significantly. For instance, between 1971 and 1974 the number of camp sites increased from 9 to 16; picnic sites from 177 to 315; and information centres from 16 to 24. Nevertheless, the Select Committee of the House of Lords have urged the Commission 'not only to open their land for recreation but to exploit it':

'The Committee consider that the Forestry Commission must be willing to stimulate demand to an extent for which they are not now ready. There may be sensitive countryside where a forest "honey-pot" (a facility intended to attract people to it, thereby diverting them from elsewhere) can contribute to the conservation of threatened areas and where a national recreation strategy shows that demand ought to be concentrated. In these circumstances the Commission should recognise the responsibility to attract visitors.'

NATURE CONSERVATION

The concept of wild life 'sanctuaries' or nature reserves is one of long standing and, indeed, antedates the modern idea of national parks. In other countries some national parks are in fact primarily sanctuaries for the preservation of big game and other wild life, as well as for the protection of outstanding physiological features and areas of outstanding geological interest. British national parks are somewhat different in concept: the emphasis is on the preservation of amenity and providing facilities for public access and enjoyment. The concept of nature conservation, on the other hand, is primarily a scientific one concerned particularly with research on problems underlying the management of natural sites and of vegetation and animal populations. Nevertheless, as the Huxley Report on *Conservation of Nature in England and Wales* pointed out, there is no fundamental conflict between these two sets of interests: 'Their special requirements may differ, and the case for each may be presented with too limited a vision: but since both have the same fundamental idea of conserving the rich variety of our countryside and sea-coasts and of increasing the general enjoyment and understanding of nature, their ultimate objectives are not divergent, still less antagonistic.' However, to ensure that recreational, economic and scientific interests are all fairly met presents some difficulties. Several reports dealing with the various problems were published shortly after the war. The outcome was the establishment of the Nature Conservancy, constituted by a Royal Charter in March 1949 and given additional powers by the National Parks and Access to the Countryside Act. (It is now the Nature Conservancy Council.)

The Conservancy's main duties are to give scientific advice, to establish and manage nature reserves and to organise and develop research. It is the question of nature reserves which has particular relevance to the subject of this book. The Conservancy have powers to acquire land or to enter into agreements with owners in order that nature reserves may be established. In agreement cases the owner remains in full possession and has responsibility for management, but he agrees to manage in accordance with the advice of the Conservancy so as to preserve the scientific interest of the particular area. Local planning authorities can also – in consultation with the Conservancy – set up local nature reserves. The 'declaration' of a reserve does not of itself confer any public right of access whatsoever. Furthermore, the powers to make access agreements or orders in 'open country' are clearly not applicable to reserves: to make such an order over a nature reserve would be a contradiction in terms. This does not mean, however, that access to reserves is generally prohibited. It is the policy of the Conservancy to allow as much access as is compatible with proper scientific management. About half of the land in national nature reserves is generally open to the public without any restriction; the remainder is open only by permit.

THE EMERGENCE OF POSITIVE PLANNING FOR LEISURE

During the last decade or so there has developed an increasing awareness on the part of government that a much more positive approach is needed to the provision of facilities for leisure, recreation and sport. This can be seen in a wide range of fields (stretching beyond the confines of this book) – from the 'arts' to waterways, from sports provision to tourism, and from urban parks to caravanning. The decade is marked, at its beginning, by the 1966 White Paper *Leisure in the Countryside* and, at its end, by the 1975 White Paper on *Sport and Recreation.* During this period a large number of reports have been issued, including that of the Scottish Committee on *Land Resource Use in Scotland,* the Lords Committee on *Sport and Leisure* and the Sandford Committee on *National Park Policies.*

Reports, White Papers and legislation now constitute an impressive library. Several new agencies have been established: some, such as the Sports Council, with wide responsibilities; some, such as the British Tourist Authority and the three Tourist Boards (for England, Scotland and Wales), with responsibilities for the provision of amenities and facilities; others, such as the Lee Valley Regional Park Authority, with specific regional development and management responsibilities. A number of existing bodies have been given new responsibilities: the Waterways Board for example and, of particular importance, the National Parks Commission which has now become the Countryside Commission.

THE COUNTRYSIDE COMMISSION

The Countryside Commission replaced the National Parks Commission in 1968. The change of name signifies an extension of function. Responsibilities in relation to national parks and areas of outstanding natural beauty remain; but to these are added the duty 'to review, encourage, assist, concert or promote the provision and improvement of facilities for the enjoyment of the countryside generally, and to conserve and enhance the natural beauty and amenity of the countryside, and to secure public access for the purpose of open air recreation'.

The Commission have an important specific duty to undertake and commission research. To assist in this and to bring together the many bodies concerned (in varying degrees) with recreation a Countryside Recreation Research Advisory Group (CRRAG) has been set up and is chaired and serviced by the Commission. The members include representatives of the British Tourist Authority, the British Waterways Board, the Nature Conservancy and the Forestry Commission.

The Group maintain a comprehensive central record of research studies in the field of countryside recreation and conservation. A *Research Register* is published periodically and a modest research programme is under way.

A particularly interesting power given to the Commission under the Countryside Act is that to initiate and assist experimental projects involving some new element of countryside planning, and designed to illustrate their appropriateness to the area in which they are carried out or to similar areas.

COUNTRY PARKS AND PICNIC SITES

Until recently, national recreational policy has been largely concerned with national parks, areas of outstanding natural beauty, and the coast. Studies undertaken by the Greater London Council in connection with the Greater London Development Plan underline the need for a positive policy in relation to metropolitan, regional and country parks. One such park is being developed in the Lee Valley under special legislation. The Lee Valley Regional Park Authority was established in January 1967 with members appointed by fifteen local authorities and with powers to precept on the GLC and the county councils of Essex and Hertfordshire. This particular area (amounting to nearly 10,000 acres) is largely derelict and has been for many years. (It is now a quarter of a century since Abercrombie's *Greater London Plan* envisaged the valley as 'an opportunity for a great piece of regenerative planning'.) It has been graphically described (by the Civic Trust) as 'London's kitchen garden, its well, its privy and its workshop . . . London's back door'. The Lee Valley Regional Park Master Plan proposes a very wide range of facilities for recreation and education including twelve major multi-purpose recreation centres as well as four major centres for youth activity, water sports, motor sports and industrial archaeology. These are to be linked by river, canal, parkland and a park road (with tolls), footpaths and bridleways.

The Lee Valley project is an ambitious scheme. It is an exercise in 'regeneration' as well as in recreational planning. It is perhaps unique. But the concept of a major 'out-of-door' recreational facility has attracted considerable discussion in recent years and is now embodied as part of contemporary wisdom in the 1967 and 1968 Countryside Acts. As the 1966 White Paper *Leisure in the Countryside* explained, 'country parks' can achieve several desirable objectives at one and the same time. Country parks 'would make it easier for town-dwellers to enjoy their leisure in the open, without travelling too far and adding to congestion on the roads; they would ease the pressure on the more remote and solitary places; and they would reduce the risk of damage to the countryside – aesthetic as well as physical – which often comes about when people simply settle down for an hour or a day where it suits them, somewhere "in the country" – to the inconvenience and indeed expense of the countryman who lives and works there'.

By September 1974, 111 country parks had been approved in England and Wales, extending over 37,000 acres.

The Countryside Act also provided new powers for local authorities in relation to picnic sites. In the words of the White Paper, these are 'places in the countryside and on the coast where a country park would not be justified, but something better than a lay-by is needed by the family who want to stop for a few hours, perhaps to picnic, perhaps to explore footpaths, or simply to sit and enjoy the view and the fresh air'. Accordingly, local authorities are empowered to provide and manage picnic sites. By September 1974, 141 picnic sites had been approved. Statistics of country parks and picnic sites are to be found in the *Annual Reports* of the Countryside Commission.

RIVERS AND CANALS

Leisure in the Countryside promised that the Government would seek to evolve, in conjunction with the river authorities, public bodies and others concerned, comprehensive plans for developing the use for recreation of the country's waterways, natural or artificial. A major problem of canals, highlighted in the British Waterways Board's 1966 Report on *The Facts About The Waterways*, is that the minimum cost of keeping non-commercial routes open is at least £600,000 a year. To keep them open for pleasure cruising would add a further £340,000.

Following extensive discussions with the various interested parties and the publication, in 1967, of a White Paper, *British Waterways: Recreation and Amenity*, the 1968 Transport Act provided a 'new charter for the waterways'. The Board's waterways are now classified into three main groups: 'commercial waterways' to be principally available for the commercial carriage of freight; 'cruising waterways' to be principally available for cruising, fishing and other recreational purposes; and 'remainder waterways'.

The effect of the new arrangements is that over 1,400 miles of waterways will remain open for pleasure cruising. The Board's annual deficits (on all operations) are borne by the Exchequer. It was originally proposed that the financial position in relation to cruising waterways would be reviewed after five years. However, the Government were persuaded that such a formal review would create uncertainty and discourage private commercial investment and development (e.g. in the building of marinas or the provision of cruising craft for hire). Instead, an Inland Waterways Amenity Advisory Council was established, one of whose functions is to consider proposals for the closure of individual waterways 'if this becomes necessary in the national interest'. The Council's functions are not, however, narrowly circumscribed; they include the consideration of 'any matter affecting the use or development for amenity or recreational purposes, including fishing, of the Cruising Waterways and any matter with respect to the provision of services and facilities for those purposes on the Cruising Waterways or the Commercial Waterways and, where they think it desirable, to make recommendations on such matters to the Board or to the Secretary of State after consulting the Board'.

NATIONAL PARKS AND LOCAL GOVERNMENT REORGANISATION

Under the 1972 Local Government Act, planning functions in a national park are largely allocated to county councils which must establish a national park committee to carry out these functions. There are, however, exceptional provisions for the Lake District and the Peak District: here new planning boards have been set up to replace the previous joint boards. In all cases, however, one third of the members are appointed by the Secretary of State.

For each national park, a national park officer must be appointed (after consultation with the Countryside Commission). A national park plan must be prepared (by April 1977) setting out the policy for the management of the park and 'the exercise of the functions exercisable' in relation to the park.

A number of functions are, however, to be carried out by district councils concurrently with a park committee or board (e.g. tree preservation, treatment of derelict land, public access and the provision of country parks). Moreover, there is provision (subject to the agreement of the Countryside Commission) for arrangements to be made with district councils to carry out any of the functions of a committee or board on an agency basis. (Full details are set out in DoE Circulars 63/73 and 65/74.)

Local government reorganisation has resuscitated debate about the administration of national parks and, in November 1975, it was announced that the Environment Sub-Committee of the Expenditure Committee would be examining this issue in the broad context of an inquiry into 'the operation of the Countryside Act 1968, the National Parks and Access to the Countryside Act 1949 and related legislation, with particular reference to the public expenditure involved, the effect of local government reorganization on the operation of the Acts, and the future development of policy on national parks and public access to the countryside in the light of the Sandford Report'.

THE MULTIPLICITY OF AGENCIES

Only a selection of leisure planning issues and the responsible organisations have been discussed in this chapter. The subject warrants a book in itself. The reader interested in further exploration of the labyrinth is referred to the Report of the Select Committee of the House of Lords on *Sport and Leisure* (and the 1975 White Paper *Sport and Recreation*). Much of the problem stems from the fact that (to quote from the Lords' report) 'recreation is often a by-product of some primary function – forestry and education are examples'). But, more fundamentally, the focus of interest and policy has changed. The matter is no longer simply one of physical planning: it is basically one of providing for a range of needs. Existing institutional arrangements are reeling under the impact, and there is no neat solution. The Lords Committee rightly stressed the primary importance of local authorities – as does the White Paper – but little development of significance can be anticipated until more resources are available for public expenditure. In the longer term, it is likely that regional organisations will assume increasing importance since it is at this level where 'planning for leisure' is most appropriate. Whether these will continue to be regional arms of national bodies or agencies of local government remains to be seen.

Chapter XI

NEW AND EXPANDING TOWNS

THE CASE FOR NEW TOWNS

In the context of post-war planning the arguments in favour of new towns were simple and overwhelming. The large cities – above all London – had grown too large: improved housing conditions had been obtained at unwarranted social and economic cost. Yet the need for more houses had not abated: on the contrary, it had been increased by the cessation of building during the war, by population growth and (at the time only dimly understood) household growth, and by the recognition and acceptance of the need for major reconstruction and thinning out of congested urban areas. Further large-scale peripheral expansion could not be countenanced: the only alternative was long-distance dispersal. Some of this could go to expanded small towns, but the scale of the problem was too great to be dealt with solely by this means. Further, it was obvious that the local government machinery was not suited to undertake building on the scale required, even if local housing situations made it politically viable that local authorities could contemplate a major building programme for non-local people. The basic solution, therefore, was the building of new towns by new *ad hoc* agencies.

The main alternatives were private enterprise and government-sponsored corporations. Private enterprise was rejected by the Reith Committee. They stated:

'While it is desirable to provide every opportunity for private development, we have come to the conclusion that in an undertaking of so far reaching and special a character as the creation of a new town, ordinary commercial enterprise would be inappropriate. Apart from the risks involved, both in matters of finance and in execution, such a policy would of necessity result in the creation of a private monopoly.'

Three essential features thus characterised early post-war new town policy:

(i) Their basic function was to relieve the housing pressures of London and other big cities.

(ii) This was to be achieved by 'the antithesis of the dormitory suburb' – by 'self-contained and balanced communities for work and living'.

(iii) New town development was to be carried out by government-sponsored corporations.

But a fourth feature needs stressing: new towns were only part of a wider policy for the distribution of population and employment. Other parts of this policy were green belts, industrial location control and expanded towns. No proper assessment of the achievements of the British new towns can be made without a parallel assessment of these other parts of the wider policy.

THE EARLIER POST-WAR NEW TOWNS

The new towns policy was thus conceived largely as a means of dealing with urban congestion. The eight London new towns have had this as their prime objective. The policy has, however, been applied to other problems. Even in the London ring of new towns, there is one – Basildon – where a primary object is rural slum clearance. (The area was one of extensive unplanned and largely unserviced shack development.)

Of the six original provincial new towns, five were in areas of regional decline – Peterlee, Aycliffe, East Kilbride, Glenrothes and Cwmbran, *Corby* was a special case, with the predominant objective of providing housing for the growing work-force of the Stewart and Lloyd's steel works. Yet, in a real sense, all of these six new town were special cases. *Peterlee*, the miners' town (built on a coalfield) aimed at concentrating, in one urban area, development which would otherwise have been scattered throughout a number of small mining villages, none of which could provide town facilities and amenities. *Aycliffe*, adjacent to a major trading estate, developed from a war-time Royal Ordnance Factory. It aimed at capitalising on this investment, but (because of intense local opposition in an area where the local MP happened to be Hugh Dalton, the Chancellor of the Exchequer) was restricted initially to a target population of a mere 10,000. *Cwmbran*, five miles from the centre of the 100,000 population county borough of Newport, but attractively placed for industry, had 8,000 existing jobs and a growing problem of journeys to work. Here the objective, as in Corby, was to serve industrial growth, but in a location which was agreed to be far from ideal, yet (to use the laconic words of the official report

Town and Country Planning 1943–51) one to which 'there was no alternative available which would not be open to still worse objections'. (The cynics were more pointed: if England and Scotland had new towns then Wales had to have one: a badly located new town was better than none at all.) *East Kilbride*, four miles 'over the hill' from the edge of Glasgow, was proposed in the Abercrombie-Matthew Clyde Valley Regional Plan: its twin aims were to take overspill from Glasgow and to act as a growth point in a favourable area of central Scotland. *Glenrothes*, again the product of a regional plan (the Mears Plan for Central and South-East Scotland), was conceived as a major plank in the policy of developing the East Fife coalfield to offset the decline of the Lanarkshire coalfields, but the disastrous failure of the Rothes Colliery led to a change in aim: Glenrothes became a centre for regional development loosely linked with Glasgow overspill.

CUMBERNAULD

Cumbernauld stands on its own – in several senses. It was the only new town designated in the fifties. Like East Kilbride it was proposed in the Clyde Valley Regional Plan, it is close to Glasgow and has a high level of commuting. Architecturally it is unique, and for this reason (rather than its location on the top of an exposed hill in central Scotland) it has proved most popular with architects: the seal of professional approval was provided when the town became the first winner of the R. S. Reynolds Memorial Award for Community Architecture. It also claims to be the safest town in Britain: road accidents are only 22 per cent of the national average, allegedly because of the advanced road design and segregation of traffic and pedestrians.

THE NEW TOWNS OF 1961–6

Cumbernauld was the one new town designated during the ten years from 1951 to 1960. Between 1961 and 1966, seven more were designated: five in England and two in Scotland. Four of the English towns are intended for overspill from two conurbations: *Skelmersdale* and *Runcorn* for Merseyside, and *Redditch* and *Dawley* for the West Midlands. They are, therefore, essentially the same in concept as the London new towns, though Dawley differs in three ways. First, whereas the other three towns have clear locational advantages, Dawley is relatively inaccessible and outside the main line of development in the midlands. Secondly, its terrain is, to put it mildly, inhospitable. Or, to use the more romantic words of

The New Towns, 1974

London Ring	Date of Designation	Population Original	At 31.12.74
Basildon	1949	25,000	84,900
Bracknell	1949	5,100	41,300
Crawley	1947	9,100	71,000
Harlow	1947	4,500	82,250
Hatfield	1948	8,500	26,000
Hemel Hempstead	1947	21,000	73,000
Stevenage	1946	6,700	74,800
Welwyn Garden City	1948	18,500	40,000
Total: London Ring		98,400	493,250
Others in England			
Aycliffe	1947	100	25,000
Central Lancs	1970	235,600	242,500
Corby	1950	15,700	53,750
Milton Keynes	1967	40,000	64,000
Northampton	1968	131,100	145,400
Peterborough	1967	81,000	98,000
Peterlee	1948	200	26,500
Redditch	1964	32,000	49,700
Runcorn	1964	28,500	48,200
Skelmersdale	1961	10,000	39,000
Telford (Dawley)	1963	70,000	94,200
Warrington	1968	122,300	133,000
Washington	1964	20,000	39,000
Total: Others in England		786,500	1,058,250
Wales			
Cwmbran	1949	12,000	43,000
Mid-Wales (Newtown)	1967	5,000	6,700
Total: Wales		17,000	49,700
Total: England and Wales		901,900	1,601,200
Scotland			
Cumbernauld	1955	3,000	38,500
East Kilbride	1947	2,400	71,500
Glenrothes	1948	1,100	32,500
Irvine	1966	34,600	50,100
Livingston	1962	2,000	22,500
Stonehouse	1973	7,200	7,800
Total: Scotland		50,300	222,900
Total: Great Britain		952,300	1,824,100

Arnold Whittick, the site is 'rich in relics of the iron industry and can justly claim to be the cradle of the industrial revolution'. Be that as it may, it is an expensive town to develop. Thirdly, its designated area was more than doubled in 1968 when its name was changed to *Telford* and its target population increased from 90,000 to 220,000. This brings it into the 'new city' class of the later sixties.

The fifth English new town of the 1961–6 period is *Washington* – some nine miles from Newcastle upon Tyne. This was the first provincial English new town to be explicitly proposed as part of a comprehensive regional programme. (See *The North-East: A Programme for Regional Development and Growth*, Cmnd 2206, HMSO, 1963.) Also of significance is the fact that it was the first new town intentionally sited as an extension of a conurbation. Other new towns (East Kilbride for example) may well eventually become extensions of conurbations but this was far from the intention. Washington is the prime example of a marked change in planning policy. Previously, new towns were conceived as a means of preventing urban growth: Washington is conceived as a means of accommodating it.

The two Scottish new towns of this period were both conceived as growth points in a comprehensive regional programme for central Scotland, though starting from very different bases: *Livingston*, some fifteen miles from Edinburgh, had a base population of 2,000, while *Irvine*, on the Ayrshire coast had 27,000.

Newtown (Montgomeryshire) is an unusual case of the adoption of the new town machinery for promoting regional development. It is situated in the largest area of rural depopulation in the country (England and Wales). Consultants reported that the case for a 'new town Newtown' was a weak one, if conceived solely in terms of a focal point for economic and social development in mid-Wales. (See *A New Town for Mid-Wales – Consultants' Proposals*, HMSO, 1966.) They concluded that designation could be justified only if overspill reception from the west midlands were incorporated into the plan. Nevertheless, optimists strongly support the view of the previous Secretary of State for Wales that the new town will stem and, ultimately, reverse the exodus of population from mid-Wales. Whether this can be achieved with an expansion of the scale envisaged – from 5,500 to 11,000 – remains to be seen.

THE NEW TOWN OF 1967-71

Apart from Newtown, five new towns were designated between 1967 and 1971. One of the most striking features of these latest new towns (like the enlargement of Dawley into Telford which was determined during the same period) is their huge size. In comparison with the Reith Committee's 'optimum' of 30,000-50,000, Telford's 220,000 and Central Lancashire's 500,000 appear massive. But size is not the only striking feature. Another is the fact that four of them are based on substantial existing towns. At the date of designation, *Peterborough* had 81,000 population, *Northampton* 131,000, *Warrington* 122,000 and *Central Lancashire* 236,000. Of course, town building has been going on for a long time in Britain and all the best sites have already been taken by what are now old towns. The time was bound to come when the only places left for new towns were the sites of existing towns.

In this situation, and given the scale of expansion, traditional terms such as 'new towns' and 'expanding towns' become inappropriate. Like the term 'overspill' they are now out of date. As with so many other aspects of town and country planning, new concepts are being embodied in old terms. Just as 'overspill' is being misleadingly applied to the accommodating of a major population increase, so the term 'new towns' is being used for major regional developments based on old towns.

Of course, few of the earlier new town were built on virgin sites (and those that were – Aycliffe and Peterlee – have had the most difficult time). Basildon had a scattered population of 25,000, while Hemel Hempstead was a substantial township of 21,000. But none of these earlier towns was in the same population class as the latest. Indeed, the original population of all the thirteen new towns designated between 1946 and 1951 was only fractionally greater (at 130,000) than that of the single 'new new' town of Warrington (at 122,000).

It would, however, be a mistake to infer that these relatively mammoth new towns were designated because the supply of alternative locations had run out. The reasoning had a number of strands. First, older towns were in need of rejuvenation and a share in the limited capital investment programme. It was not self-evident that economic sense or social justice was to be achieved by another round of traditional-type new towns. Related to this was the old economic argument that nothing succeeds like success; or, to be more accurate and precise, a major development with a population base of 80,000 to 130,000 or more has a flying start over one which has a mere 5,000–10,000. A wide range of facilities is already available, and (hopefully) can be expanded at the margin. There are numerous other advantages such as the much more varied housing market. On the other hand, the disadvantages are yet to be assessed.

It is also noteworthy that every one of these five newest towns is on excellent communications routes for both road and rail – four of them on the electrified rail line to Euston. This is 'linear planning' on a grand scale.

But perhaps too much should not be made of common features. These newer new towns are as varied as the old ones. Probably the only strictly valid common denominator is that they were all intended to assist in the accommodation of population increase. Three – Milton Keynes, Peterborough and Northampton – are linked with London overspill, while Warrington and Central Lancashire are linked with Merseyside and south-east Lancashire, though the links are somewhat tenuous.

STONEHOUSE

Stonehouse has the distinction of being the latest, the most precarious and possibly the last of the new towns. The case for Stonehouse was set out in a *Memorandum* by the Secretary of State for Scotland in 1972. Its main *raison d'être* was to meet the overspill requirements of Glasgow, while at the same time 'acting as a springboard for industrial expansion and renewal'. There is little doubt about the inherent attractiveness of the site – close to the junction of the M74 and A71 roads; but (at least with hindsight) there must be serious doubts about its relevance to the rapidly declining economy of Clydeside. Indeed, at the time of writing, the Strathclyde Regional Council are pressing the Secretary of State to abandon the new town – on the grounds not only that it is not needed, but that it will accelerate the decline of urban Clydeside and divert resources which are urgently needed to rejuvenate this old area.

In an extreme form, the position of Stonehouse mirrors doubts which are currently being expressed about the purpose of a new towns programme in current (and forecast) conditions. This is an issue which is touched upon further at the end of this chapter.

THE SELECTION OF SITES

The selection of sites for 'new' towns is very difficult in a small country such as Britain. The requirements are numerous: an adequate water supply (but avoiding the sterilisation of a material part of the catchment area for the water supplies of the region); good drainage; a reasonably flat site – not too hilly (which would be expensive) nor too flat (which would detract from the interest and potentialities of the site); near main roads and a through railway line (but not too close since this might involve extra costs for bridging, underpasses, relief roads and so on); a reasonable distance from existing large urban developments; not forgetting the avoidance of areas of 'outstanding natural beauty', of great historical interest, of mining subsidence or large surface workings, and of first-class agricultural land. Clearly these ideal requirements can rarely be met: the problem then becomes one of balancing costs and benefits.

Of the ten sites proposed in Abercrombie's Greater London Plan, only two – Stevenage and Harlow – were actually designated. Four were rejected on the grounds that they were too close to existing towns and therefore unlikely to survive as separate entities: Redbourn (near Hemel Hempstead, St Albans and Harpenden); Stapleford (near Hertford); Margaretting (near Chelmsford); and Holmwood (near Dorking – and in a particularly beautiful piece of countryside). Ongar was rejected partly because of its inadequate rail service (and the high cost of making it adequate) – a difficulty which applied also to Redbourn. White Waltham was situated in an area of valuable agricultural land and, furthermore, would have put a nearby airfield out of use. Growhurst was considered unattractive to industry and too near Crawley, which had been proposed to take the place of Holmwood.

In the provinces, the problem of the risk of subsidence has been acute. A proposed new town at Mobberley in Cheshire, though near to Manchester, was seriously considered but rejected because of liability to subsidence due to salt mining. In South Wales attempts to find a suitable site for a new town which could serve workers on the trading estate at Treforest, near Pontypridd, proved abortive.

There is, additionally, the political context within which decisions on new sites are made: this may exacerbate the physical problems or, alternatively, reduce the importance which is attached to them.

DESIGNATION

Once a site has been chosen the first formal step is designation. This is accomplished by means of a draft order, following which there are consultations with interested parties – particularly the local authorities concerned. If any objections cannot be settled administratively, a public local inquiry must be held. This is not a judicial one; it is a step in the administrative process by means of which objections are publicly stated and the minister is made aware of the extent to which his proposals are opposed. Before any case comes to inquiry, the proposed site and possible alternatives will have been exhaustively investigated, 'so that it is unlikely that the inquiry will disclose any major factor of which the Minister is not aware'.

Unfortunately, though such an attitude may be realistic, it is not one likely to be welcomed by local opponents: at the very least there is a clear need for an enlightened public relations policy. This was notably lacking in the early days of the new towns programme and considerable opposition – and litigation – resulted.

Objections to earlier new towns generally resulted at most in the exclusion of certain areas of agricultural land from the designated area: 317 acres at Crawley, 394 at Harlow, 763 at Bracknell, 1,050 at Corby and 2,020 at Hemel Hempstead. The designated area can, however, be extended at a later date, in which case – unless there are no objections – a further public inquiry is held. Bracknell, for instance, had its designated area increased by over 1,500 acres in 1961 and 1962.

THE NEW TOWN DEVELOPMENT CORPORATIONS

The New Towns Act (now consolidated for England and Wales in the Act of 1965, and for Scotland in the Act of 1968) provides for the setting up of development corporations to plan and create new towns wherever the Secretary of State is satisfied 'that it is expedient in the national interest' to do so. The corporations have powers 'to acquire, hold, manage and dispose of land and other property, to carry out building and other operations, to provide water, electricity, gas, sewerage and other services, to carry on any business or undertaking in or for the purposes of the new town, and generally to do anything necessary or expedient for the purposes of the new town or for the purposes incidental thereto'.

This followed the recommendations of the Reith Committee that a new and separate agency (with no other responsibilities) should be created for each new town. The justification for this was that the creation of a new town was not simply a matter of erecting buildings: it also involved 'the development of a balanced community enjoying a full social, industrial and commercial life'.

The corporations are not, however, the sole agency in new town development. Despite the apparently all-embracing character of their powers, they are not local authorities: education and local health services, for example, remain the responsibility of the normal local government machinery. Water, sewage disposal, gas and electricity, and hospitals are likewise the responsibility of the normal local or public authority. Nevertheless, where the necessary provision is beyond the technical or financial resources of the local authority, the development corporations can assist by undertaking the work themselves or by making a financial contribution: this applies particularly to water, sewerage and sewage disposal facilities. This provides a useful degree of flexibility, though it has often been a source of friction between the development corporations and local authorities. Much time and effort has had to be spent on determining the allocation of expenditure between these two types of authority. The problem is aggravated by their very different characters. As the former General Manager of Stevenage (A. C. Duff) has put it:

'. . . relations between the New Town Corporation and the Urban District (or Borough) Council are likely to require careful handling, even granted that there is goodwill on both sides, and unfortunately goodwill has been the exception rather than the rule. The Councillors are aware that the members of the Corporation devote less of their time to the business of the New Town than do the Councillors: that the members are paid but the Councillors are not; that the members are for the most part "strangers from London", while the Councillors are all local residents; and that the members are nominated by a Minister while the Councillors are elected by the ratepayers. The Councillors would be rather more than human if they did not on occasion feel some measure of both envy and resentment.'

FINANCE

Development corporations also differ from a local authority in that they are wholly financed from the Exchequer: advances are made from the Consolidated Fund. The New Towns Act of 1946 authorised issues up to £50 million to cover the needs of the first few years, but this total has been successively increased by later Acts. (The present total is £1,750 million, and may be further extended to £2,250 million by affirmative order of the House of Commons.) Exchequer advances are payable over sixty years, with interest at the rate prevailing at the date on which the advance is made. There is no concealed subsidy in the form of a concessionary rate of interest: the loans are made at a rate which reflects the current rate for government credit. The Reith Committee had recommended that all finance should be found by the State by way of loan but, in fact, the administration of these loans has proved to be very different from the Reith conception. The Reith Committee argued that it was 'most important that the financial autonomy and responsibility of the corporation shall be assured, and that development shall not be delayed or restricted by discussions of policy arising over applications for public advances'. This posited a degree of freedom for the corporations which it would be difficult to reconcile with public accountability. The balance is not easy to achieve, particularly where expenditure is proposed on risky ventures or developments for which there is no financial return. Since it is public money which is being invested, the Treasury have to ensure that each proposal is reasonable. But the Act goes further: it specifically requires that before approval is given to any proposal the Secretary of State must be satisfied that 'having regard to all the circumstances' a reasonable financial return can be expected. This gives the central departments a very large degree of control over the operations of the development corporations. In fact, new towns policy – both generally and in relation to individual towns – is framed by the Department of the Environment, not by the development corporations. Since it is the central government which is providing the capital it is difficult to see how this can be otherwise.

The position may well be different in the newer 'partnership' towns where the local authorities will be playing a major, not a subordinate, role. How this will work out in practice remains to be seen.

ASSESSING NEW TOWN ACHIEVEMENTS

Twenty-nine new towns with a current population of nearly 2 million; ranging in original size from less than 100 to 250,000 and in ultimate size from a possible 11,000 (Newtown) to 500,000 (Central Lancashire); differing in density, character, location and economic potential; and with various, and sometimes changing objectives – what criteria can be used for assessing their achievements? And is the assessment to be in terms of the adequacy of provision (however that is interpreted) or in terms of alternatives forgone? If the former, what is more significant: reduction in commuting, architectural merit, range of amenities, 'balance', impact on conurbation housing problems, financial profit and loss, reduction in road accidents, satisfaction of residents . . .? If the latter (alternatives forgone), would it have been a better economic investment (or a better social policy) to facilitate a larger amount of development on the periphery of the conurbations or, at the other extreme, to plan major developments in central Wales, the Borders or the Highlands? And how far should the new towns be judged by reference to their original objectives – as distinct from those which now seem to be more relevant?

No apology is needed for not embarking on even a superficial assessment here. Space permits only a brief account of progress in relation to employment and housing.

Unfortunately, even a summary of physical achievements is

difficult to provide since there is no comprehensive statistical return of the progress of development in the new towns (though the 1975 Report from the Expenditure Committee now provides a relative feast of data). More generally (to the bewilderment and astonishment of foreign visitors) incredibly little attempt has been made to learn from the experience gained in the new towns: government have taken an attitude which can only be described as nonchalant. Further, few serious academic studies have been undertaken.

The Reith Committee recommended the establishment of a Central Advisory Commission – both for 'harmonizing policy and practice' and for 'pooling information and experience'. This recommendation was never implemented, and such research, monitoring and statistical work which has been done within government has, at least until recently, been on an extremely limited scale. Furthermore, it has only been in recent years that any attempt has been made to undertake a comprehensive review of the new towns programme – and even this has been in terms mainly of regional planning policies and national public expenditure.

The figures in the following account are taken from the summaries provided annually in *Town and Country Planning* – the Journal of the Town and Country Planning Association.

EMPLOYMENT

The basic conception underlying the new towns was that they should be 'balanced' communities within which the majority of the inhabitants would both live and work. It follows that (to the extent to which this objective is attained) the rate of development will be determined by the growth of local employment. Industrial location in new towns is subject to the same control as exists over the country generally. The need to steer industry away from the high employment area of the south to areas of unemployment in the north proved difficult in the early years to reconcile with the need to stimulate industrial development in the London new towns, but once they became established these towns rapidly achieved boom conditions – to such an extent, in fact, that it became difficult to build houses at an adequate rate. Less favoured new towns – particularly Peterlee – have found the attraction of industry to be a longer-term difficulty. Generally speaking, however, the new towns have been able to offer sites and an environment which have proved most attractive to industrialists.

Development corporations are free to either build factories themselves and let them to firms, or lease sites on which the firms can build their own factories. (In a few exceptional cases the central government have agreed to the freehold disposal of sites.) It is generally felt that a balance of the two is desirable: letting produces a greater profit to the corporations, but the leasing of sites is thought to provide a welcome degree of stability and insurance against the effect of an economic crisis.

By the end of 1974, over 68 million square feet of factory space had been built in the new towns, of which 30 million were in the London ring, 15½ million in Scotland and 22½ million in the other new towns of England and Wales. (Aycliffe is excluded from these figures: adjacent to this new town is an industrial estate employing some 9,000 people.)

These statistics refer in the main to manufacturing industry: they exclude service industries which account for between 20 and 40 per cent of total employment. Service employment increases in response to local demands as the new towns grow: though provision can be – and is – made for them, they cannot be stimulated in the same way as can manufacturing industry. By 31 December 1974, some 4,000 shops (comprising over 10 million square feet) had been completed since the dates of designation.

Office employment, of course, can be encouraged, particularly as the large school populations enter the juvenile market. At the end of 1974, nearly 8 million square feet of new offices had been completed and a further 3 million square feet were under construction. Several government departments have offices in the new towns – the Stationery Office at Basildon, the Meteorological Office at Bracknell, the General Post Office at Hemel Hempstead, as well as the usual local offices of the Department of Health and Social Security and the Inland Revenue.

HOUSING

Nearly two-thirds of the capital expenditure incurred by development corporations has been for housing (£835 million out of a total of £1,400,000). The corporations have built some 220,000 houses and have been the main provider in all the new towns. They are not, however, the only house-building agency: local authorities have provided over 35,000 houses for renting, and private builders some 50,000 for owner-occupation. Increasing emphasis is being placed on owner-occupation, partly because of the rising demand for this form of tenure and partly because of the need to attract more private capital into the new towns. In 1967 the minister advised development corporations that in new towns started since 1961 the aim should be to achieve 50 per cent owner-occupation by the end of the planned build-up period. In the older new towns the aim is to achieve this proportion in new building.

The overwhelming demand in all the new towns has been for houses with gardens. Development has, therefore, been at low densities. This has led to the criticism that they lack 'urban character' – an aesthetic view which seems at variance with the principle of providing the type of dwellings which people want. In fact, great ingenuity and skill has been shown by the development corporations in planning a wide variety of architectural types, a range of interesting layouts and a generally high standard of landscaping. Of course, by no means all the schemes have been successful (though opinions will differ on which these are), but the general standard of new town housing is undoubtedly superior to the generality of post-war housing.

Unlike local authorities, development corporations have no pool of low-cost pre-war housing nor can they meet any deficiencies on their housing accounts from rate subventions. Their rents thus reflect the high costs and interest rates of the post-war period. There are, however, significant differences between different new towns, and between older and newer (Parker Morris standard) houses within individual towns.

THE COMMISSION FOR THE NEW TOWNS

The New Towns Act of 1946 envisaged that the new towns would eventually be transferred from the development corporations to local authorities. This was in line with Howard's principle that there should be local control and that profits (particularly those resulting from increases in land values) should accrue to the benefit of the towns themselves. It did, however, depart from the Reith Committee's majority view that it was unwise for the functions of (virtually monopoly) land ownership and local government to be combined in a single body.

In fact, as the time for the transfer approached it became clear – to the Conservative Government, if not to the Opposition – that ownership and management should remain in the hands of a body which was independent of the local authority. The New Towns Act of 1959 set up an *ad hoc* public body for this purpose – the New Towns Commission. To date, the Commission have taken over all the assets and liabilities of Crawley, Hemel Hempstead, Hatfield and Welwyn Garden City. (At the time of writing, the Government have announced that a Bill will be introduced during the present session to transfer housing to the local authorities.) The Commission are charged with the duty 'to maintain and enhance the value of the land held by them and the return obtained by them from it' while, at the same time, having 'regard to the purpose for which the town was developed and to the convenience and welfare of the persons residing, working, or carrying on business there'. They have powers to make contributions towards the cost of providing amenities for the town or of providing water supplies, sewerage or sewage disposal services. They can purchase land by agreement (but not compulsorily) either in or near the towns, and promote or assist business activity. Local committees must be set up in each town to manage residential property.

The Commission were established in October 1961, and the assets and liabilities of four new towns have so far been transferred to them. Apart from the local committee (who have full delegated powers for housing management), a local executive has been set up in each of the towns. These, in fact, consist almost entirely of officers transferred from the development corporations, and deal with the bulk of the committee's executive functions. Only a small headquarters staff is maintained in London.

Although the new towns for which the Commission are now responsible have reached the stage at which large-scale planned immigration is being reduced, they have a high rate of natural growth. House-building, therefore, continued at a high level for several years, but the local authorities are now responsible for the needs of second-generation families (the newly-wed children of present tenants). As a matter of government policy, the Commission are currently allowed to build only a limited number of dwellings for elderly people.

EXPANDING TOWNS

The New Towns Act was the first instalment of the 'overspill' plan: the second was to be an Act to facilitate town expansion by local authorities. This, however, was deferred until the immediate post-war housing shortage had been met. It was contrary to the political facts of life to expect local authorities to build houses for families from other areas while they still had severe housing problems of their own. It was, therefore, not until 1952 that the Town Development Act was passed.

The essential difference between the New Towns Act and the Town Development Act is apparent from their full titles. The New Towns Act is 'an Act to provide for the creation of new towns by means of development corporations'; the Town Development Act is 'an Act to encourage town development in county districts for the relief of congestion or overpopulation elsewhere'. The former set

up special agencies to deal with a problem which was, by implication, beyond the competence of local authorities. The latter did
precisely the opposite: it provided 'encouragement' to local
authorities to meet the overspill problem themselves 'by agreement
and co-operation'. As Macmillan (then Minister of Housing)
stressed (during the Second Reading debates), 'the purpose of the
Bill is that large cities wishing to provide for their surplus population shall do so by orderly and friendly arrangements with neighbouring authorities . . . it is our purpose that all these arrangements
should be reached by friendly negotiation and not imposed by
arbitrary power'. Such financial help was to be provided as would be
'necessary to get the job going'. At the present time this consists of a
housing subsidy and a grant towards the cost of main sewerage,
sewage-works and water-works required for the development.

Actual development can be undertaken by the receiving authority themselves; or by the exporting authority acting either as an
agent for the receiving authority or on their own account; or by the
county council in whose area the receiving authority are situated.
Tenants can be selected either from the housing list of the exporting
authority or by means of an industrial selection scheme. In the latter
case only families who secure employment in the receiving area are
eligible for rehousing there.

Town development is very widely defined, as:

'Development in a district (or partly in one district and partly in
another) which will have the effect, and is undertaken primarily for
the purpose, of providing accommodation for residential purposes
(with or without accommodation for the carrying on of industrial or
other activities, and with all appropriate public services, facilities
for public worship, recreation and amenity, and other requirements) the provision whereof will relieve congestion or overpopulation outside the county comprising the district or districts in which
the development is carried out.'

This description of the Act serves to show how flexible its provisions
are. Since town development is undertaken by local authorities with
widely different problems and of varying size and wealth, this
flexibility is essential.

A town expansion scheme can operate successfully only if all the
local authorities concerned – the 'exporting' authority, the 'reception' authority and the county council – are able and willing to
co-operate, and if the Department of Industry are likewise able and
willing to assist in persuading industry to move into the expanding
town. There are big difficulties – technical, administrative, finan-

cial, social and political – to be overcome. These constitute a severe strain on the local government machine. However, given a fortuitous combination of circumstances, experience has shown that town expansion schemes can operate to the great benefit of small towns.

Haverhill (now, following local government reorganisation, St Edmundsbury) is a case in point: situated in the south-east corner of West Suffolk, this small town saw in the Town Development Act a means of arresting its economic decline and obtaining modern urban facilities which it so clearly lacked. Blessed with a local government machine of a calibre hardly to be expected in such an area, a co-operative and forward-looking county council, and considerable technical and financial assistance from both this county council and the exporting authority (the Greater London Council), the town has already provided over 2,500 houses and 1,300,000 square feet of factory space.

Schemes operated in conjunction with the Greater London Council have the advantage of very favourable financial and technical aid which an authority of this size and wealth can provide. Nevertheless, their contribution to the solution of the London overspill problem has not been impressive. In an attempt to increase the provision, the former London County Council proposed to undertake the building of a new town in Hook, Hampshire. This was strongly opposed by Hampshire County Council, who proposed alternative areas for expansion. These alternative proposals (at Basingstoke and Andover) were accepted and, since Hampshire County Council are an active participant in the scheme, have proceeded at a faster speed than is usual with town expansion. They are also on a larger than normal scale: Basingstoke, in particular, had provided 5,800 houses and over 3 million square feet of factory space by the end of 1973.

PROVINCIAL SCHEMES

In the schemes for provincial conurbations progress has been very slow. Several factors are responsible for this. The exporting authorities have not been so well organised as the Greater London Council to make the Town Development Act work. They have not been so convinced of the necessity of attempting to make it work or, at the least, they have maintained that the scale of their problems requires direct central government action by way of new towns rather than the small-scale assistance to their problems likely to be achieved by 'fiddling around with the Town Development Act'. Then there is the problem of attracting industry to provincial town expansion schemes. For the small number of towns which have welcomed the idea of expansion this has proved the crucial problem.

More frequently, however, there is considerable local opposition to expansion. Apart from the technical and financial difficulties and the strong force of inertia, receiving authorities are generally small, vulnerable and highly disinclined to take risks. There is a fear that expansion will do more harm than good, that it will change the social as well as the physical character of the town – and that it may have unwelcome political consequences. The public inquiry into the proposals for an expansion scheme for Westhoughton was opened with the recorded voice of Vera Lynn singing 'Land of Hope and Glory' as 500 objectors slowly marched in procession to the town hall. Before the inquiry opened, prayers were said in local churches against the scheme; 9,000 out of the 11,000 people on the electoral roll had signed a petition; 1,400 objections had been lodged; and two local coach proprietors laid on free day-trips to Bolton, where the inquiry was held.

Though an extreme case, this does illustrate the difficulties facing town expansion proposals. Nevertheless, by the end of 1973, some 70,000 houses and 12 million square feet of factory space had been provided in provincial town expansion schemes (in addition to the 93,000 dwellings and 30 million square feet of factory space for London overspill). In Scotland (by 31 March 1974), some 11,000 houses had been built for Glasgow overspill.

THE END OF DISPERSAL?

The heading for this final brief section is taken from an article by Maurice Ash in the February 1975 issue of *Town and Country Planning*. Major changes in the economy and in population growth, together with the first indications of an inner city problem familiar in the USA, have brought about some major doubts (a prelude to some radical rethinking?) about overspill policies. The case of Stonehouse (designated to assist Clydeside – which is now de-populating at an alarming rate) has already been mentioned. But this is merely an extreme case. That this is cause for concern, even in the most prosperous conurbation, is evidenced by the study, directed by Lomas, of inner London (*The Inner City*, 1974).

Clearly, a new and expanding towns programme conceived when population forecasts envisaged over 70 million people in Britain by the turn of the century is hardly likely to be appropriate for a situation in which the outcome is projected at 58 million. This remarkable change in population projections has focused attention on the rapidly increasing problems of the inner cities. As Ash has pointed out (in the article referred to above):

'We have failed to grasp "Ebenezer's other half": the problem of re-ordering the cities whose populations were thinning out and whose relief had been the ultimate, but forgotten, purposes of Ebenezer Howard's garden cities policy. We took it for granted that lower densities were enough: that cities could virtually re-order themselves. Ebenezer never heard of the ghetto.'

Planning policies for inner cities are inherently much more difficult to forge and operate than those which have been established for new towns. (And it should not be forgotten that the majority of the overspill from the urban areas has gone to developments in areas other than those designated as new and expanding towns.) New and expanded towns cannot be legitimately blamed for 'creating' the inner city problem: what is at fault is the inadequacy of policies aimed at dealing directly with the problems of the inner city. It is this 'other half' which now demands urgent attention.

Chapter XII

SLUM CLEARANCE AND IMPROVEMENT

INADEQUATE HOUSING

Britain has a very large legacy of old housing which is inadequate by modern standards. This results from the relatively early start of the industrial revolution in this country and the rapid urban development which took place in the nineteenth century. (The contrast in Scandinavian countries, whose industrial revolutions came later when wealth was greater and standards higher, is marked.) As a result, British policies in relation to clearance and redevelopment are of long standing. But it was the Greenwood Housing Act of 1930 which heralded the start of the modern slum clearance programme. Over a third of a million houses were demolished before the Second World War brought the programme to an abrupt halt.

By 1938 demolitions were running at the rate of 90,000 a year: had it not been for the war, over a million older houses would (at this rate) have been demolished by 1951. The war, however, not only delayed clearance programmes: it resulted in enforced neglect and deterioration. War damage, shortage of building resources and (of increasing importance in the period of post-war inflation) crude rent restriction policies increased the problem of old and inadequate housing.

It was not until the mid-fifties that clearance could generally be resumed, and some 1½ million slum houses have been demolished since then. But the problem is still one of large dimensions. The 1971 House Condition Survey (England and Wales) showed that, though the number of unfit houses had fallen by a third since the 1967 Survey, the total still exceeded 1,200,000. An additional 1,800,000 *fit* dwellings lacked one or more of such basic amenities as an internal w.c. or a bath.

These figures (and similar ones for Scotland) are, of course, a product of the standards employed. This is only partly a matter of definition: it is also a matter of interpretation. A striking illustration of this is provided by a comparison of the 1968 and the 1973 Welsh House Condition Surveys. Though the number of dwellings lacking amenities decreased, the number of unfit dwellings *rose* from 92,000 to 147,000: from 10·4 per cent of the stock to 15 per cent. The reason why such a result is possible can be seen from an examination of the statutory standard of unfitness.

STANDARDS

The size of the slum problem is of course essentially related to the standards adopted. A 'slum' is more easily recognised than defined. The quality of housing has a number of different dimensions. The Denington Committee drew attention to five:

  (i) the structure and condition of housing (stability, damp, natural lighting, etc.);
 (ii) the equipment and services built into housing (w.c., water supply, drainage, artificial lighting, etc.);
(iii) the quality of the surrounding environment (air pollution, noise, open space, traffic conditions, etc.);
(iv) the space available to individual households (persons per room, bedroom requirements, etc.);
 (v) the privacy available in dwellings occupied by more than one household (sharing accommodation and facilities, sound insulation, etc.).

The assessment and quantification of these is no easy matter, and there is considerable scope for area variation and personal judgement. This is particularly clear when an overall assessment is required of the need for slum clearance or improvement.

Statutory definitions relate predominantly to structure, physical condition and plumbing. In England and Wales, the legislation lists a number of matters which have to be taken into consideration, but a house is deemed 'unfit for human habitation' only 'if it is so far defective in one or more of the said matters that it is not reasonably suitable for occupation in that condition'. There is thus considerable scope for judgement.

The 'said matters' are:

repair
stability
freedom from damp
internal arrangement
natural lighting
ventilation
water supply

drainage and sanitary conveniences
facilities for the preparation and cooking of food and for the
disposal of waste water.

In Scotland, following the Scottish Housing Advisory Committee's 1967 Report on *Scotland's Older Houses*, the new legislation attempted a greater degree of objectivity. Dispensing with the concept of 'unfitness' it introduced a *tolerable standard*. A house is held to meet this if it:

(a) is structurally stable;
(b) is substantially free from rising or penetrating damp;
(c) has satisfactory provision for natural and artificial lighting, for ventilation and for heating;
(d) has an adequate piped supply of wholesome water available within the house;
(e) has a sink provided with a satisfactory supply of both hot and cold water within the house;
(f) has a water closet available for the exclusive use of the occupants of the house and suitably located within the house;
(g) has an effective system for the drainage and disposal of foul and surface water;
(h) has satisfactory facilities for the cooking of food within the house;
(i) has satisfactory access to all external doors and outbuildings.

Despite the greater clarity and objectivity of the Scottish standard, it is apparent that the subjective element cannot be completely eliminated. The SHAC Report suggested that it could, however, be further reduced by the use of a 'housing defects index'. Considerable work has been undertaken on this both north and south of the Border. (See e.g. SDD, *Slum Clearance and Improvements*, HMSO, 1969.)

SLUM CLEARANCE IN ENGLAND AND WALES

Local authorities in England and Wales have a duty under the Housing Acts 'to cause an inspection of their district to be made from time to time' with a view to dealing with a wide range of unsatisfactory housing conditions. So far as unfit housing is concerned, they can require individual owners to repair, close or demolish. For *areas* of unfit housing, however, a 'clearance area' procedure is used. An area can be declared a clearance area if the houses are unfit or badly arranged, and if the local authority are satisfied 'that the most satisfactory method of dealing with the conditions in the area is the demolition of all the buildings in the area'. Before declaring a clearance area the local authority must also satisfy themselves that the persons to be displaced from residential accommodation can be adequately rehoused. Usually this is interpreted as meaning that the local authority are able to rehouse the displaced families: indeed it is often referred to as an 'obligation to rehouse'. In fact, however, local authorities are statutorily required to provide accommodation only in so far as suitable dwellings do not already exist. There are parts of the country where there is no great shortage of housing and where a significant number of displaced families do rehouse themselves: this applies particularly in the case of those owner-occupiers who receive full market value compensation for their houses.

To be included in a clearance area a house must be unfit or dangerous or injurious to health, but it need not be incapable of being made fit at reasonable cost. Other buildings – factories, schools, shops: indeed, *any* building – can also be included so long as they are so badly arranged as to be 'dangerous or injurious to health'.

Having declared a clearance area the local authority proceeds to purchase the properties (either by agreement or by compulsory purchase order).

It is useful to know the jargon which is used in relation to clearance areas. Maps have to be prepared as part of the formal procedure for submitting CPOs to the Secretary of State. On these, different categories of property have to be identified either by hatching and stippling or by colour. The names of the colours are frequently used as a shorthand description of the different categories of property. Thus, *pink* houses are those which are unfit for human habitation; *pink hatched yellow* are buildings included because of their bad arrangement; and *grey* properties are those which, though not in either of the other categories, are needed for the satisfactory redevelopment of the cleared area.

This categorisation is important for two reasons. First, the compensation which an owner receives for his property will depend upon whether or not it is 'pink'. If it is, he normally receives only cleared site value (though there is provision for 'well maintained' payments); if it is not, he will receive market value for the site with the house on it. Secondly, the matters about which the local authority have to be satisfied vary. With a 'pink' house they must be satisfied that the house is unfit according to the criteria set out in the Housing Acts. These in fact make no reference to the effect of the conditions on the health of the occupants – though objectors commonly use the argument that there is no evidence that their houses cause ill-health. With 'pink hatched yellow' properties it is legally necessary to prove that there is danger to health. This is difficult to do, at least in a manner which would be acceptable to a logician. The cynic might legitimately comment that all this is a legal fiction which – though relevant to nineteenth-century conditions – is now quite archaic. Nevertheless, it is accepted that severe lack of light and air space; narrow, cramped courts, yards and alleys; and similar overshadowed and congested buildings do fall within the legal definition. In practice, these conditions are commonly found in conjunction with internal inadequacies which render the house unfit. So far as 'grey' properties are concerned, the only matter at issue is whether their acquisition is reasonably necessary for the satisfactory redevelopment of the area. It is not necessary to prove that it is *impossible* to achieve a layout without them. It is sufficient to show that acquisition is reasonable.

During the years 1970 to 1973, rather more than 50,000 houses in or adjacent to clearance areas were demolished in England and Wales each year (a further 10,000–15,000 unfit houses were dealt with individually). The annual figure, however, has been falling, and in 1974 it dropped to 37,000 in clearance areas and 4,800 outside clearance areas: a total of around 42,000. This compares with 68,000 in 1970, 69,000 in 1969, and 71,000 in 1967 and 1968. This large fall reflects a major shift in policy from demolition to improvement (which is discussed in the following section).

HOUSE IMPROVEMENT POLICIES

A major change in policy has taken place in recent years – away from large-scale clearance and redevelopment, and towards improvement as a less disruptive, more socially desirable, and cheaper means of dealing with inadequate housing. Though an improvement grants policy was introduced in 1949, it was not until the mid-fifties that it got under way. Since then, the emphasis has gradually shifted from individual house improvements, first to the improvement of streets or areas of sub-standard housing, and later to the improvement of the total environment.

Initially it was assumed that houses could be neatly divided into two groups: according to the 1953 White Paper, *Houses: The Next Step*, there were those which were unfit for human habitation and those which were 'essentially sound'. As experience was gained, the 'improvement philosophy' broadened and it came to be realised that there was a very wide range of housing situations related not only to the presence or otherwise of plumbing facilities and the state of repair of individual houses, but also to the varying socio-economic character of different areas and the nature of the local housing market. A house 'lacking amenities' in Chelsea was, in important ways, different from an identical house in Rochdale: the 'appropriate action' was similarly different. Later, it was better understood that 'appropritate action' defined in housing market terms was not necessarily equally appropriate in social policy terms. A middle-class 'invasion' might restore the physical fabric and raise the quality (and 'tone') of a neighbourhood, but the social costs of this were borne by displaced low-income families. The problem thus became redefined.

Growing concern for the environment also led to an increased awareness of the importance of the factors *causing* deterioration. It is clear that these are more numerous and complex than housing legislation has recognised. Through traffic and inadequate parking provision was quickly recognised as being of physical importance. The answer – in physical terms – was the re-routing of traffic, the closure of streets and the provision of parking spaces (together with cobbled areas and the planting of trees). More serious causes of physical blight such as obnoxious industries were obviously more difficult to deal with. But most difficult of all is to assess the social function of an area, the needs it meets and the ways in which conditions can be improved for (and in accordance with the wishes of) the people living in an area. Until recently this issue was dealt with largely by ignoring it. The latest legislation – the 1974 Housing Act – brings it to the fore.

The 1974 Act represents a major reorientation of housing policy. To quote from DoE Circular 13/75, *Renewal Strategies*:

'The housing activity of many urban local authorities was, for many years, dominated by the need to clear and redevelop areas of old housing for which no other solution was available, a process which often enabled extra homes to be built for families on the waiting list. Not unnaturally, run-down areas not already in the clearance programme were often assumed to be suitable only for demolition and redevelopment in due course. Residents of privately rented dwellings were usually believed to be content to change their tenancy for that of a council house or flat; adverse blighting effects of clearance and the dispersal of communities were seen as being more than outweighed by the benefits conferred by the improvement in housing standards. Within the last few years, however, the position has altered significantly. Except in a few cities the programme of large-scale slum clearance should now be drawing to a close. Where authorities have been seeking to clear housing, especially dwellings which are fit or owner-occupied, it has proved much less easy to demonstrate that redevelopment is the best course, and resistance to such action has been increasing from residents of all kinds. Moreover, in the face of serious housing shortage in London and other major cities, wholesale demolition is increasingly criticised because it means that the total housing stock is reduced for a number of years while rebuilding takes place.'

Emphasis is laid on a comprehensive strategy on an area basis implementing a policy of 'gradual renewal'. A further quotation from this most important Circular is appropriate:

'Gradual renewal is a continuous process of minor rebuilding and renovation which sustains and reinforces the vitality of a neighbourhood in ways responsive to social and physical needs as they develop and change. Rehabilitation should take place to varying standards to match the effective demand of individual occupiers. Successful management of rehabilitation, in particular, will call for a more flexible attitude by local authorities towards the rate at which desirable standards of renovation are adopted. It must be accepted – and willingly – that some houses of low quality meet a real need for cheap accommodation, a need which might not otherwise be satisfied. It would not always be sensible to press for the immediate rehabilitation of all dwellings in an area to the full ("ten-point") standard or more, or to clear them, until they cease to fulfil their present social function. For example, sub-standard dwellings occupied by elderly persons could, *if this were the residents' wish*, remain largely undisturbed for the time being, except for the carrying out of basic repairs and elementary improvements (e.g. hot water supply, better heating) with the help of the new grants where appropriate. Authorities should also consider the possibility of selective acquisition of dwellings, or rehousing of certain residents, to prevent the undue deterioration of a neighbourhood or enable better use to be made of the housing stock.

Renewal similar to that described above has traditionally taken place in areas able to attract private investment, but has rarely been an explicit aim of local authority housing policy. Authorities have tended to see the normal life cycle for housing areas as one of development, decay, clearance and redevelopment, with rehabilitation postponing the necessity for clearance, notwithstanding the fact that individual houses were in different stages of obsolescence. Policies of comprehensive redevelopment have, however, blighted all the dwellings in the area uniformly and experience has shown that social conflicts and tensions can arise as the point of demolition is reached. Gradual renewal, on the other hand, can serve to minimise the disruption of established communities in a variety of housing areas.'

The new powers (and duties) conferred by the 1974 Housing Act centre upon areas of particular housing stress. Local housing authorities are now required to consider the need for dealing with these as Housing Action Areas. (Confusingly this is the term used in Scotland for the different purposes described in the following section.)

Housing Action Areas in England and Wales are areas where 'the living conditions are unsatisfactory and can most effectively be dealt with within a period of five years so as to secure – (a) the improvement of the housing accommodation in the area as a whole, and (b) the well-being of the persons for the time being residing in the area, and (c) the proper and effective management and use of that accommodation'. Physical conditions are to be measured by traditional indices, but particular importance is to be attached to social conditions, including not only the proportion of households lacking amenities or living in overcrowded conditions, but also the proportion living in privately rented accommodation, and 'the concentration in the area of households likely to have special housing problems – for instance old-age pensioners, large families, single parent families, or families whose head is unemployed or in a low income group'. (Further details are given in DoE Circular 14/75, *Housing Act 1974: Parts IV, V, VI – Housing Action Areas, Priority Neighbourhoods, and General Improvement Areas*, HMSO, 1975. See also DoE Area Improvement Note 10, *The Use of Indicators for Area Action*, HMSO, 1975.)

It should be noted that, in a Housing Action Area, *action* is of the essence – 'within a period of five years'. To achieve this, there is a range of powers: for acquisition, rehabilitation, protection from eviction, environmental improvement – indeed, for any action which is required to remove the underlying causes of housing stress in the area, to arrest and reverse deterioration, and to effect real improvements in the living conditions of those living in the area. But 'a basic – and novel – feature of HAAs is the statutory provision which makes the well-being of the people living in them one of the requirements for, and objects of, declarations. This means involving people and groups, in the scale, nature, and timing of proposed action programmes.' There is thus an explicit role for neighbourhood groups and such organisations as tenants' co-operatives and housing associations. Local authorities have extensive powers to compel private landlords to repair or improve properties in an

HAA, and a miscellany of grants is available for improvement, repairs and 'environmental works'.

In areas adjacent to HAAs, local authorities can declare Priority Neighbourhoods (PNs) where the objective is 'to prevent the housing position in or around stress areas from deteriorating further and to stop stress from rippling out from areas which are the subject of concentrated action, normally by use of HAA powers; and may also serve to pave the way for later, more intensive, action by HAA treatment if still needed, or by GIA action of a kind which cannot be undertaken immediately'. (GIAs – General Improvement Areas – are discussed below.)

Despite its title, a Priority Neighbourhood is essentially one which is suitable for HAA (or GIA) treatment, but where this is, for the time being, impracticable. As with HAAs, there is a great deal of flexibility, and policies can be elaborated in accordance with the specific needs of the area. In the longer term, HAA or Priority Neighbourhood treatment may be followed by clearance, designation as a GIA, or 'no further special treatment'.

General Improvement Areas (which were originally provided for by the 1969 Housing Act) are envisaged as being areas 'of fundamentally sound houses capable of providing good living conditions for many years to come and unlikely to be affected by known redevelopment or major planning proposals'. There are fewer powers of compulsion available to local authorities in a GIA: reliance is predominantly on voluntary action, but there are larger Exchequer grants for environmental improvement.

Local authorities now have a wide range of powers to deal sensitively and appropriately with the specific problems which arise in their areas. What started initially as an improvement grant policy (based essentially on the offer of grants to individual owners) has developed into a complex of provisions to deal comprehensively with widely differing environmental problems.

Between 1969 (when GIAs were introduced) and the end of 1973, nearly 800 GIAs were declared – covering nearly half a million dwellings, for which some 60,000 improvement grants were approved. During the same period, the total of improvement grants in England and Wales amounted to well over 1,100,000. It is, of course, too soon for any figures to be given on HAAs and PNs. What is involved here, however, is illustrated by the London Borough of Haringey's report on *First Steps Towards a Housing Action Area.*

SCOTTISH POLICIES

Scottish housing is different from that south of the Border in significant ways. There is a high proportion of tenemental properties, dwellings tend to be smaller, rents are lower, and over a half of the housing stock is owned by public authorities. Building costs and standards – but not space standards – are also higher. These and other differences reflect history, economic growth and decline, and climate.

Scottish housing legislation and policies are similarly different, and are becoming more so as the quantitative housing shortage is falling to small proportions. Above all, Scotland faces a major problem of tenemental slums. Though some 300,000 dwellings have been demolished since the war, there still remain a very large number of slums. The most recent (though crude) estimate, given in the 1973 Scottish White Paper, *Towards Better Homes,* puts the figure in the range 180,000–190,000: some 10 per cent of the stock. The clearance (or improvement) of these slums constitutes the major housing problem in Scotland.

As in England and Wales, increasing emphasis is being placed on improvement as distinct from clearance as the generally preferred policy. But with much of the older tenemental properties, particularly in central urban areas, the scope for improvement is severely restricted by the decayed fabric of the buildings, the internal physical layout of the tenements, and the high cost of alterations – not to mention the severe practical problems created by multiple ownership. The tenemental problem in Scotland is of a totally different physical and financial nature from that of terraced housing in England and Wales. (A detailed account is given in the 1967 Report of the Scottish Housing Advisory Committee on *Scotland's Older Houses.*)

Nevertheless, the social issues are very similar, and the current legislation – the Housing (Scotland) Act 1974 – is aimed at providing procedures and subsidies which will (to quote SDD Circular 67/1975) 'enable authorities to ensure that as much as possible of their sub-standard housing stock is improved to an acceptable standard, while houses which cannot effectively be improved are demolished'.

All area policies are dealt with under Housing Action Area procedures. (Though the term is the same as in England and Wales the meaning is quite different.) There are three types of HAA: for demolition, for improvement or for a combination of the two. For an area to be declared a 'housing action area for demolition', more than half of the houses* must be below the tolerable standard. A 'housing action area for improvement', or 'for demolition and improvement' can be declared where more than half the houses are either below the tolerable standard or lack one or more of the standard amenities.

It is not possible here to detail all the provisions relating to Scottish HAAs: the following is merely a brief summary.

The most striking feature of the new system is the power given to local authorities for the *compulsory improvement* of houses in areas where most of the houses lack one or more of the standard amenities. The need for this (certainly in tenemental property – where the biggest problem lies) stems from the fact that the improvement of *some* of the houses in a tenement cannot normally be carried out without affecting the other houses. To put the matter crudely: it frequently is a case of 'all or nothing'. The declaration of an improvement HAA is, however, in essence a declaration of intent: it is a clear and definite proclamation by the local authority that the future of the area is to be safeguarded and that marked improvements are to be made – to the environment as well as to the houses.

Given the peculiar characteristics of tenemental property, it is typically necessary to ensure that improvements are planned *as one operation* to all the houses (at least in a close or stair, if not in the block as a whole). Concerted action of this kind can sometimes be done by the landlords or, more frequently, their factors (agents), but in any case some 'external organisation' is necessary. One method of doing this is by the establishment of *ad hoc* housing associations. Experiments in this direction are under way (particularly in Glasgow) with the assistance of the Housing Corporation.

Higher rates of improvement grant are available – and mandatory – in these areas: 75 per cent instead of the normal 50 per cent (rising to 90 per cent where this is justified by the financial circumstances of the owner). Discretionary grants are also available, on a similar basis, for repairs. Expenditure to be met by owners can be financed by loans from the local authority.

These provisions also include a new requirement that the local authority must allow two months 'for representations from the people affected and must take account of these before making a final resolution declaring a housing action area'. This is a legalistic formulation of an obligation on local authorities to act sensitively in

---

* The English reader should note that the Scots use the term 'house' to mean the same as the English 'dwelling', i.e. it embraces a flat or tenement.

accordance with the wishes of the people living in HAAs. As SDD Circular 67/1975 explains:

'The Secretary of State attaches particular importance to this requirement, and he would urge local authorities to make the fullest use of this period to consult those affected, explaining and discussing the proposals with them. He considers that full consultation with the residents and a sensitive and sympathetic response to their wishes for the future of the area will go far to obviate opposition or resistance to what is proposed, and to ensure that once a final resolution is made the work which it entails will proceed as quickly as possible.'

By contrast with the elaborate statutory provisions for improvement in England and Wales, the Scottish system appears remarkably simple. This is not the place to speculate on the reasons for this difference (which can equally be seen in the planning field): suffice it to say that while the English try to attain flexibility by a complex range of powers to be *adopted* by local authorities according to their various circumstances, the Scots prefer broad powers within which flexibility can be attained by local *adaptation*.

But both approaches are characterised by more sensitivity. It would be an exaggeration to say that the 'bulldozer' has been banished: given the foul conditions in some areas no alternative is possible. But clearly the relevance of this approach now has to be much more carefully assessed before it is employed.

Chapter XIII

REGIONAL PLANNING

AGENCIES OF REGIONAL PLANNING

In previous editions of this book, this chapter has opened with the statement that there is no executive machinery for regional physical planning in Britain: though there are a large number of agencies undertaking responsibility for particular services and development on a regional scale, there is no organisation responsible for co-ordinated programming, development and control.

This is still the case in England and Wales, though the position in Scotland has been transformed by the establishment of multi-purpose regional authorities who are now responsible for producing regional reports and, significantly, have taken over responsibility for water services which, south of the Border, have been transferred to new *ad hoc* authorities. Indeed, there are now more regional planning authorities for specific services than there were before local government reorganisation. Both Wales and Scotland now have Development Agencies charged with very broad development responsibilities, while Wales also has its Land Development Agency for the purposes of the Community Land Act.

In short, there is a multiplicity of regional planning machines, some of which are purely advisory (such as the regional economic planning councils) while others have important executive functions (such as the Highlands and Islands Development Board). Additionally there are the nationalised industries and bodies ranging from the Nature Conservancy Council to the Tourist Boards which have their own regional organisations and, of course, the regional offices of government departments.

It follows that a succinct account of 'regional planning' is impracticable – unless it were to be a mere directory of agencies. In this chapter, attention is focused on a selection of regional economic and physical problems and the development of machinery to deal with them.

REGIONAL THINKING

A number of strands can be identified in the evolution of thinking on regionalism. Two are of particular relevance in this book – the physical planning and the economic planning strands. Some account of the former from the local end has already been given. It is now necessary to supplement this with an outline of the situation as it has developed at the centre.

At the end of Chapter II, some stress was laid on the lack of a regional tier of planning between local authorities and the central departments. This lack did not seem (and was not) as important in the mid-forties as it appeared when population growth, economic growth, increased personal mobility, a rising standard of living and a host of other related factors conspired in the fifties to increase pressures on land and the machinery of land planning control. In any case, it was not possible to go further at the time. For a period, the framework of regional advisory plans (particularly in the London and Glasgow regions) had to suffice. They had some impact: they enabled some broad planning objectives to be communicated to and, more important, to be acknowledged by local planning authorities. Informal arrangements, professional contacts and a generally shared planning philosophy also helped.

By the end of the fifties, it became clear that something more was needed. Development plans had become hopelessly out of date due to cumbersome procedures and the great change in the underlying forces with which they were supposed to cope. Furthermore, in England the disbandment of the regional organisation of the Ministry of Housing in 1954–6 had (according to the department's former Permanent Secretary in her book *The Ministry of Housing and Local Government*) the opposite effect to that intended. 'There was a strong feeling at headquarters that the divisions did not know their regions or their authorities as well as they should; and that it would be better if headquarters staff could be enabled to devote more time to travelling out. It was thought that the abolition of the regional organization would improve Whitehall's knowledge of, and contacts with, the North, the Midlands, the East and the South West to the benefit of all; and that officers and representatives of local authorities might be encouraged to come more frequently to Whitehall, as they had done in pre-war years. It did not come off.' And so the problems changed in character and increased in complexity at the very time when the central department were in insufficient touch with local government.

REGIONAL STUDIES

The turn of the tide came in the early sixties in three areas for three different reasons. In 1962 a Northern Housing Office of the ministry was opened in Manchester to assist the large programme of slum clearance and redevelopment in the north and north-west. In 1963 another regional office, with both housing and planning functions, was set up in Newcastle in connection with the 'Hailsham Plan' for the north-east, to which there was a clear political commitment. Probably of greater importance was the beginning, in 1961, of a series of regional studies. These resulted from the awareness within the department of the inadequacy of the development plans and land allocations to meet the rising pressures for development. These studies started, in traditional manner, as 'regional conferences' and 'land studies' undertaken jointly by officers of local authorities and the department. In the south-east and the west midlands they developed into new-style regional studies covering unprecedentedly large areas.

The *South East Study* was published in March 1964 and included regionally based proposals of a kind and on a scale which had not been seen since the wartime and immediate post-war period of optimistic planning. New cities (*sic*) were suggested in the Southampton-Portsmouth area, the Bletchley area (later to become Milton Keynes) and the Newbury area. New towns were considered for Ashford and Stansted. Large-scale expansions were proposed for Ipswich, Northampton, Peterborough and Swindon. Consultants were appointed to consider, with the local authorities concerned, many of these proposals.

The next clearly identifiable step in this period of intense examination and thinking came with the decision of the Labour Government in 1964 to set up regional economic planning machinery. The trend towards this was already in evidence. Early in 1964 the President of the Board of Trade was made responsible for 'trade, industry and regional development'. The White Paper, *South East England*, outlining the Government's reaction to the *Study*, was published jointly by the department and the board. Indeed, *The South East Study* was the only one to bear the imprint of the Ministry of Housing and Local Government. Before the next studies were completed (on the west midlands and the north-west) the Department of Economic Affairs had been set up (taking over the regional development division of the Board of Trade). During its lifetime (1964–9) the DEA had responsibility for the direction and publication of regional studies. (This now rests with the Department of the Environment.)

REGIONAL PLANNING COUNCILS

There are ten regional economic planning councils – eight in England and one each in Wales and Scotland. These planning councils are advisory bodies and consist of a chairman and about twenty-five members all appointed by the appropriate Secretary of State. The members are appointed as 'individuals having a wide range of knowledge and experience in their regions'. they are not delegates or representatives of particular interests. The councils' main functions are 'to study and advise on the needs and potentialities of their regions and on the development of a long-term planning strategy for their regions, and to advise central government on aspects of national policy which have a bearing on regional development'.

Alongside each council is a board consisting of senior civil servants from the main government departments concerned with regional planning. In the English regions, the chairmen of the boards are all senior officials of the DoE. The functions of the boards are 'to co-ordinate the regional economic planning work of Departments, and to co-operate with the Economic Planning Councils in developing the long-term planning strategies for the regions'.

The functions of this regional advisory machinery were officially stated in 1965 as being:

(i) to work out broad objectives for each region and so provide a comprehensive framework within which decisions in particular sectors can be taken;
(ii) to advise on the formulation of national policies where these can significantly affect the regions;
(iii) to advise on the application in the regions of national policy;
(iv) to stimulate interest within each region and build up a common approach within each region to its problems.

Initially the work was of a kind which might be described as being 'regional stocktaking'. The primary objective was to assemble the facts and figures relating to the regions which could form the basis for an overall assessment and for a broad regional strategy. Attention was concentrated on preparing 'studies' on the lines of *The South East Study*. The first two were published in 1965 for the north-west and the west midlands. Both of these were undertaken by 'a group of officials from Government Departments concerned with regional planning', and were 'referred' to the planning councils for the respective regions (without any commitment on the part of government to the studies' findings or to the proposals which might be made by the councils). Following the establishment of the regional councils, further studies were undertaken and published. Unlike the earlier two, these were reports by the councils themselves. But they were not 'regional plans'; indeed they both specifically disclaimed any pretension to be. As the foreword to *The East Midlands Study* puts it, the objective was 'to present to the public an account of the region as it is, and as it is changing; it draws attention to problems and opportunities, with an indication of what is involved in them. It is hoped that the study will form an adequate basis for the public discussion out of which the main lines of the region's planning will emerge; until adequate opportunity for that discussion has been provided it would be presumptuous to go further'.

This approach stemmed from two important factors. First, the essential information and research needed for an adequately based system of regional planning was lacking. Secondly (and this remains of preponderant importance now that the former inadequacy is being rectified), the regional councils have no executive powers and no authority over either the central government or local authorities. They 'represent' the regions only in a very indirect way. They have to tread warily between the cautiousness of Whitehall and the sensitivities of the county and town halls. It could hardly be expected that they would rapidly resolve the conflicts between the constituent local authorities (and particularly between town and county) which have for so long frustrated attempts to plan on any scale other than that circumscribed by local authority boundaries. Essentially the regional councils constitute an experiment in forging new, and wider, loyalties – loyalties to a region rather than to a locality. The studies and reports are thus not sets of policies agreed by the regions and submitted to the central government for consideration and action; rather are they the interim findings and thoughts of a group of individuals with experience of and interest in the regions, submitted to all concerned (government at all levels, and public and private bodies) as a first exercise in regional thinking.

REGIONAL STRATEGIES

What then is the function of the regional studies? Probably the clearest statement is to be found in the 1967 report of the South West Economic Planning Council, significantly entitled *A Region with a Future: A Draft Strategy for the South West*:

'It has come to be recognised that it is too soon in the experience of regional planning to aim at achieving a set of Government-approved plans for all regions which will neatly dovetail with each other and which, in numbers of population, distribution of man-power, growth and location of industry, scale and disposition of public investment, etc., will in aggregate coincide with the fore-casts, intentions and capabilities envisaged by the Government for the economy as a whole. The immediate aim should be for each Council to provide themselves with a "regional strategy" by which recommendations can be made on decisions affecting their regions which cannot wait, and advice be given immediately on the implica-tions for their regions of national and local policies.'

The truth of the matter, however, is that the present regional machinery is a temporary makeshift – though there are no proposals afoot to supersede it. Two important points need to be stressed. First, the councils have no executive powers whatsoever: they can comment or rant and rage but they can *do* nothing – they are purely advisory bodies. Secondly, the creation of the boards in no way affects the existing powers and responsibilities of local authorities and central government departments. Advice and co-ordination: these are the essential functions of the councils and the boards.

Though it would be difficult to establish a clear causal relation-ship, the regional economic planning machinery has probably stimulated the coming-together of local authorities in loose group-ings on a regional scale. Typically these have been termed – in an ungainly but innocuous way – 'standing conferences'. In some regions these have operated independently of (if not aloofly from) the regional planning councils. In others it has been possible to achieve close collaboration.

Thus in the west midlands yet another *West Midlands Study* has been carried out by the Standing Conference of Local Planning Authorities. This is a purely local government undertaking: it is quite independent of the West Midlands Economic Planning Coun-cil, though advice was rendered by the regional staffs of central government departments. At the other extreme is the South East Joint Planning Study Team which reported in 1970. This was commissioned in May 1968 *jointly* by the then Secretary of State for Economic Affairs, the Minister of Housing and Local Government and the Minister of Transport, and by the chairmen of the Standing Conference on London and South East Regional Planning (a body which dates from 1962) and the South East Economic Planning Council.

The *Strategic Plan for the South East* has set the pattern for later 'strategic plans' produced jointly by *ad hoc* teams recruited from central and local government. Following the establishment of the

DoE (which gave this department the leading responsibility for
regional policy as a whole and for the English regional economic
planning machinery), a 'Planning Regional Plans Directorate' was
set up to co-ordinate the preparation of regional strategies. The
purposes of these are to provide a regional framework for local
authority land use planning and a guide to major investment
decisions for government, the nationalised industries and the larger
private firms. The role of the DoE is to assist the strategy teams by
advice on the information needs, statistics, techniques, policy assumptions and monitoring system to be used in regional planning,
to draw together regional planning work into coherent and acceptable national relationships, and to advise on the regional planning
implications of national policies and developments. The costs are
shared between central and local government. Examples of the new
strategic plans are *Strategic Plan for the North West* and *Strategic
Choice for East Anglia.*

In Scotland, the Scottish Economic Planning Board (set up, like
the English boards, in 1965) was preceded by the Scottish Development Group (set up in 1963). The White Paper on the Scottish
Economy 1965-7 was based on analysis of five broad sub-regions:
central Scotland, the Highlands, the Borders, the south-west and
the north-east. In an attempt to bridge the gap between the responsibility for 'planning' and execution, the Scottish Office encouraged
the establishment of sub-regional 'local consultative groups'. (In
the Highlands there is also the Highlands and Islands Development
Board set up by statute in 1965 with the objective of stimulating the
economic and social development of the seven crofting counties.)

In their evidence to the Royal Commission on Local Government
in Scotland, the Regional Development Division of the Scottish
Office stated that one of the purposes of these local consultative
groups was 'to create a new sense of participation in national
planning; but more specifically they are designed to create an
awareness of the problems and potentials of the sub-regions looked
at as coherent units, and to promote co-operation among all concerned within the sub-regions'. They warned, however, that it
remained to be seen how well the groups could cope with 'internal
tensions' within sub-regions. Particular difficulty was experienced
in even establishing a group to serve central Scotland which has
particularly intractable planning problems of a sub-regional
character.

THE WEST CENTRAL SCOTLAND PLAN

What was termed 'a significant step forward' was, however, made in
1970 when a West Central Scotland Plan Steering Committee was

established. This was representative of central government, local government and industrial and economic expertise in the region. Its remit was to prepare and keep up to date an advisory economic and physical plan for west central Scotland which would serve as a guide to local planning authorities in preparing their development plans. The resultant plan, *West Central Scotland: A Programme of Action*, was published in May 1974. It was diplomatically labelled 'consultative draft report', partly because of the opposition of some of the constituent authorities to the unfavourable impact which implementation of the plan would have on their areas. Thus the first lessons of regional planning were learned: that effective regional policies imply that some desirable developments have to be abandoned in favour of others; that limited resources have to be allocated to specific purposes and areas; and that while some areas will particularly benefit others will particularly lose.

With the establishment of the Strathclyde Regional Council this debate is now firmly placed on an appropriate platform, and the elected regional councillors will have to face up to the regional planning problems of their huge area. Some hard decisions will have to be made – but this is what regional planning is about.

The West Central Scotland Plan highlighted the crucial importance of the economic base of planning (of which the indicator was a *net* loss of 360,000 people during the fifties and sixties). Before discussing this further, it is necessary to sketch the development of post-war economic planning policies in Britain.

ECONOMIC PLANNING POLICIES

Employment and economic change lie at the heart of regional planning. This, indeed, was the starting-point for the Barlow inquiry thirty-five years ago. Post-war industrial location policies have been directed towards reducing unemployment in the development areas and restraining new industrial building in 'congested' areas. This has been the interpretation given to the phrase 'a proper distribution of industry'. For most of the post-war period, however, this has been regarded, in the main, as a *social* policy running alongside, but not supporting, *economic* policies. A classic exposition of this view was given by the President of the Board of Trade (R. Maudling) in the Second Reading debates on the Local Employment Bill (*HC Debates*, 9 November 1959):

'We should start from the assumption that the economic and industrial expansion of the country should proceed freely in response to growing and changing consumer demand, and that it should proceed on the principle of the most effective use of our national resources. . . . This principle of the most effective use of our resources must clearly be mitigated in some cases by Government action to deal with certain social consequences which the nation does not regard as acceptable.'

During the sixties, however, there was an increasing awareness that a maldistribution of employment had serious economic effects on the national economy. The 1963 Report of the National Economic Development Council on *Conditions Favourable to Faster Growth* provides a good illustration of this new thinking:

'The level of employment in different regions of the country varies widely, and high unemployment associated with the lack of employment opportunities in the less prosperous regions is usually thought of as a social problem. Policies aim, therefore, to prevent unemployment rising to politically intolerable levels, and expenditure to this end is often considered a necessary burden to the nation, unrelated to any economic gain that might accrue from it. But the relatively low activity rates in these regions also indicates considerable labour reserves. To draw these reserves into employment would make a substantial contribution to national employment and national growth.'

This argument, it should be noted, was put forward not by physical planners but by economists. It differs very markedly from the traditional type of economic argument; and it rejects the idea that the long-term solution to regional economic decline lies in migration to the prosperous areas. Apart from the social cost of large-scale migration that this would involve, there are two other significant objections. First it would add to the problems of congestion in the south-east and the midlands – problems which are already straining to the utmost the machinery of town and country planning. Secondly, it would be quite impracticable for these prosperous areas to absorb the required number of migrants. Furthermore, if the less prosperous regions were allowed to run down, their future problem would become even more difficult to solve. The objective should be to employ a regional development policy which would aim at achieving self-sustaining regional growth. It is here that the relationship between economic planning and town and country planning is most clearly seen: potential industrial developers are concerned not only with labour supply and good sites, but also with adequate services, educational provision, and so on. In short, if industrialists are to be attracted to the less prosperous regions then these regions have to be made both economically and socially attractive. In the words of the White Paper on *The North East*: 'even generous assistance to enterprise may not be fully effective unless it is backed by faster progress in making towns and villages more pleasant, in improving communications, and in removing scars on the industrial countryside'.

The problems can thus be seen as a compound of the economic and the social. The promotion of industrial activity has to be accompanied by a modernisation of the general environment. This is not merely a question of providing a 'bait' to industrialists: it is also a matter of economic efficiency – 'to ensure that the scale of the public services and facilities match the needs of a modern society'. The problem is in part one of historic legacies: the regions where economic growth is comparatively slow are the regions where there is a concentration of physical obsolescence. Indeed, some observers have spoken of a geographical division of the country into two nations – separated roughly by the River Trent. The 'fortunate regions' of the south have a high level of employment, a large amount of private investment, a high standard of health, a relatively high standard of social service and social amenity. On the other hand, the 'unfortunate regions' of the north, of Wales and of Scotland – the boom areas of the coal age – have an enormous legacy of obsolete social capital, a slower rate of economic growth, an accompanying higher rate of unemployment, a poorer standard of health and social service, and a not unrelated migration of population.

This image of the two nations is clearly overdrawn and false in many respects (even when the current problems of the west midlands and inner London are ignored), but the essential point is valid: the regions with a slow rate of economic growth have acute environmental problems which are difficult to cope with in the context of their relatively low level of economic activity and which, in turn, present obstacles to an increased growth rate. It is for this reason that so much emphasis is now being given to improving 'infrastructure'.

Nevertheless, it does not follow that all existing towns and settlements should be modernised. Some areas have lost their economic *raison d'être* and have little or no potentiality for growth. In any case, a policy of promoting growth is most effective when it is applied to carefully selected areas where the potentialities are particularly good. Since 1960, industrial location policy has been mainly aimed at relieving high unemployment in development districts. This was a major departure from the previous policy of promoting growth more generally in regions. The 'selection' of development districts was made, however, on the basis of un-employment rates. The application of the 'growth point' idea, on the other hand, involves selection on the basis of potentialities. To quote again from *Conditions Favourable to Faster Growth*:

'Better results might be secured for the slowly expanding regions as a whole by identifying their natural growth points and seeking to attract industry to them. Within the bigger areas a wider choice of location than at present would be available to incoming firms. This would increase the likelihood of attracting a larger number and a greater variety of firms, and of stimulating the development of industrial complexes. Firms would then benefit from the presence of kindred industry. These complexes and other places especially attractive to industry could be developed into growth points within the less prosperous regions. It could be expected that the benefit of new growth in any part would repercuss fairly quickly throughout the region.'

The two regional programmes for Scotland and north-east England represented the first essays in comprehensive regional planning by central government. Their importance lies not so much in the actual proposals made, but in the advance in thought and policy which they represent. They (like the Welsh report, *Wales: The Way Ahead*) do, however, differ from succeeding reports – or 'studies' as they are typically called. They involved a degree of government commitment which is notably absent from their successors, even when they have been prepared by central government. (The 'official' preface to *The South East Study* underlines that its main purpose is 'to provide a basis for discussion'; the point is rubbed home even more clearly in the preface to *The West Midlands* regional study where it is stated that the Government 'are not in any way committed by the Study Group's findings'.)

The point is, of course, that regional planning is not simply a matter of planning *within* a region. It has to take place within a framework of national policies which can be translated into decisions about the allocation of resources *between* regions. The White Papers on Scotland and the north-east proposed increases in public service investment which would have involved (for 1964-5) Scotland receiving 11 per cent of the Great Britain total (for a country with less than 10 per cent of the population) and the north-east receiving 7 per cent (with $5\frac{1}{2}$ per cent of the population). These proposals were drawn up on the basis of a political assessment of the needs of these regions, but clearly there are problems in continuing with this approach for all regions.

THE 'INTERMEDIATE AREAS'

Indeed, as aid to the development areas has increased, there has been mounting political pressure from 'intermediate areas' (or 'grey areas', to use the more popular term). It was this pressure which led to the setting up of the Hunt Committee, whose Report, *The Intermediate Areas*, was published in April 1969. The terms of reference of this Committee were 'to examine in relation to the economic welfare of the country as a whole and the needs of the development areas, the situation in other areas where the rate of economic growth gives cause (or may give cause) for concern, and to suggest whether revised policies to influence economic growth in such areas are desirable and, if so, what measures should be adopted'.

The Committee quickly found that it was no easy matter to judge the presence and severity of 'causes for concern'. In the present state of regional knowledge and analysis, political judgement has a very large role to play. Nevertheless, a brave and useful attempt was made. The major 'cause for concern' was 'slow economic growth . . . where it is associated with unused or under-used labour resources, low earnings, a concentration of industries with a declining labour force, poor communications and a run-down physical environment making areas unattractive for new economic growth, and net outward migration'. The chosen criteria were:

(a) Sluggish or falling employment   } as the major indicators
(b) A slow growth in personal incomes   } of slow growth.
(c) A slow rate of addition to industrial and commercial premises – as indicating a low level of industrial and commercial investment and a slow rate of economic growth.
(d) Significant unemployment – as the most obvious measure of wasted human resources.
(e) Low or declining proportions of women at work – as indicating a particular under-use of resources, especially in areas with a tradition of female employment.
(f) Low earnings – as throwing some light on the efficiency of the use of labour and as one of the factors relevant to the economic opportunity of individuals.
(g) Heavy reliance on industry whose demand for labour was growing slowly or falling and was likely to continue to do so – as an indication of vulnerability to economic change resulting in possible under-utilisation of labour resources.
(h) Poor communications as material to slow growth in the recent past and to the potential for growth.

(i) Decayed or inadequate environment, including dereliction as material to slow growth in the recent past and to the potential for growth.

(j) Serious net outward migration – as a pointer to the danger of accelerating decline, and as a summing up of the reactions of individuals to a complex of social and economic factors such as the local range of employment opportunities, educational and social activities and the state of the social and physical environment.

They concluded that the severest problems were undoubtedly in the development areas and that there was not a clear-cut and well-defined category of 'intermediate area'. Rather there were 'symptoms of concern' present to a varying extent and a varying degree in different parts of the country. Nevertheless, they felt that the north-west and Yorkshire & Humberside stood in the greatest need of a new impetus and recommended special assistance for these regions, and more limited assistance to the Notts-Derbyshire coalfield and to north Staffordshire.

In recommending help to such a large area of the country (containing a fifth of the population of Great Britain) there was no suggestion that the 'growth-area' policy should be abandoned. On the contrary, the Committee were simply following the logic which underlay the setting up in 1966 of broad development areas in place of the former narrower and relatively scattered development districts, chosen on the basis of high unemployment: 'as a result of inducements being made available to industry throughout these wider areas, industrialists are not tied to locations of greatest need, which may not be the most viable long-term locations for industry'. It followed that the recommended aid might go to relatively prosperous parts of an intermediate area, but this was in principle no different from the position in the development areas.

This, however, ignores the political difficulties. Any aid to intermediate areas which is effective in increasing new industrial development must (at least in the short run) have an effect on the development areas. As the Hunt Committee ruefully point out at the beginning of their report, 'the supply of mobile industry available to stimulate economic growth is, taken as a whole, insufficient at present to meet the needs of the development areas and overspill towns, let alone areas of slow growth. We recognize that remedial measures for areas of slow growth may hold back progress elsewhere.'

The reaction of the Government of the day was that assistance should be concentrated in more narrowly defined localities within the regions concerned. The selection of these intermediate areas was to be governed strictly by 'criteria of need', in particular the level and character of unemployment, the rate of outward migration, and the scope for industrial growth. On this basis, seven intermediate areas were designated: the Yorkshire coalfield, northeast Lancashire, the Nottingham/Derbyshire coalfield, north Humberside, Plymouth, part of south-east Wales, and Leith.

Intermediate area status was extended to other areas in 1971, 1972 and 1974. Any listing is rapidly outdated: at the time of writing the latest position was detailed in the November 1974 issue of the *Department of Employment Gazette*.

Throughout this continuing debate on the allocation of resources between regions there has been little attention paid to the impact on planning *within* regions – except in very broad, generalist terms such as that the movement of industry from London and the west midlands will 'relieve congestion'. The Hunt Committee, however, did discuss as a 'possible cause for concern' the flow of industry to overspill areas in the south-east, East Anglia and the west midlands, and in particular the difficulties being experienced by Telford New Town.

The essential argument here is that the high level of development area incentives is jeopardising the overspill programme for London and the west midlands, and throws into question the viability of the future programmes which are based on the premise that the transfer of employment from the two conurbations will be on a substantially increased scale. The three Economic Planning Councils (South East, East Anglia and West Midlands) all put up a case for relaxation of IDC control and additional finance inducements in overspill areas. The Hunt Committee favoured the former but not the latter. Conurbation firms, should, in their view, be allowed to move to an overspill location provided that the Board of Trade (now the Department of Industry) has advised the firm of the incentives and attractions of the development areas and provided that the movement is within the planned growth programme of the overspill area. Financial inducements, on the other hand, 'might divert a much needed amount of new work away from areas of high unemployment'.

But is it possible to implement current regional physical planning strategies within the context of the present economic policies of giving priority to development areas? If there is not sufficient mobile industry for the areas of high unemployment and for the overspill areas, something has to give way. Nowhere is this clearer than in the west midlands.

It is here that we see the unresolved dilemma of present regional policies. Regional planning means different things to central and local government. As Senior has put it (in his 'memorandum of dissent' to the Redcliffe-Maud Report):

'What *central* government means by "regional planning" is primarily the correction of economic imbalance *between* one "region" and another; and it is only with reluctance that central government is reconciling itself to the fact that this purpose – crucial to its central function in the economic field – necessarily involves the making of investment decisions *within* "regions" on a territorial as well as a functional basis. What *local* government means by "regional planning", on the other hand, is primarily the expression of national policies in terms of a comprehensive long-term strategy for economic and physical development *within* each provincial-scale "region", in the context of which local planning authorities can work out meaningful structure plans for their own areas.'

This gap cannot be bridged until there is a regional planning machine designed for the job. At present central government can channel (or block) resources to regions, but there is no machinery (in England and Wales) for rationally distributing resources *within* regions on the basis of a comprehensive strategy. The Department of the Environment have a role and powers quite inadequate for this; and in any case, it is not a proper task for central government – it is essentially a regional matter. Any plan involves the submerging of some interests in favour of others. At national level the priority given to development areas is a clear case in point. But at the regional level there is no system for determining policies. Each local authority have the interests of their ratepayers at heart, and development needed for a wider benefit is jeopardised. Thus (for instance), if a conurbation authority see industrial overspill as having undesirable effects on their rateable value and a potentially good overspill authority see development as an intolerable local burden, an overspill policy is killed at birth, even if it is in the wider interests of the region as a whole. To quote Senior again:

'Any plan which seeks to guide development in the interest of the region as a whole must call for the concentration of investment in particular parts of it and the prevention of development in others. But so long as the region is divided between different implementing authorities, one of them is bound to find that it is being called upon to bear more than its share of the cost and get less than its share of the benefit of giving effect to particular provisions of the overall plan: if this were not so there would be no need for such a plan. And it would be not only altruistic, but positively undemocratic, for that authority thus to subordinate its own ratepayers' interests to that of its neighbour's ratepayers. It is quite unreasonable to expect a wrongly organized local government structure to behave as it would automatically tend to do if it were rightly organized, when the wrong organization automatically produces a different incidence of the costs and benefits of acting in the interest of the region as a whole.'

NEW REGIONAL PLANNING MACHINES

The problem thus cannot be adequately approached without new and appropriate instruments of regional government. These must be able to bring together economic, physical and social issues. Some functions must of course be carried out by specialised *ad hoc* agencies (the railways for example) but, given broadly based and sensibly delineated regional authorities, arrangements for co-ordination with these can be effective. At the very least, some machinery is needed (as suggested in *Strategic Choice for East Anglia*) to provide a forum in which the multiplicity of specialised executive agencies are required to come together for mutual reconciliation of their objectives and activities. This is not the place to outline a possible scheme: there is an abundance of proposals in the Reports of the Redcliffe-Maud Commission and the Royal Commission on the Constitution. In any case, it may well be politically impossible to consider further local government reorganisation so soon after the recent trauma – though the prospects of devolution to Scottish and Welsh Assemblies may well raise the question within the framework of devolution to English provinces or regions. But the fact remains that until the appropriate machinery is devised, regional planning will remain largely a central government activity concerned with 'balance' and the location of major investments. The library of regional and sub-regional studies will increase, but the effective co-ordinated action will be impossible to achieve.

In the meantime the experience of the Scottish regional councils will be watched with interest. It remains to be seen whether they present a model to be copied and developed south of the Border.

Chapter XIV

PLANNING AND THE PUBLIC

PUBLIC OPINION

'Public opinion – your opinion – is of the utmost importance in the making of planning decisions. Elected members and officers go to considerable lengths to find out what you think about the issues and problems facing us in planning and to discover your reaction to the proposed solutions. The City does not belong to the Council much less the Planning Committee. It is your City and your views matter.'

This passage comes from the foreword to *Planning for Leicester*, a publication of the Leicester City Council, which is aimed at explaining the planning process and seeking the participation of the Leicester citizens in it. Such publications, though once rare, are now a common means of enlisting public support for, and involvement in, the making of planning policies. This stems from an increased realisation of the essentially political nature of the planning process and the crucial importance of public acceptability. It was this lack of public acceptability which was one of the main reasons for the failure of the compensation-betterment provisions of the 1947 Act and the short-lived Land Commission. And it is a major purpose of the new planning system to achieve a greater flexibility and sensitivity than had proved possible under the earlier system.

Part of the difficulty lies in the fact that much planning is regulative, and there is a natural tendency to forget or to fail to see the real gains that have been made, for instance, in protecting the countryside from unsightly advertising hoardings. But the issue goes much deeper. Throughout the fifties and sixties, planning proposals were generally presented to the public as a *fait accompli*, and only rarely were they given a thorough public discussion. Though there was (and still is) machinery for objections and appeals, this quasi-judicial process was devised for use by a restricted range of interested parties. As will be shown later in this chapter, it was modified in its operation in response to increasing public pressures, but the general attitude to this system was (and remains) less favourable than to the normal judicial system with which it is frequently – though inappropriately – compared. However, the important issue is not that of the scope for registering 'objections', but that of the extent to which planning involves active public participation. This in turn demands a high degree of political sophistication and understanding on the part of the public.

This is more than a matter of jolly public relations. The public need to understand the problems with which planning is concerned and the constraints under which planners work. To quote again from *Planning for Leicester*, 'planners work within the tight limits of the law and they are not the all-powerful gods that they are sometimes thought to be'. Moreover, the effect of planning decisions on land values must not be forgotten. Advance knowledge of planning proposals can markedly affect the value of the land concerned. This may lead to land speculation or to premature objections on the part of owners who expect to be adversely affected. As a result, a planning department often have to operate under a veil of secrecy. This can only serve to increase public suspicion. Strangely this situation is itself in part the result of previous lack of public support. As already suggested, though it is by no means the full explanation, there can be no doubt that the divorce between planners and the public is one of the factors which has led to the curious half-dismantled planning legislation which we now have – what Lord Holford has called 'a set of spare parts'. It must be axiomatic that compensation for acquisition of land or restriction on its use must be at a level which is publicly acceptable. This is so not merely on grounds of equity but also because 'inadequate' compensation will arouse such opposition as to inhibit public authorities from using their powers. This was the position under the 1947 Act. Each amendment of this Act has been designed to remove further injustices. But injustices still remain and will continue to do so until a scheme is devised which will at one and the same time be adequate for achieving planning objectives and prove publicly acceptable. How far the Community Land Act (outlined in Chapter VII) will meet the needs of the situation remains to be seen.

The point is basically a simple one: the planners cannot effectively move too far ahead of public opinion. This does not apply only to town and country planning: it applies equally to the social services, to the nationalised industries, and indeed to any form of public or private monopoly or near-monopoly. It goes to the root of democratic government in modern industrial society; and it thus leads far from the central questions which form the subject matter of this book. All that can be attempted here is a discussion of a selection of relevant topics.

PLANNING APPLICATIONS

Some two-thirds of a million applications for planning permission are made each year to local planning authorities in Britain, of which about four-fifths are granted. This enormous spate of applications involves great strains on the local planning machinery which, generally speaking, is not adequately staffed to deal with them and at the same time undertake the necessary work involved in preparing and reviewing development plans. Yet full consideration by local planning staffs is needed if planning committees – the elected members who have the responsibility for granting or refusing applications – are to have the requisite information on which to base their decisions. The importance of this is underlined by the fact that planning committees often have remarkably little time during a meeting in which to come to a decision. Agendas for meetings tend to be long: an average of five to six minutes for consideration of each application is nothing unusual, and in some cases the time may be as little as two minutes. It cannot, therefore, be surprising that in a large proportion of cases (in the bigger authorities at least) the recommendations of the planning officer are approved *pro forma*. This may, of course, result in part from the harmonious relationship which commonly exists between local authority representatives and their officers; and, in any case, lay members tend to accept the technical expertise of their officials, while, on the other hand, the officials well know the minds of their political masters. Yet the point remains that both the elected representatives and the planning officials are hard pressed to cope with the constant flood of applications. Several important implications follow from this. First, and most obvious, is the danger that decisions will be given which are 'wrong' – i.e. which do not accord with planning objectives. Secondly, good relationships with the public in general and unsuccessful applicants in particular are difficult to attain: there is simply not sufficient time. Thirdly, this lack of time corroborates the view of many (unsuccessful) applicants that their case has never had adequate consideration: a view which is further supported by the manner in which refusals are commonly worded. Phrases such as 'detrimental to amenity' or 'not in accordance with the development plan', and so on, mean little or nothing to the individual applicant. He suspects that his case has been considered in general terms rather than in the particular detail which he naturally thinks is important in his case. And he may be right: understaffed and overworked planning departments cannot give each case the individual attention which is desirable.

This, of course, is not the whole picture. For instance, individuals who may wholly agree with a general planning principle will tend to see it in a different light when it is applied to their own applications. As Grove has pointed out (in *Planning and the Applicant*): 'The man who has his home in one part of a green belt and owns what an estate agent would call "fully ripe building land" in another part, is as vociferous in relying on green belt principles to oppose building near his home as he is in denouncing the extreme and ridiculous lengths to which those principles have been carried when he is refused planning permission on his other land, and frequently seems to achieve this without any conscious hypocrisy.' This normal human failing is encouraged by the curious compromise situation which currently exists in relation to the control of land. On the one hand it seems to be generally accepted in principle (as it definitely is in law) that no one has a right to develop his land as he wishes unless the development is publicly desirable (as determined by a political instead of a financial decision). On the other hand, though the allocation of land to particular uses is determined by a public decision, the motives for private development are financial – and the financial profits which result from the development constitute private gain (though subject to capital gains tax). This unhappy circumstance (which is discussed at length in Chapter VII) involves a clash of principles which the unsuccessful applicant for planning permission experiences in a particularly sharp manner. It follows that local planning officials may have a peculiarly difficult task in explaining to a landowner why, for example, the field which he owns needs to be 'protected from development'.

Nevertheless, the success which attends this unenviable task does differ markedly between different local authorities. (The Dobry Report, summarised in Chapter VI, illustrates the range of current practices.) The question is not simply one of the great variations in potential land values in different parts of the country or in the relative adequacy of planning staffs. Though these are important factors, there remains the less easily documented question of attitudes towards the public. All that can be said is that in some local authorities a great effort is made to assist and explain matters to an applicant, whereas in others the impression one gains is that of a bureaucratic machine which displays little patience and no kindness towards the individual applicant who does not understand 'planning procedures'.

DELEGATION OF PLANNING DECISIONS TO OFFICERS

The 1968 Planning Act (now consolidated in the 1972 Act) made provision for the delegation to officers of planning decisions. This is in line with the recommendations of the Maud Report on *Management of Local Government*, the Mallaby Report on *Staffing of Local Government*, and the report of the *Management Study on Development Control*.

The background to this is that 70 per cent of all planning applications are of 'a simple nature'. The *Management Study on Development Control* found that a large proportion of these 'simple' applications were determined by a committee or by the council without presentation of details, without discussion and in accordance with the recommendations of the officers. They concluded that very many development control applications were already effectively delegated to officers for decision but were required to go through a formal procedure for ratification by a body of members. This created unnecessary work for the local authority and unnecessary delay for the applicant. Consideration was given to the possibility of a system which allowed for *approvals only* to be issued by a planning officer on certain clearly defined classes of application:

(a) construction of one house in a residential area;
(b) construction of blocks of private garages;
(c) changes of use not conflicting with the development plan and not requiring advertising;
(d) erection of temporary buildings and extension of existing temporary permissions;
(e) construction of vehicular access on other than trunk roads;
(f) construction of extensions to existing residential properties.

It was estimated that this would reduce by up to 50 per cent the number of cases needing to go to committee, 'would save committee time for more important work, would save a considerable amount of administrative work and time, and would speed up the issue of decision notices to applicants'. The Mallaby Committee added that greater delegation would provide more attractive and challenging official careers, and thus stimulate recruitment. In this way a better service would be rendered to the public.

The statutory provisions go further than the proposals of the *Management Study*. They enable local authorities to delegate decisions on all kinds of planning application except those for listed building consent. The power is entirely discretionary: it is for local

authorities to decide which officers, if any, should be given delegated powers and for which kinds of application. A decision of an
officer exercising delegated powers has the same standing as one
given by the council itself.

This streamlining at the local level reflects the principle underlying the current legislation – that the planning system should be so
organised that decisions are taken at the appropriate level. Thus
the department are responsible for broad policy issues, the local
authority for local plans, and officials for detailed administrative
issues which do not warrant committee involvement. In this way a
real attempt is being made to reduce the bureaucratic, cumbersome
and unwieldy system which has been paralysing the machinery. The
relationships with, and the service to, the public should improve
considerably. But much will depend on the more subtle factors than
formal rearrangements of power: an issue to which we return
shortly.

MALADMINISTRATION AND THE 'OMBUDSMAN'

Most legislation is based on the assumption that the organs of
government will operate efficiently and fairly. This is not always the
case, but, even if it were, provision has to be made for the citizen
who feels aggrieved by some action (or inaction) to complain, have
his complaint investigated, and be satisfied that the investigation is
impartial. As modern industrial society becomes more complex the
pressures for a machinery of protest, appeal and restitution grow –
as is evidenced in such widely differing fields as social security, race
relations and press publicity.

At the parliamentary level, the case for an 'ombudsman' was
reluctantly conceded by the Government, and a Parliamentary
Commissioner for Administration was appointed in 1967. He is an
independent statutory official whose function is to investigate complaints of maladministration referred to him through Members of
Parliament. His powers of investigation extend over all central
government departments and he has the right of access to all
departmental papers.

Only a small fraction of the Parliamentary Commissioner's cases
relate to planning matters and, of course, his concern is with
administrative procedures, not with the merits of planning decisions. His quarterly report (issued as a House of Commons Paper)
gives the full but anonymised texts of reports of all the cases which
he has investigated. In his fourth report for 1974–5, for instance
(HC 405, June 1975), he reports on cases involving a complaint that
the Secretary of State for the Environment failed to understand the

grounds on which he had been requested to intervene in (i.e. to use his default powers in relation to) a redevelopment scheme; a complaint by a Motorways Action Committee that, following a motorway inquiry, the inspector called for further evidence from the DoE (much of which, the committee submitted, was 'highly dubious and contentious, and contained a number of misleading assumptions') on which they were not given the opportunity to cross-examine the department's witness; a complaint by a group of local residents that an appeal decision to allow a gypsy caravan site paid little heed to local residents' objections, ignored important relevant facts, and was taken on the basis of inconsistent attitudes; and a complaint that an appeal refusal to allow the replacement of a coach house was unfair and improper in that the reasons given in the decision letter were not in accordance with the facts and that the decision could not be reconciled with the policies followed by the local planning authority or with planning permissions they had given for other development in their area. In all these cases the Parliamentary Commissioner concluded that the complaint could not be upheld. This is not always the case, however; the Commissioner has had occasion to criticise some aspects of the department's handling of particular cases and has led to changes in internal administrative procedures.

The Commissioner has, in a number of cases, noted that part of a complaint is against the actions of a local authority. He has no jurisdiction in this area and any reference made to local authorities is simply 'to provide background, and place in context the actions of the Department'. The position is now, of course, changed by the establishment of the 'local government ombudsman' – or, to be more precise, the Commission for Local Administration. Separate Commissions have been set up (under the provisions of the Local Government Act 1974 and the Local Government (Scotland) Act 1975) for England, for Wales and for Scotland. Complaints about local 'maladministration' must be referred to the Local Commissioner through a councillor.

It is early days yet to assess the likely achievements of this new institution, but it is noteworthy that a high proportion of complaints concern planning matters. This is briefly documented and illustrated in the Commission's first annual report. One of the Local Commissioners also added the comment:

'It is reasonable to conclude that, given my present terms of reference, complaints about planning matters are likely always to form a large proportion of those received. I would hope that in due course the Local Commissioners will be able to offer from their experience some comment on changes in procedures which might help to reduce cause for complaint in this area of local government work and on the different practices of local authorities in, for instance, the amount of publicity given to the public about planning applications which have been received.'

Where maladministration is found, it is for the local authority to take such action as they think appropriate in the light of the Commissioner's report. If the Commissioner is not satisfied with the action taken, he can make a further report, but he has no powers to impose legal enforcement. In the words of one Commissioner, 'we assume that the local publicity and the council's good sense will be enough'.

LOCAL GOVERNMENT AND THE ELECTORATE

The innovation of a local ombudsman is of interest in a wider context. By comparison with the position of Parliament (and through Parliament, the taxpayer) *vis-à-vis* central government, the ratepayer is badly placed *vis-à-vis* local government. There is little at the local level to compare with such institutions as those of the Parliamentary Question, the Public Accounts Committee, the Expenditure Committee and the Comptroller and Auditor General. There are, of course, the provisions for district audit in England and Wales, and in Scotland, a new institution termed the Commission for Local Authority Accounts (the chairman of which – Tom Fraser, a former Labour Minister of Transport – is on record as saying that they are interested 'in more than balancing the books': they would 'ensure that the ratepayers get value for money; that there was no unnecessary duplication of services between region and district; that rents and charges for local authority services were regularly reviewed').

In such ways local government is beginning to come under unprecedented scrutiny, though still on a modest scale. This trend is a most healthy one and promises to make local government more sensitive and responsive to its electorate.

A full examination of these issues is obviously beyond the scope of this book, but sufficient has been said to indicate the broader framework within which planning is operating and by which it will be judged.

PLANNING APPEALS

An unsuccessful applicant for planning permission can, of course, appeal to the Secretary of State and, as noted in Chapter III, a large number do so. Each case is considered by the department on its merits. This allows a great deal of flexibility, and permits cases of individual hardship to be sympathetically treated. But, at the same time, it can make the planning system seem arbitrary – at least to the unsuccessful appellant. Although broad policies are set out in such publications as the *Development Control Policy Notes*, the general view in the department is that a reliance on precedent could easily give rise to undesirable rigidities. As Mandelker has pointed out:

'Conditions vary so fundamentally from case to case and from one part of the country to another that it would be impossible, if not wrong, to draft rules that would hold good uniformly. The basic problem is that a variety of factors operate in a planning case; the art of making a decision lies in the striking of a proper balance. Under the circumstances, there is little that the Department can do beyond listing those factors which it considers crucial, and expressing rules of thumb which will help select those which should preponderate.'

Other issues relevant to this view are the traditional local-central government relationship (in which local authorities are considered as equal partners in the processes of government) and the particular character of town and country planning in this country. The flexibility of the development plan, the wide area of discretion legally allowed to the planners in the operation of planning controls, and the very restricted jurisdiction of the courts, necessitate a judicial function for the department. But this function is only quasi-judicial: decisions are taken, not on the basis of legal rules as in a court of law or in accordance with case-law, but on a judgement as to what course of action is, in the particular circumstances and in the context of ministerial policy, desirable, reasonable and equitable. By its very nature this must be elusive, and the unsuccessful appellant may well feel justified in believing that the dice are loaded against him. The very fact that public inquiries on planning appeals are heard by ministerial 'inspectors' (and probably in the town hall of the authority against whose decisions he is appealing) does not make for confidence in a fair and objective hearing. The contrast with the courts is striking; to quote Grove again:

'The usual complaint of the civil litigant is not that his case is not fairly and impartially heard and determined, but that, owing to the complexity of the system, the delay and expense are excessive. The views of the planning applicant, except when he is successful, are quite different. He rarely complains of the cost (though quite often of the delay) but frequently takes the view that the inquiry or hearing was nothing more than an opportunity for him to "let off steam".'

Of course, part of the expressed dissatisfaction comes from those who are compelled to forgo private gain for the sake of communal benefit: the criticisms are not really of procedures, and they are not likely to be assuaged by administrative reforms or good 'public relations'. They are fundamentally criticisms of the public control of land use – in particular, if not in principle.

Nevertheless, the appeals procedure has had shortcomings which have attracted strong and relevant protest. For example, the department used not to publish the reports prepared by their inspectors on appeal inquiries. Their main argument against publication was that this would cause misunderstanding and embarrassment. In their evidence to the Franks Committee on *Administrative Tribunals and Inquiries*, they stated:

'The objection in principle that we should see to publication is that our inspectors really act in a dual capacity. They act first of all as the inspector who goes down to see the site and who, being a technical man, can give us an appreciation of the soundness of the authority's proposals; they hear the arguments and report to the Minister what took place, what impression is made upon them, what view they take of the site and so on. Then they make a recommendation and in that capacity they are acting as officers of the Department because their recommendation is essentially what should be the application of policy to the facts they found. That is why you can have identical facts but different decisions. They have got to be *au fait* with current policy and say what they think that the Minister, his policy being what it is, would wish to do in the particular case as they found it. We think that publication of the recommendation would cause embarrassment.'

This passage clearly illustrates how a public inquiry is different from a judicial review. It is usual to apply the phrase 'quasi-judicial', but this is not very satisfactory, as the Franks Committee implied. They saw the problem essentially as one of finding a reasonable balance between conflicting interests:

'On the one hand there are Ministers enjoined by legislation to carry out certain duties. On the other hand there are the rights and feelings of individual citizens who find their possessions or plans interfered with by the administration. There is also the public interest, which requires both that Ministers and other administrative bodies should not be frustrated in carrying out their duties and also that their decisions should be subject to effective checks or controls.'

The Franks Committee argued that inspectors' reports should be published, and this view was accepted by the Government. It is interesting to note that in the great majority of cases (on planning appeals) the minister's decision has been 'broadly in line' with the recommendations of the inspector.

This is not the place to discuss all the issues relevant to these procedures: the interested reader is referred to the Report of the Franks Committee. The immediate point is simply that neither the statutory provisions, nor the arguments on administrative inquiries, are concerned primarily with the encouragement of public participation in the planning process. To achieve this a local authority have to forge their own procedures.

Nevertheless, significant changes have been made in recent years to broaden the scope and to change the character of public inquiries on planning appeals, particularly in the case of proposals of major importance. Before outlining these, however, it is necessary to consider the statutory position of 'third parties'.

'THIRD PARTY' INTERESTS

The rights of 'third parties' – those affected by planning decisions but having no legal 'interest' in the land subject to the decision – were highlighted in the so-called Chalk Pit case.* This, in brief, concerned an application to 'develop' certain land in Essex by digging chalk. On being refused planning permission, the applicants appealed to the Minister of Housing, and a local inquiry was held. Among those who appeared as objectors at the inquiry some were substantial landowners, including a Major Buxton, whose land was adjacent to the appeal site and was being used for agricultural and residential purposes. The inspector's recommendation was that the appeal should be dismissed, mainly because there was a serious danger of chalk dust being deposited on the land of Major Buxton and others in quantities which would be 'detrimental to the user of the land'; and that there was no present shortage of chalk in the locality. The minister disagreed with the inspector's recommendations and allowed the appeal. Major Buxton then appealed to the High Court, partly on the ground that in rejecting his inspector's

* Buxton and Others v. Minister of Housing and Local Government (1960), 3 WLR 866. The account given here of this case is based on a summary contained in Public Law, Summer 1961, pp. 121-8.

findings of fact, the minister had relied on certain subsequent advice and information given to him by the Minister of Agriculture without giving the objectors any opportunity of correcting or commenting upon this advice and information. But Major Buxton now found that he had no legal right of appeal to the courts: indeed he apparently had had no legal right to appear at the inquiry. (He only had what the judge thought to be a 'very sensible' administrative privilege.) In short, Major Buxton was a 'third party': he was in no legal sense a 'person aggrieved'. Yet clearly in the wider sense of the phrase Major Buxton was very much aggrieved, and at first sight he had a moral right to object and to have his objection carefully weighed. But should the machinery of town and country planning be used for this purpose by an individual? Before the town and country planning legislation, any landowner could develop his land as he liked, provided he did not infringe the common law which was designed more to protect the right to develop rather than to restrain it. The law of nuisance and trespass was not a particularly strong constraint on the freedom to use land. But, as the judge stressed, the planning legislation was designed 'to restrict development for the benefit of the public at large and not to confer new rights on any individual members of the public'.

This, of course, is the essential point. It is the job of the local planning authority to assess the public advantage or disadvantage of a proposed development – subject to a review by the Secretary of State if those having a legal interest in the land in question object. Third parties cannot usurp these government functions. Nevertheless, it might be generally agreed that those affected by planning decisions should have the right to make representations for consideration by a planning committee. The present position is that third parties have an 'administrative privilege' to appear at a public inquiry, but generally no similar privilege in relation to a planning application.

There is one group of exceptions to this. The Town and Country Planning Act of 1959 introduced a provision designed to give an opportunity for the public ventilation of objections to certain planning proposals of an 'unneighbourly' character. Such developments are advertised, and objectors allowed to make written 'representations' to the local planning authority. If the planning application is granted, there is no further opportunity for objections – however much the objectors may be affected. But, if the application is refused and the applicant appeals, the objectors have the normal privilege of appearing and being heard at the public inquiry. In short, the only new provision here is the requirement for publicity and the formal right to make representations. The types of develop-

ment covered by these provisions are very limited – public conveniences, refuse disposal and sewerage works, slaughterhouses
and theatres, dance halls, skating rinks, etc. It might be possible to
extend this list somewhat (to include, for example, fish and chip
shops and petrol stations), but to extend it to cover all applications
would, quite apart from any objections on principle, lead to the
danger of a breakdown in planning procedures. The machinery of
planning is already overburdened with development applications
and appeals. An extension of the opportunities for representations,
objections and appeals would slow down procedures and make
them dangerously cumbersome. This is a practical issue of importance, but the fundamental point is that it is the job of local planning
authorities to assess what is publicly desirable. Measures designed
to make the system open and fair are all to the good. Openness and
fairness were two of the principles which the Franks Committee
sought to apply to administrative tribunals and inquiries. Their
third principle – impartiality – cannot be applied without qualification to planning procedures (as the Committee pointed out). If a
local planning authority were merely a judicial body seeking to
achieve a fair balance between conflicting private interests, many of
the arguments for extending the rights of individuals to be heard
and to object could be accepted. But the local planning authority
are not an impartial body: they are an agency of government
attempting to secure what they believe to be the best development
for its area. In short, they have a fundamentally political responsibility.

THE CHANGING NATURE OF PUBLIC INQUIRIES

This fundamental political responsibility, however, has to be sound-
ly based, and an increasingly articulate and 'environmentally aware'
public has forced changes even within the narrow confines of an
inquiry on a planning appeal, particularly where major development proposals are at issue (and even more so in the case of
called-in applications and motorway proposals, where the inquiry is
concerned with whether planning permission should be given,
rather than with whether the decision of a planning authority should
be upheld or reversed).

The purpose of a public inquiry is to enable the Secretary of State
to decide whether a planning authority have been correct in refusing
permission for a particular development.* Originally, the main

* The discussion is focused on inquiries on an appeal against a decision of a local
planning authority to refuse planning permission for a particular development. It
applies also to other inquiries, e.g. on an appeal against conditions imposed by a local
authority in granting planning permission. Inquiries on structure plans have now
been replaced by 'examinations in public': these are discussed in Chapter V.

emphasis in the inquiry procedure was on the strength (or otherwise) of the objections made by the appellant, though even here the Secretary of State was concerned with the intrinsic merits of the case. But increasingly, public inquiries on major issues have become more searching, a larger number of third parties have been involved, and the department have been at pains to ensure that all the relevant issues have been covered. The most explicit statement of this development of the public inquiry system is to be found in a *Memorandum of Guidance on the Procedure in Connection with Statutory Inquiries* and Circular 14/1975 issued by the Scottish Development Department in 1975. This was issued as a code of guidance for reporters (as 'inspectors' are called in Scotland) *and for all parties to inquiries*. Though it was envisaged that the recommended procedures would be adopted as a whole, the covering Circular drew particular attention to five points:

(i) The importance on the one hand of applicants giving full, public explanations of their proposals and their effect and, on the other hand, of planning authorities discussing the proposals thoroughly with applicants and with objectors to improve public understanding, open the way to compromise and perhaps even avoid the need for an inquiry at all.

(ii) The need to circulate in advance of the inquiry as much written evidence as possible and to discourage the use, for tactical advantage, of surprise evidence, with reserve sanction to treat such action as unreasonable behaviour to be taken into account for the purpose of award of expenses.

(iii) The avoidance of repetitious cross-examination.

(iv) The importance of the role of the reporter in directing the proceedings. He should not necessarily be a silent listener to the proceedings: he should be free to seek any clarification he deems necessary or to direct questions to issues which he thinks will be important to the Secretary of State's decision, but which may not have been adequately covered in the evidence.

(v) The desirability of the maximum informality of procedure, so that the ordinary interested person does not feel inhibited from making a contribution without professional representation.

DISSATISFACTION WITH ROAD INQUIRIES

In contrast with the positive approach of the Scottish Development Department is the current disarray in connection with road inquiries. Some of the problems here (such as the forced postponement of the inquiry into the Airedale Trunk Road and the disruption at the inquiries on road proposals in Epping Forest and in Cornwall) are the result of pressure groups who are opposed to the building of any road anywhere, irrespective of the merits (or otherwise) of particular projects. The arena for much of this debate should be Parliament: it is nonsensical at every local inquiry. On the other hand, national transport policy is (at the time of writing) in a state of some confusion – to say the least. Objectors have made the most of this, and no solution is possible until some clear guidelines are laid down (after appropriate national debate). This in turn means that policy should be clear and broadly acceptable. So far as roads are concerned, this is certainly not the case at present. As a result, public confidence in the appeal process has been seriously weakened, and this problem has been exacerbated by the sheer volume of inquiries. Frank Layfield's paper on *The Role of Inquiries in Land Planning* neatly sets out the relevant considerations in a broader context, but until road policies in general are settled and generally accepted, there is a real danger that the public inquiry process will be thrown into widespread disrepute.

It may be that the answer (as suggested by a *Times* leader of 3 December 1975) is for a two-stage process, with one inquiry concerned with the need (or otherwise) for a road, and a later inquiry concerned with the detailed routing. Be that as it may, a continuation of the present unsatisfactory situation would have serious repercussions on a much wider range of planning issues.

STATUTORY PROVISION FOR PUBLIC PARTICIPATION

Road inquiries are one exception to the general trends in relation to public participation. The wider changes in the character of major public inquiries reflect increasing concern on the part of central government for the public acceptability of planning and, at the same time, increased pressure for more information on and involvement in the planning process. But the major landmark in this changing philosophy of planning is the 1968 Planning Act (and its Scottish equivalent of 1969) which makes public participation a statutory requirement in the preparation of structure plans.

The main stimulus for this came, not from the grass-roots (still less from local government), but from central government themselves. Under the old development plan system, the department were becoming crippled by what a former Permanent Secretary called 'a crushing burden of casework'. The concept of ministerial responsibility was clearly shown to be inapplicable over the total field of development plan approval and planning appeals. Not only was much of this work inappropriate to a central government department: its sheer weight prevented central government from fulfilling their essential function of establishing major planning policies. A new system was therefore required which would remove much of the detailed work of planning – including approval of local plans – from central to local government. But this necessitates public confidence in local government: hence the importance of public participation. This now becomes, not a desirable adjunct to the planning process, but a fundamental basis. If public participation does not work, the system will collapse.

The legislation provides only the barest sketch of the new system: public participation is much more than adherence to formal procedures. It is merely provided that, in drawing up a structure plan, a local authority must:

(i) give 'adequate' publicity to the report of the survey on which the plan is based, and to the policy which they propose to include in the plan;

(ii) provide publicity for their proposals and 'adequate opportunity' to enable representations to be made by the public;

(iii) take into account these representations in drawing up the structure plan;

(iv) place the plan on deposit for public inspection, together with a statement of the time within which objections may be made to the Secretary of State;

(v) submit the plan to the Secretary of State, together with a statement of the steps which have been taken to comply with the above requirements, and of consultations which have been carried out with 'other persons'.

A local plan is drawn up within the policy framework of an approved structure plan and does not normally have to be submitted to the Secretary of State for approval (though a copy has to be sent to him and, exceptionally, he can direct that it 'shall not have effect unless approved by him'). It follows the same procedure as a structure plan, but if there are any objections these are sent to the local authority (not the Secretary of State) and are heard at a public inquiry which is held by an independent inspector who reports to the authority. The Secretary of State will not normally be concerned with local plans (though he will presumably check that they do properly reflect the policy approved in the structure plans).

At first sight it might appear that local authorities are to be judges in their own case, particularly since there is provision for inspectors to be appointed by local authorities. Indeed, much has been made of this 'unfair judicial process'. But the fact is that the process is not

a judicial one: it is essentially administrative and political. This is
why citizen-participation is so crucial. If local authorities do not
succeed in carrying their citizenry with them the new system will
fail: public opposition will necessitate a move back to the previous
system.

LOCAL GOVERNMENT AND PUBLIC PARTICIPATION

Concern with – and even interest in – public participation has not
been a particularly obvious strength of British local government,
and it will be even more difficult to achieve with the new larger local
authorities. With little experience to build on, it was perhaps
inevitable that a Committee should be appointed 'to consult and
report on the best methods, including publicity, of securing the
participation of the public at the formative stage in the making of
development plans for their area'. The Committee were set up
under the chairmanship of the late Arthur Skeffington (then Joint
Parliamentary Secretary to the Minister of Housing and Local
Government) in March 1968 and published their report *People and
Planning* in July 1969.

The Skeffington Report made a number of rather obvious recommendations which do not carry us a great deal further, for example:

'people should be kept informed throughout the preparation of a
structure or local plan for their area';
'local planning authorities should seek to publicize proposals in a
way that informs people living in the area to which the plan relates';
'the public should be told what their representations have achieved
or why they have not been accepted';
'people should be encouraged to participate in the preparation of
plans by helping with surveys and other activities as well as by
making comments'.

The mundane nature of many of the recommendations is testimony
to the distance which British local government has to go in making
citizen-participation a reality.

Unfortunately, the Report does not discuss many of the really
crucial issues, though passing references suggest that the Committee were aware of some of them. For instance, it is rightly stated that
'planning' is only one service 'and it would be unreasonable to
expect the public to see it as an entity in itself'. The Report
continues: 'public participation would be little more than an artificial abstraction if it became identified solely with planning procedures rather than with the broadest interests of people'. This has
major implications for the internal organisation and management of

local authorities. So have the proposals for the appointment of 'community development officers . . . to secure the involvement of those people who do not join organizations' and for 'community forums' which would 'provide local organizations with the opportunity to discuss collectively planning and other issues of importance to the area', and which 'might also have administrative functions, such as receiving and distributing information on planning matters and promoting the formation of neighbourhood groups'.

What is conspicuously lacking in this debate on public participation is an awareness of its political implications. The Skeffington Report noted that it was feared that a community forum might become the centre of political opposition: but the only comment made was 'we hope that that would not happen; it seems unlikely that it would, as most local groups are not party political in their membership'. The issue is not, however, one of *party politics*: it is one of local policies, pressures and interest. Public participation implies a transfer of some power from local councils to groups of electors. It is power which is the crucial issue – not in any sinister sense, but simply in terms of who is to decide local issues. The department do not want to be concerned with these (except where they have ramifications over a larger front: hence central approval of structure plans). This will be a matter of intimate concern for local councillors – and officials as well.

The transfer of considerable statutory powers from central to local government will show only too clearly that planning is essentially a political process – a fact which has been confused by the semi-judicial procedures with which the department have been so preoccupied.

None of this is to argue that the philosophy underlying the new legislation is misplaced: far from it. The intention is to demonstrate that the real problem of citizen-participation and local democratic control go far deeper than issues of formal procedures, of social surveys and public exhibitions. If the new system works it will have a major impact on British political processes; and it will not be confined to 'town and country planning'.

Curiously, it was not the Skeffington Committee but the Seebohm Committee (in their Report on *Local Authority and Allied Personal Social Services*) which highlighted another related issue (and one which the proposed community development officer would particularly face):

'the participants may wish to pursue policies directly at variance with the ideas of the local authorities, and there is certainly a difficult link to be forged between the concepts of popular participation and traditional representative democracy. The role of the social worker in this context is likely to give rise to problems of conflicting loyalties. The Council for Training in Social Work suggest in evidence that if community work is to be developed by the local authority, then the authority "will need to recognize the fact that some of its staff may be involved in situations which lead to criticism of their services or with pressure groups about new needs. The workers themselves will need to be clear about their professional role and this will depend upon their training and the organizational structure within which they work".... Participation provides a means by which further consumer control can be exercised over professional and bureaucratic power.'

A further problem in public participation is that of determining how representative are the views expressed by participating citizens. As the Skeffington Report implies, the views of 'the non-joiners and inarticulate' are as important as those of 'the actively interested and organized'. And as American experience shows, public participation can lead to strong demands to keep an area 'white', to exclude public authority housing, and to safeguard local amenities at a high cost to the larger community. It is not every community which is best placed to assess its needs in relation to a wider area.

Finally, reference needs to be made to the tricky problem of planning blight. The best way of avoiding this is to maintain the utmost secrecy until definite plans can be presented to the public as a *fait accompli.* Obviously this is not easy to reconcile with a greater degree of public participation. There is no easy answer to this. Indeed, the Skeffington Committee were probably right in saying that 'some increase in planning blight may have to be accepted if there is to be increased participation by the public'. Whether the compensation provisions for planning blight are adequate is another matter.

The essential ingredient of effective public participation is a concern on the part of elected members and professional staffs to make participation a reality. But it cannot be effective unless it is organised'. This, of course, is one of the fundamental difficulties. Though a large number of people may feel vaguely disturbed in general about the operation of the planning machine (and particularly upset when they are individually affected), it is only a minority who are prepared to do anything other than grumble. The minority may be growing, and with the general rise in educational levels it can be expected to continue to do so. It has to be recognised, however, that public participation will, as far as can be seen, always be restricted. In the words of Maurice Broady: 'the activity of responsible social criticism is not congenial to more than a minority. Most of us for most of the time are content to remain complacently acquiescent in our social niche . . . The activist, the social critic, the reformer will always be a small section of any society. Their activities require not only extra effort which few are willing to expend, but also the ability to criticise and organize which comparatively few possess.'

The minority is, nevertheless, an important one and, as the success of the Consumers' Association and similar bodies has shown, it can be instrumental in activating widespread interest and support (even if this stops short of actual participation). A little official encouragement might have surprisingly widespread effects. At the local level this could be on the lines suggested by the Coventry experiment (summarised in an Appendix to the Skeffington Report). At the national level it might take the form of financial assistance from the Exchequer towards the administrative overheads of a central agency – as is done with the Civic Trust and the National Federation of Housing Societies. But the leadership role and concern for wider community interests must always remain the responsibility of the local authority.

IN CONCLUSION

The debate on public participation (like that on local government reorganisation and regional devolution) raises the fundamental question of whether the machinery of government is deploying its resources in the most effective way. The issue is important not only in the interests of the mental health of the central administration, but also because their overcommitment with detailed aspects of planning and issues which are of purely local concern means that there are insufficient human resources left for a consideration of the broader planning issues which should be their particular responsibility. Fogarty in his book *Under-Governed and Over-Governed* has put this argument in general terms. Ministers, top management and trade union leaders, he argues, 'have over-committed themselves to settling detailed problems, and as a result have left themselves with too little time and energy to deal competently with the broader issues of overall government and management. By doing so they have also defeated even their immediate purpose and have made it harder to find sound solutions to problems of detail. . . . [Town and country planning] has fiddled with details. But it has succeeded neither in promoting timely action over such major features of regional development as the reshaping of the older conurbations or the building of new motorways, nor in creating a satisfactory urban landscape in newly developing areas, nor in bringing home to people in particular localities what they themselves might do to improve their neighbourhood amenities on the lines of the well-known schemes of the Civic Trust.'

The argument does not have to be accepted in full for its major point to be appreciated. Now that regional planning is beginning to move into the realm of practical politics, it is becoming increasingly important to reduce the amount of effort consumed by details. Broad regional policy-making is a more fitting task for central government than considering appeals on the design of suburban bungalows. It is in this context that the question of public support and participation needs to be considered. In the long run it may well prove to be a fundamental issue in adapting the planning machine to meet the problems of the second half of the twentieth century. It represents a bold step towards a realignment of political forces in the field of town and country planning. If it succeeds it will not stop there.

REFERENCES AND FURTHER READING

Abercrombie, P., *Greater London Plan*, HMSO, 1945.

Addison Report: *Report of the National Park Committee*, Cmd 3851, HMSO, 1931.

Aldous, T., *Battle for the Environment*, Fontana, 1972.

Aldridge, H. R., *The Case for Town Planning*, National Housing and Town Planning Council, 1915.

Allison, L., *Environmental Planning: A Political and Philosophical Analysis*, George Allen & Unwin, 1975.

Alonso, W., 'What Are New Towns For?', *Urban Studies*, Vol. 7, No. 1, February 1970.

Ancient Monuments Boards for England, Wales and Scotland, *Annual Reports*, (published in one volume), HMSO.

Arvill, R., *Man and Environment*, Penguin Books, revised edition, 1969.

Ashworth, W., *The Genesis of Modern British Town Planning*, Routledge, 1954.

Bains Report: *The New Local Authorities – Management and Structure*, HMSO, 1972.

Barlow Report: *Report of the Royal Commission on the Distribution of the Industrial Population*, Cmd 6153, HMSO, 1940.

Barr, J., *Derelict Britain*, Penguin Books, 1969.

Bayliss, B. T. and Edwards, S. L., *Transport for Industry (Summary Report)*, Ministry of Transport, HMSO, 1968.

Beaver Report: Committee on Air Pollution, *Interim Report*, Cmd 9011, HMSO, 1953; *Report*, Cmd 9322, HMSO, 1954.

Best, R. H., *Land for New Towns*, Town and Country Planning Association, 1964.

Beveridge Report: *Social Insurance and Allied Services*, Cmd 6404, HMSO, 1942.

Bigham, D. A., *The Law and Administration Relating to Protection of the Environment*, Oyez Publications, 1973.

Bonham-Carter, V., *The Survival of the English Countryside*, Hodder & Stoughton, 1971.

Bowley, M., *Housing and the State 1919–1944*, George Allen & Unwin, 1945.

Briggs, A., *History of Birmingham*, Vol. 2, Oxford University Press, 1952.

British Road Federation, *Basic Road Statistics*, published annually by the Federation (26 Manchester Square, London W1).

British Waterways Board, *Annual Reports*, HMSO.

British Waterways Board, *The Future of the Waterways*, HMSO, 1964.

British Waterways Board, *The Facts About the Waterways*, HMSO, 1966.

British Waterways Board, *Leisure and the Waterways*, HMSO, 1967.

Broady, M., *Planning for People*, National Council of Social Service, Bedford Square Press, 1968.

Brown, A. J., *The Framework of Regional Economics in the United Kingdom*, Cambridge University Press, 1972.

Brown, H. J. J., *The Land Compensation Act 1973*, Sweet & Maxwell, 1973.
Browne Report: *Refuse Storage and Collection*, HMSO, 1967.
Buchanan, C. D., *The State of Britain*, Faber, 1972.
Buchanan, Colin and Partners, *The Conurbations*, British Road Federation, 1969.
Buchanan Report: *Traffic in Towns*, HMSO, 1963. (Also published in shortened form by Penguin Books, 1964.)
Button, K. J., 'Transport Policy in the United Kingdom', *Three Banks Review*, No. 103, September 1974.
Buxton, R., *Local Government*, Penguin Books, 2nd edition, 1973.
Buxton, R., 'Planning in the New Local Government World', *Journal of Planning and Environment Law*, February 1974.
Cameron, G. C. and Wingo, L., *Cities, Regions and Public Policy*, Oliver & Boyd, 1973.
Central Housing Advisory Committee, *The Needs of New Communities: A Report on Social Provision in New and Expanding Communities*, HMSO, 1967.
Central Land Board, *Annual Reports (1948/49 to 1958/59)*, HMSO.
Central Office of Information, *Regional Development in Britain*, HMSO, 2nd Edition, 1974.
Central Office of Information, *Towards Cleaner Air: A Review of Britain's Achievements*, HMSO, 1973.
Central Statistical Office, *Abstract of Regional Statistics*, HMSO, annual.
Central Water Planning Unit, *First Annual Report 1975*, CWPU, 1975.
Centre for Environmental Studies, *Progress in Structure Planning: Integration of Local Government Services*, CES Conference Paper 8, 1974.
Chartered Institute of Public Finance and Accountancy, *Local Government Trends*, published annually by the Institute.
Cherry, G. E., *Urban Change and Planning: A History of Urban Development in Britain since 1750*, Foulis, 1972.
Cherry, G. E., *The Evolution of British Town Planning*, Leonard Hill, 1974.
Chester, D. N. and Willson, F. M. G., *The Organisation of British Central Government, 1914–1964*, George Allen & Unwin, 2nd edition, 1968.
Clawson, M. and Hall, P., *Land Planning and Urban Growth: An Anglo-American Comparison*, Johns Hopkins University Press, 1973.
Commission for Local Administration in England, *Report for the year ended 31 March 1975*, published by the Commission (21 Queen Anne's Gate, London, SW1).
Commission for Local Administration in England, *Your Local Ombudsman*, (published by the Commission).
Commission for the New Towns, *Annual Reports*, HMSO.
Confederation of British Industry, *Reshaping Regional Policy*, CBI, 1972.
Corfield, F. V., *Compensation and the Town and Country Planning Act 1959*, Solicitors' Law Stationery Society, 1959.
Council for the Protection of Rural England, *Annual Reports*, CPRE.
Council on Tribunals, *Annual Reports*, HMSO.
Countryside Commission, *Annual Reports*, HMSO.
Countryside Commission, *Regional Coastal Reports* (HMSO, 1967–8):
    1. The Coasts of Kent and Sussex.
    2. The Coasts of Hampshire and the Isle of Wight.
    3. The Coasts of South-West England.
    4. The Coasts of South Wales and the Severn Estuary.
    5. The Coasts of North Wales.
    6. The Coasts of North-West England.
    7. The Coasts of North-East England.

8. The Coasts of Yorkshire and Lincolnshire.

9. The Coast of East Anglia.

Countryside Commission, *The Coasts of England and Wales: Measurements of Use, Protection and Development*, HMSO, 1968.

Countryside Commission, *Coastal Recreation and Holidays*, HMSO, 1969.

Countryside Commission, *Picnic Sites*, HMSO, 1969.

Countryside Commission, *The Coastal Heritage*, HMSO, 1970.

Countryside Commission, *The Planning of the Coastline*, HMSO, 1970.

Countryside Commission, *Nature Conservation at the Coast*, HMSO, 1970.

Countryside Commission, *National Parks: The Challenge to the New Authorities*, published by the Commission, 1974.

Countryside Commission for Scotland, *A Park System for Scotland*, published by the Commission, 1974.

Countryside Commission for Scotland, *Annual Reports*, HMSO.

Cowan, P. (ed.), *The Future of Planning*, Heinemann, 1973.

Cox, H. and Morgan, D., *City Politics and the Press*, Cambridge University Press, 1973.

Craven, E. (ed.), *Regional Devolution and Social Policy*, Macmillan, 1975.

Crowe, S., *Tomorrow's Landscape*, Architectural Press, 1956.

Crowe, S., *The Landscape of Roads*, Architectural Press, 1960.

Cullingworth, J. B., *Housing in Transition*, Heinemann, 1963.

Cullingworth, J. B., *Housing and Local Government*, George Allen & Unwin, 1966.

Cullingworth, J. B., *Scottish Housing in 1965*, HMSO, 1967.

Cullingworth, J. B., *Report to the Minister of Housing and Local Government on Proposals for the Transfer of GLC Housing to the London Boroughs*, 2 vols, MHLG, 1970.

Cullingworth, J. B., *Problems of an Urban Society*, 3 vols, George Allen & Unwin, 1972.

Cullingworth, J. B., *Environmental Planning 1939–1969, Vol. I: Reconstruction and Land Use Planning*, HMSO, 1975.

Cullingworth, J. B. and Karn, V. A., *The Ownership and Management of Housing in the New Towns*, HMSO, 1968.

Cullingworth, J. B. and Watson, C. J., *Reports on a Household Survey and a House Condition Survey in the Central Clydeside Conurbation*, HMSO, 1971.

Daniels, P. W., 'Office Decentralisation from London – Policy and Practice', *Regional Studies*, Vol. 3, No. 2, September 1969, pp. 171–8.

Davison, R. C., *British Unemployment Policy: The Modern Phase Since 1930*, Longmans Green, 1938.

Denington Report: *Our Older Homes: A Call for Action*, HMSO, 1966.

Dennis, N., *Public Participation and Planners' Blight*, Faber, 1972.

Department of Economic Affairs, *The Task Ahead: Economic Assessment to 1972*, HMSO, 1969.

Department of Economic Affairs, *Economic Planning in the Regions*, HMSO, 2nd edition, 1968.

DoE, *Management Networks: Structure Plans*, HMSO, 1971.

DoE, *Long Term Population Distribution in Great Britain*, HMSO, 1971.

DoE, *Report of a River Pollution Survey of England and Wales 1970*, HMSO, Vol. I, 1971, Vol. II, 1972.

DoE, *Getting the Best Roads for our Money: the COBA Method of Appraisal*, HMSO, 1972.

DoE, Reports of four working parties in preparation for the UN Conference on the Human Environment, HMSO, 1972:

Human Habitat: How Do You Want To Live?

Pollution: Nuisance or Nemesis?
Organisation and Youth: 50 Million Volunteers.
Natural Resources: Sinews for Survival.
DoE, *Report of the Working Party on Local Authority/Private Enterprise Partnership Schemes,* HMSO, 1972.
DoE, *House Condition Survey 1971, England and Wales,* DoE, 1973.
DoE, *The New Water Industry: Management and Structure,* HMSO, 1973.
DoE, *Making Towns Better* (the 'Urban Guidelines' Studies), HMSO, 1973:
  The Sunderland Study, I: Tackling Urban Problems – A Basic Handbook.
  The Sunderland Study, II: Tackling Urban Problems – A Working Guide.
  The Oldham Study: Environmental Planning and Management.
  The Rotherham Study, I: A General Approach to Improving the Physical Environment.
  The Rotherham Study, II: Technical Appendices.
DoE, *Participation in Road Planning: A Consultation Paper,* DoE, 1973.
DoE, *A Background to Water Reorganization in England and Wales,* HMSO, 1973.
DoE, *Report of a Survey of the Discharges of Foul Sewage to Coastal Waters of England and Wales,* HMSO, 1973.
DoE, *Local Government in England and Wales: A Guide to the New System,* HMSO, 1974.
DoE, *Neighbourhood Councils in England: A Consultation Paper,* DoE, 1974.
DoE, *Miscellaneous Local Government and Planning Statistics, 1973,* DoE, 1974.
DoE, *The Water Services: Economic and Financial Policies,* 1st Report 1973; 2nd Report 1974; 3rd Report 1974, HMSO.
DoE, *Selected Enforcement and Allied Appeals (October 1974),* HMSO, 1974.
DoE, *The Monitoring of the Environment of the United Kingdom,* HMSO, 1974.
DoE, *Housing Land Availability in the South East: A Consultants' Study,* HMSO, 1975.
DoE, *Survey of Derelict and Despoiled Land in England 1974,* 3 vols, DoE, 1975.
DoE, *Census of Urban Deprivation* (Working Note No. 6), DoE, 1975.
DoE, *DoE And Its Work,* DoE, 1975.
DoE, *Planning Appeals: A Guide to Procedure,* DoE, 1975.
DoE, *The Manning of Public Services in London: A Study by a Joint Group of Officials of the Department of the Environment, the Department of Employment, the Greater London Council, and the London Boroughs Association,* DoE (LGP2), 1975.
DoE, *Control of Office Development: Annual Reports by the Secretary of State for the Environment,* House of Commons Papers, HMSO, annual.
DoE *Area Improvement Notes,* HMSO.
  1. *Sample House Condition Survey,* 1971.
  2. *House Condition Survey within a Potential General Improvement Area,* 1971.
  3. *Improving the Environment,* 1971.
  4. *House Improvement and Conversion,* 1972.
  5. *Environmental Design in Four General Improvement Areas.* 1972.
  6. *The Design of Street and Other Spaces in General Improvement Areas,* 1972.
  7. *Parking and Garaging in General Improvement Areas,* 1972.
  8. *Public Participation in General Improvement Areas,* 1973.
  9. *Traffic in General Improvement Areas,* 1974.
  10. *The Use of Indicators for Area Action,* 1975.
DoE, *Development Control Policy Notes,* HMSO, 1969–75.
  1. *General Principles.*
  2. *Development in Residential Areas.*
  3. *Industrial and Commercial Development.*

4. *Development in Rural Areas.*
5. *Development in Town Centres.*
6. *Road Safety and Traffic Requirements.*
7. *Preservation of Historic Buildings and Areas.*
8. *Caravan Sites.*
9. *Petrol Filling Stations and Motels.*
10. *Design.*
11. *Amusement Centres.*
12. *Hotels.*
13. *Out of Town Shops and Shopping Centres.*
14. *Warehouses.*
15. *Hostels and Homes.*

Dobry Reports: *Control of Demolition*, 1974; *Review of the Development Control System, Interim Report*, 1974; *Final Report*, 1975, HMSO.

Donnison, D. V., 'The Economics and Politics of the Regions', *Political Quarterly*, Vol. 45, No. 2, April–June 1974.

Donnison, D. V. and Eversley, D., *London: Urban Patterns, Problems and Policies*, Heinemann, 1973.

Dower Report: *National Parks in England and Wales*, Cmd 6628, HMSO, 1945.

Duncan, T. L. C., *Measuring Housing Quality: A Study of Methods*, Occasional Paper 20, Centre for Urban and Regional Studies, University of Birmingham, 1971.

Duncan, T. L. C., *Housing Improvement Policies in England and Wales*, Research Memorandum No. 28, Centre for Urban and Regional Studies, University of Birmingham, 1974.

Estimates Committee, Session 1961–2, *Classified Roads*, HC 227, HMSO, 1962.

Estimates Committee, Session 1968–9, *Motorways and Trunk Roads*, HC 475, HMSO, 1969.

Evans, H. (ed.), *New Towns: The British Experience*, Charles Knight, 1972.

Eversley, D., *The Planner in Society*, Faber, 1973.

Expenditure Committee, Session 1972–73, *Urban Transport Planning*, HC 57 (3 vols), HMSO, 1972. (See also *Government Observations*, Cmnd 5366, HMSO, 1973.)

Expenditure Committee, Session 1972–73, *House Improvement Grants*, HC 349, HMSO, 1973.

Expenditure Committee, Session 1972-73, *Regional Development Incentives*, HC 327, HMSO, 1973; and *DTI*, HC 42, HMSO, 1973.

Expenditure Committee, Session 1974–75, *New Towns*, HC 616 (5 vols), HMSO, 1975.

Fairbrother, N., *New Lives, New Landscapes*, Penguin Books, 1972.

Fedden, R., *The Continuing Purpose: A History of the National Trust, Its Aims and Work*, Longmans, 1968.

Foley, D., *Governing the London Region: Reorganization and Planning in the Sixties*, University of California Press, 1972.

Forestry Commission, *Annual Reports*, HMSO.

Forestry Commission, *Forestry in the Landscape*, HMSO, 1966.

Forestry Commission, *Forestry in the British Scene*, HMSO, 1968.

Forshaw, J. H. and Abercrombie, P., *County of London Plan*, Macmillan, 1943.

Franks Report: *Report of the Committee on Administrative Tribunals and Enquiries*, Cmnd 218, HMSO, 1957.

Freight Transport Association, *Planning for Lorries*, FTA, 1974.

Frost, D. and Sharman, N., 'Participation in Urban Renewal: The Swinbrook Project', *GLC Intelligence Unit Quarterly Bulletin*, No. 25, December 1973.

Fuerst, J. S., *Public Housing in Europe and America*, Croom Helm, 1974.

Garner, J. F., *Control of Pollution Act 1974*, Butterworths, 1975.

Geddes, P., *Cities in Evolution*, London, 1915.

Gee, F. A., *Homes and Jobs for Londoners in New and Expanding Towns*, HMSO, 1972.

GISP Report: *General Information System for Planning*, HMSO, 1972.

Gillis, J. D. S. *et al.*, *Monitoring and the Planning Process: Some Conclusions from the Development of the Notts-Derbys. Monitoring and Advisory System*, Institute of Local Government Studies, University of Birmingham, 1974.

Gosling Report: *Report of the Footpaths Committee*, HMSO, 1968.

Greater London Council, *Surveys of the Use of Open Space*, GLC, 1968.

Greater London Council, *Greater London Development Plan: Statement; Report of Studies; Tomorrow's London*, GLC, 1969.

Greater London Council, *Traffic and the Environment*, GLC, 1972.

Green, G., 'Politics, Local Government and the Community', *Local Government Studies*, June 1974.

Green Paper, *War on Waste: A Policy for Reclamation*, Cmnd 5727, HMSO, 1974.

Grieve, R., 'Regional Planning in Scotland', *The Planner*, Vol. 59, November 1973.

Griffith, J. A. G., *Central Departments and Local Authorities*, George Allen & Unwin, 1966.

Grove, G. A., 'Planning and the Applicant', *Journal of the Town Planning Institute*, Vol. 49, May 1963, p. 130.

Gunningham, N., *Pollution, Social Interest and the Law*, Martin Robertson, 1974.

Gwilliam, K. M. and Mackie, P. J., *Economics and Transport Policy*, George Allen & Unwin, 1975.

Haar, C. M., *Land Planning Law in a Free Society*, Harvard University Press, 1951.

Hall, P. (ed.), *Land Values*, Sweet & Maxwell, 1965.

Hall, P., *The Theory and Practice of Regional Planning*, Pemberton, 1970.

Hall, P. *et al.*, *The Containment of Urban England: Vol. I – Urban and Metropolitan Growth Processes; Vol. II – The Planning System*, George Allen & Unwin, 1973.

Hall, P., *Urban and Regional Planning*, Penguin Books, 1974.

Hammond, E., 'Dispersal of Government Offices: A Survey', *Urban Studies*, Vol. 4, No. 3, November 1967, pp. 258–75.

Hammond, E., *London to Durham: A Study of the Transfer of the Post Office Savings Certificate Division*, University of Durham, Rowntree Research Unit, 1968.

Hardman Report: *Dispersal of Government Work from London*, Cmnd 5322, HMSO, 1973. (See also Working Party on the Hardman Report, *The Unanswerable Case for the Dispersal of Civil Service Jobs from London to Glasgow and the West of Scotland*, Corporation of Glasgow, 1973.)

Haringey London Borough Council, *First Steps Towards a Housing Action Area*, Haringey LBC, 1975.

Harloe, M., Issacharoff, R. and Minns, R., *The Organization of Housing: Public and Private Enterprise in London*, Heinemann, 1974.

Hayward, J. and Watson, M., *Planning, Politics and Public Policy – The British, French and Italian Experience*, Cambridge University Press, 1975.

Heap, D., *Introducing the Land Commission Act*, Sweet & Maxwell, 1967.

Heap, D., *An Outline of Planning Law*, Sweet & Maxwell, 6th edition, 1973.

Heap, D., *Encyclopedia of the Law of Town and Country Planning*, Sweet & Maxwell (continuously updated by supplements).

Heap, D., *The Land and the Development, or The Turmoil and the Torment* (The Hamlyn Lectures 1975), Stevens, 1975.

Herbert Report: *Report of the Royal Commission on Local Government in Greater London*, Cmnd 1164, HMSO, 1960.

Herrmann, P. G., *Forecasts of Vehicle Ownership in Counties and County Boroughs in Great Britain*, Road Research Laboratory (Crowthorne, Berkshire), 1968.

Hill, D. M., *Participating in Local Affairs*, Penguin Books, 1970.

Hillman, J., *Planning for London*, Penguin Books, 1971.

Hillman, M. et al., *Personal Mobility and Transport Policy*, PEP Broadsheet 542, 1973.

Historic Building Councils for England, Wales and Scotland, *Annual Reports* (published separately), HMSO.

Hobday Report: *Prevention of River Pollution*, HMSO, 1949.

Hobhouse Report: *Report of the National Parks Committee (England and Wales)*, Cmd 7121, HMSO, 1947.

Howard, E., *Garden Cities of Tomorrow*, ed. F. J. Osborn, Faber, 1946.

Hunt Report: *The Intermediate Areas*, Cmnd 3998, HMSO, 1969.

Hutcheson, A. M. and Hogg, A., *Scotland and Oil*, Oliver & Boyd, 1975.

Huxley Report: *Conservation of Nature in England and Wales*, Cmd 7122, HMSO, 1947.

Jackson, J. N., *The Urban Future: A Choice Between Alternatives*, George Allen & Unwin, 1972.

Jeger Report: Report of the Working Party on Sewage Disposal, *Taken for Granted*, HMSO, 1970.

Jenkins, S., 'The Press as Politician in Local Planning', *Political Quarterly*, Vol. 44, No. 1, January–March 1973.

Jenkins, S., 'The Politics of London Motorways', *Political Quarterly*, Vol. 44, No. 3, July–September 1973.

Johnson, W. A., *Public Parks on Private Land in England and Wales*, Johns Hopkins University Press, 1971.

Jones, G. W., 'The Local Government Act 1972 and the Redcliffe–Maud Commission', *Political Quarterly*, Vol. 44, No. 2, April–June 1973.

Jones, T. L., 'Public Participation in the Countryside: An Experiment in Hertfordshire', *Journal of Planning and Environment Law*, August 1973.

Journal of Planning and Environment Law, Occasional Papers, *Planning Inquiry Practice*, Sweet & Maxwell, 1974.

Jowell, J., 'Development Control' (review article on the Dobry Report), *Political Quarterly*, Vol. 46, No. 3, July–August 1975.

Karn, V. A., *Housing Surveys of Crawley, Stevenage, Aycliffe and East Kilbride*, Occasional Papers 8–11, Centre for Urban and Regional Studies, University of Birmingham, 1970.

Key Report: *Pollution of Waste by Tipped Refuse*, HMSO, 1961.

Kimber, R., Richardson, J. J. and Brooke, S. K., 'British Government and the Transport Reform Movement', *Political Quarterly*, Vol. 45, No. 2, April–June 1974.

Kirwan, R. M., Martin, D. B. et al., *The Economics of Urban Residential Renewal and Improvement*, Centre for Environmental Studies, Working Paper 77, 1972.

Klein, R., 'The Case for Elitism: Public Opinion and Public Policy', *Political Quarterly*, Vol. 45, No. 4, October–December 1974.

Land Commission, *Annual Reports*, HMSO.

Layfield, F., 'The Role of Inquiries in Land Planning', RTPI, *Town and Country Planning Summer School 1974: Report of Proceedings*.

Lee Valley Regional Park Authority, *Lee Valley Regional Park*, 1969 (published by the Authority, Myddleton House, Bulls Cross, Enfield, Middlesex).

Leicester City Planning Department, *Planning for Leicester*, Leicester City Council, 1975.

Lervez, J., *Economic Planning and Politics in Britain*, Martin Robertson, 1975.

Ling, A., 'Skyscrapers and their Siting in Cities', *Town Planning Review*, Vol. 34, No. 1, April 1963.

Llewelyn-Davies, Weeks, Forestier-Walker and Bor, and Ove Arup and Partners, *Motorways in the Urban Environment*, British Road Federation, 1971.

Local Government Chronicle, *Corporate Management in Action*, Brown, Knight and Truscott, 1975.

Local Government Manpower Committee, *1st Report*, 1950; *Second Report*, 1951, HMSO.

Location of Offices Bureau, *Annual Report* (obtainable from the Bureau, 27 Chancery Lane, London WC2).

Lomas, G., *The Inner City: A Preliminary Investigation of the Dynamics of Current Labour and Housing Markets with Special Reference to Minority Groups in Inner London*, London Council of Social Service, 1974.

London County Council, *The Planning of a New Town* (Hook), LCC, 1961.

Long, J. R., *The Wythall Inquiry*, Estates Gazette, 1962.

Lutyens, E. and Abercrombie, P., *A Plan for Kingston upon Hull*, A. Brown & Sons, 1945.

McCrone, G., *Regional Policy in Britain*, George Allen & Unwin, 1969.

Mackintosh, J. P., *The Devolution of Power*, Penguin Books, 1968.

McLoughlin, J., *The Water Act 1973*, Sweet & Maxwell, 1973.

Mallaby Report: *Staffing of Local Government*, HMSO, 1967.

Mandelker, D. R., *Green Belts and Urban Growth*, University of Wisconsin Press, 1962.

Marriott, O., *The Property Boom*, Hamish Hamilton, 1967. (Pan Books 1969.)

Masser, I., 'Methods of Sub-Regional Analysis: A Review of Four Recent Studies', *Town Planning Review*, Vol. 41, No. 2, April 1970.

Maud Report: *Management of Local Government*, HMSO, 1967.

Mayo, M., *Community Development and Urban Deprivation*, Bedford Square Press, 1974.

Megarry, R. E., *Lectures on the Town and Country Planning Act 1947*, Stevens, 1949.

Meynell, A., 'Location of Industry', *Public Administration*, Vol. 37, Spring 1959.

Midland Bank Review, 'Government Policy and the Regional Problem', *Midland Bank Review*, November 1975.

Miller, B., 'Citadels of Local Power', *The Twentieth Century*, Vol. 162, October 1957.

Ministry of Agriculture, Fisheries and Food, *Forestry Policy*, HMSO, 1972.

MHLG, *Design in Town and Village*, HMSO, 1953.

MHLG, *Report for the Period 1950/51 to 1954*, Cmd 9559, HMSO, 1955.

MHLG, *Trees in Town and City*, HMSO, 1958.

MHLG, *Caravans as Homes* (Arton Wilson Report), Cmnd 872, HMSO, 1959.

MHLG, *The Control of Mineral Working*, HMSO, revised edition, 1960.

MHLG, *New Life for Dead Lands: Derelict Areas Reclaimed*, HMSO, 1963.

MHLG, *The Future of Development Plans: A Report by the Planning Advisory Group*, HMSO, 1965.

MHLG, *The Deeplish Study: Improvement Possibilities in a District of Rochdale*, HMSO, 1966.

MHLG, *Gypsies and Other Travellers*, HMSO, 1967.

MHLG, *Historic Towns: Preservation and Change*, HMSO, 1967.

MHLG, *Management Study on Development Control*, HMSO, 1967.

MHLG, *Bath: A Study in Conservation*, HMSO, 1968.

MHLG, *Chester: A Study in Conservation*, HMSO, 1968.

MHLG, *Chichester: A Study in Conservation*, HMSO, 1968.

MHLG, *York: A Study in Conservation*, HMSO, 1968.

MHLG, *Report for 1967 and 1968*, Cmnd 4009, HMSO, 1969.
MHLG, *Living in a Slum: A Study of St. Mary's, Oldham*, Design Bulletin 19, HMSO, 1970.
MHLG, *Moving out of a Slum: A Study of People Moving from St. Mary's, Oldham*, Design Bulletin 20, HMSO, 1970.
MHLG, *Preservation Policy Group: Report to the Ministry of Housing and Local Government, May 1970*, HMSO, 1970.
MHLG, *Development Plans: A Manual on Form and Content*, HMSO, 1970.
MHLG, *Bulletin of Selected Planning Appeals*, No. 1–13, HMSO, 1947–58; *Selected Planning Appeals (Second Series)*, No. 1–5, 1959–63, HMSO.
Ministry of Local Government and Planning, *Town and Country Planning 1943–1951: Progress Report by the Minister of Local Government and Planning on the Work of the Ministry of Town and Country Planning*, Cmd 8204, HMSO, 1951.
Ministry of Town and Country Planning, *Footpaths and Access to the Countryside: Report of the Special Committee (England and Wales)*, Cmd 7207, HMSO, 1947.
Ministry of Transport, *Roads in England* (Annual Report), HMSO.
Ministry of Transport, *Passenger Transport in Great Britain* (Annual Statistics), HMSO.
Ministry of Transport, *British Waterways: Recreation and Amenity*, Cmnd 3401, HMSO, 1967.
Ministry of Transport, *How Fast? A Paper for Discussion*, HMSO, 1968.
Ministry of Transport, *Transport in London*, Cmnd 3686, HMSO, 1968.
Ministry of Transport, *Roads for the Future: A New Inter-Urban Plan*, HMSO, 1969.
Ministry of Transport, *Roads for the Future: The New Inter-Urban Plan for England*, Cmnd 4369, HMSO, 1970.
Moore, V., 'The Taxation of Development Gains', *Journal of Planning and Environment Law*, November 1974, pp. 634–41.
Mowat, C. L., *Britain Between the Wars, 1918–1940*, Methuen, 1955.
Mukherjee, S., *There's Work To Be Done*, Manpower Services Commission, HMSO, 1974.
Mutch, W. E. S., *Public Recreation in National Forests: A Factual Study*, Forestry Commission, HMSO, 1968.
National Economic Development Council, *Conditions Favourable to Faster Growth*, HMSO, 1963.
National Economic Development Office, *New Homes in the Cities: The Role of the Private Developer in Urban Renewal in England and Wales*, HMSO, 1971.
National Parks Commission, *Annual Reports*, HMSO. (The National Parks Commission was superseded by the Countryside Commission in 1968. See *Nineteenth Report of the National Parks Commission* and *First Report of the Countryside Commission for the Year Ended September 30th, 1968*, HC 33, HMSO, 1968.)
National Water Council, *First Annual Report and Accounts 1974/75*, NWC, 1975.
Nature Conservancy, *The Nature Conservancy: Progress 1964–1968*, HMSO, 1968.
Nature Conservancy Council, *Statement of Policies*, NCC, 1974.
Nature Conservancy Council, *First Report 1 November 1973 – 31 March 1975*, HC 499, HMSO, 1975.
Nettleford, J. S., *Practical Town Planning*, St Catherine Press, London, 1914.
New Town Development Corporations, *Annual Reports*, HMSO.
Nicholson, J. H., *New Communities in Britain*, National Council of Social Service, 1961.
Nicholson, M., *The Environmental Revolution*, Hodder & Stoughton, 1970.
Noise Advisory Council Reports (HMSO):
  Neighbourhood Noise, 1971.
  Aircraft Noise, 1971.

Traffic Noise, 1972.

Noise in Public Places, 1974.

Noise in the Next Ten Years, 1974.

North East of Scotland Joint Planning Advisory Committee, *The Regional Report: Function and Uses*, Summary and Conclusions, NESJPAC, 1974.

North West Economic Planning Council, *Derelict Land in the North West*, NWEPC, 1969.

Ogilvy, A. A., 'The Self-Contained New Town', *Town Planning Review*, Vol. 39, No. 1, April 1968.

Organisation for Economic Co-operation and Development, *Streets for People*, OECD, 1974.

Organisation for Economic Co-operation and Development, *The Polluter Pays Principle*, OECD, 1975.

Orlans, H., *Stevenage*, Routledge & Kegan Paul, 1954.

Osborn, F. J. and Whittick, A., *The New Towns: The Answer to Megalopolis*, Leonard Hill, revised edition, 1969.

Outdoor Recreation Resources Review Commission, *Outdoor Recreation for America*, US Government Printing Office, 1962.

Oxenham, J., *Reclaiming Derelict Land*, Faber, 1966.

Pahl, R. E., *Whose City?*, Longmans, 1970.

Paterson Report: *The New Scottish Local Authorities – Organisation and Management Structures*, HMSO, 1973.

Pilcher Report: *Commercial Property Development: First Report of the Advisory Group*, HMSO, 1975.

Pippard Report: *Pollution of the Tidal Thames*, HMSO, 1961.

Political and Economic Planning, *Location of Industry*, PEP, 1939.

Political and Economic Planning, *Solving Traffic Problems – I: Lessons from America*, Planning Broadsheet No. 402, 1956.

Porter, E., *Pollution in Four Industrialised Estuaries: Four Case Studies undertaken for the Royal Commission on Environmental Pollution*, HMSO, 1973.

Professional Institutions Council for Conservation, *The Urban Road in Relation to the Conservation and Renewal of the Environment*, PICC, 1974.

Professional Institutions Council for Conservation, *Dereliction of Land*, PICC, 1974

Public Participation in Structure Planning: 'Linked Research Project', *Interim Papers* (from Department of Extramural Studies, University of Sheffield).

Ramsay Report: *Report of the Scottish National Parks Survey Committee*, Cmd 6631, HMSO, 1945.

Rapoport, R. and R. N., *Leisure and the Family Life Cycle*, Routledge & Kegan Paul, 1975.

Redcliffe-Maud Report: Royal Commission on Local Government in England, *Vol. 1. Report*, Cmnd 4040; *Vol. 2. Memorandum of Dissent by Mr. D. Senior*, Cmnd 4040-I; *Vol. 3. Research Appendices*, Cmnd 4040-II; Summary *Local Government Reform*, Cmnd 4039, HMSO, 1969.

Redcliffe-Maud, Lord and Wood, B., *English Local Government Reformed*, Oxford University Press, 1974.

Reith Reports: *New Towns Committee: Interim Report*, Cmd 6759; *Second Interim Report*, Cmd 6794; *Final Report*, Cmd 6876, HMSO, 1946.

Reith, Lord, *Into the Wind*, Hodder & Stoughton, 1949.

Reynolds, J. P., 'Public Participation in Planning', *Town Planning Review*, Vol. 40, No. 2, July 1969, pp. 131–48.

Rhodes, G., *Administrators in Action: British Case Studies, Vol. II* ('The Wentworth By-Pass'), George Allen & Unwin, 1965.

Rhodes, G., *The New Government of London: The First Five Years*, Weidenfeld & Nicolson, 1972.

Richards, P. G. *The Reformed Local Government System*, George Allen & Unwin, 2nd edition, 1975.

Richardson, H. W. and West, E. G., 'Must We Always Take Work to the Workers?', *Lloyds Bank Review*, January 1964.

Robson, W. A., *The Development of Local Government*, George Allen & Unwin, 2nd edition, 1948; 3rd edition, 1954.

Robson, W. A., *The Governors and the Governed*, George Allen & Unwin, 1964.

Rodwin, L., *The British New Towns Policy*, Harvard University Press, 1956.

Rowe, A., *Democracy Renewed: The Community Council in Practice*, Sheldon Press, 1975.

Royal Commission on the Constitution, *Vol. I: Report*, Cmnd 5460; *Vol. II: Memorandum of Dissent by Lord Crowther-Hunt and Professor A. J. Peacock*, Cmnd 5460-I, HMSO, 1973.

Royal Commission on Environmental Pollution, *First Report*, Cmnd 4585, HMSO, 1971; *Second Report: Three Issues in Industrial Pollution*, Cmnd 4894, HMSO, 1972; *Third Report: Pollution in Some British Estuaries and Coastal Waters*, Cmnd 5054, HMSO, 1972; *Fourth Report: Pollution Control – Progress and Problems*, Cmnd 5780, HMSO, 1974.

Royal Fine Art Commission for England and Wales, *Periodic Reports*, HMSO.

Royal Fine Art Commission for Scotland, *Periodic Reports*, HMSO.

Royal Town Planning Institute, *The Land Question*, RTPI, 1974.

Royal Town Planning Institute, *Planning Aid*, RTPI, 1974.

Royal Town Planning Institute, *The Urban Crisis: Transport Problems of Cities*, RTPI, 1975.

Ryan, M. and Isaacson, P., 'Structure Planning in Dockland', *Political Quarterly*, Vol. 45, no. 3, July–September 1974.

Ryan, P., *The National Trust*, Dent, 1969.

Sandford Report: *Report of the National Park Policies Review Committee*, HMSO, 1974.

Schaffer, F., *The New Town Story*, MacGibbon & Kee, 1970. (Paladin, 1972.)

Schon, D. A., *Beyond the Stable State*, Temple Smith, 1971. (Penguin Books, 1973.)

Scott Report: *Report of the Committee on Land Utilisation in Rural Areas*, Cmd 6378, HMSO, 1942.

Scottish Council of Social Service, *Community Councils*, SCSS, 1974.

SDD, The New Scottish Housing Handbook, Bulletin 2, *Slum Clearance and Improvements*, HMSO, 1969.

SDD, *Scotland's Historic Buildings: A Guide to the Legislation which Protects Them*, SDD, 1970.

SDD, *Scotland's Travelling People*, HMSO, 1971.

SDD, *Draft New Town (Stonehouse) Designation Order 1972: Memorandum by the Secretary of State*, HMSO, 1972.

SDD, *Towards Cleaner Water: Report of a Rivers Pollution Survey of Scotland*, HMSO, 1972.

SDD, *The Water Service in Scotland: Report of the Scottish Water Advisory Committee*, HMSO, 1972.

SDD, *North Sea Oil and Gas: Interim Coastal Planning Framework – A Discussion Paper*, SDD, 1973.

SDD, *Community Councils: Some Alternatives for Community Council Schemes in Scotland*, HMSO, 1974.

SDD, *Annual Reports*, HMSO.

Scottish Housing Advisory Committee, *Scotland's Older Houses*, HMSO, 1967.

Seebohm Report: *Report of the Committee on Local Authority and Allied Personal Services*, Cmnd 3703, HMSO, 1968.

Select Committee on Estimates, Session 1955–56, *Development Areas*, HC 139, HMSO, 1955.

Select Committee on Estimates, Session 1958–59, *Trunk Roads*, HC 223, HMSO, 1959.

Select Committee on Scottish Affairs, *Land Resource Use in Scotland*, HC 511 (5 vols), HMSO, 1972. (See also *Government Observations on the Report of the Select Committee on Scottish Affairs*, Cmnd 5428, HMSO, 1973.)

Sharp, D., *Living with the Lorry: A study of the Goods Vehicle in the Environment*, Freight Transport Association and Road Haulage Association, 1973.

Sharp, E., *The Ministry of Housing and Local Government*, George Allen & Unwin, 1969.

Sharp, T., *Town and Townscape*, John Murray, 1968.

Sharp, T., 'Dreaming Spires and Teeming Towers', *Town Planning Review*, Vol. 33, No. 4, January 1963.

Sharp, T., *Exeter Phoenix*, Architectural Press, 1946.

Silkin, Lord, 'Third Party Interests in Planning', *Report of the Proceedings of the Town and Country Planning Summer School, 1962*, Town Planning Institute, pp. 40–9.

Sillitoe, K. K., *Planning for Leisure: An Enquiry into the Present Pattern of Participation in Outdoor and Physical Recreation and the Frequency and Manner of Use of Public Open Spaces, Among People Living in the Urban Areas of England and Wales*, Government Social Survey, HMSO, 1969.

Skeffington Report: Committee on Public Participation in Planning, *People and Planning*, HMSO, 1969.

Smeed Report: *Road Pricing: The Economics and Technical Possibilities*, HMSO, 1964.

Smith, B. C., *Regionalism in England*, 3 volumes:
  Vol. 1: *Regional Institutions: A Guide* (1964).
  Vol. 2: *Its Nature and Purpose 1905–1965* (1965).
  Vol. 3: *The New Regional Machinery* (1965).
  Acton Society Trust.

Smith, B. C., *Advising Ministers: A Case Study of the South-West Economic Planning Council*, Routledge & Kegan Paul, 1969.

Smith, P. M., 'What Kind of Regional Planning? A Review Article', *Urban Studies*, Vol. 3, November 1966, pp. 250–7 (a review of the North-West and the West Midlands regional studies and the 1966 White Paper on the Scottish economy).

Socialist Commentary, *Transport Policy: the Report of a Study Group*, published in *Socialist Commentary*, April 1975, and separately.

Society of County Borough Treasurers, *Public Transport in Urban Areas*, 1972.

Solesbury, W., 'Ideas about Structure Plans: Past, Present and Future', *Town Planning Review*, Vol. 46, no. 3, July 1975.

Sports Council, *The Sports Council: A Review 1966–69* (with bibliography), Central Council for Physical Recreation, 1969.

Standing Conference on London and South East Regional Planning, *London and South East England Regional Planning 1943–1974*, SCLSERP, 1974.

Standing Conference on London and South East Regional Planning, *A History of the Conference and Its Work 1962–1974*, SCLSERP, 1973.

Standing Conference on London and South East Regional Planning, *Lorry Routing*, SC 264, SCLSERP, 1975.

Starkie, D. N. M., *Transportation Planning and Public Policy* (*Progress in Planning*, Vol. 1, Part 4), Pergamon, 1973.

Stewart, J., *Corporate Management in Action*, Local Government Chronicle, 1975.

Strathclyde Regional Council, *Strathclyde Region: The Context of the Regional Report*, Strathclyde Regional Council, 1975.

Surveyor, 'An Inter-round Commentary on the First TPPs', *The Surveyor*, 20 September 1974.

Tanner, J. C., *Revised Forecasts of Vehicles and Traffic in Great Britain*, Road Research Laboratory (Crowthorne, Berkshire), 1967.

Tanner, J. C., *Forecasts of Vehicles and Traffic in Great Britain: 1974 Revision*, TRRL Report LR 650, 1974.

Taylor, R., *Noise*, Penguin Books, 1970.

Taylor, R., Cox, M. and Dickins, I., *Britain's Planning Heritage*, Croom Helm, 1975.

Tetlow, A. and Goss, A., *Homes, Towns and Traffic*, Faber, revised edition, 1968.

The Times, 'Places without a Future', *The Times*, 20, 21 and 22 March 1934.

Thomas, R., *London's New Towns: A Study of Self Contained and Balanced Communities*, PEP Broadsheet 510, 1969.

Thomas, R., *Aycliffe to Cumbernauld: A Study of Seven New Towns in their Regions*, PEP Broadsheet 516, 1969.

Thomson, J. M., 'An Evaluation of Two Proposals for Traffic Restraint in Central London', *Journal of the Royal Statistical Society*, Series A, Vol. 30, Part 3, 1967.

Thorpe Report: *Report of the Departmental Committee of Inquiry into Allotments*, Cmnd 4166, 1969.

Titmuss, R. M., *Problems of Social Policy*, HMSO and Longmans, 1950.

Titmuss, R. M., 'War and Social Policy', *Essays on 'The Welfare State'*, George Allen & Unwin, 1958.

Town and Country Planning: special issue, January–February 1968, 'New Towns Come of Age'.

Town and Country Planning Association, *London under Stress*, 1970.

Tudor Walters Report: *Report of the Committee on Questions of Building Construction in Connection with the Provision of Dwellings for the Working Classes*, Cd 9191, IIMSO, 1918.

Tulpule, A. H., *Forecasts of Vehicles and Traffic in Great Britain: 1972 Revision*, TRRL Report LR 543, 1973.

Turvey, R., *The Economics of Real Property*, George Allen & Unwin, 1957.

United Nations, Department of Economic and Social Affairs, *Urban Land Policies and Land-Use Control Measures*, (ST/ECA/167), 7 vols, UN, 1973.

Unwin, R., *Town Planning in Practice: An Introduction to the Art of Designing Cities and Suburbs*, T. Fisher Unwin, 1909.

Urban Motorways Committee, *New Roads in Towns*, HMSO, 1972.

Uthwatt Report: *Report of the Expert Committee on Compensation and Betterment*, Cmd 6386, HMSO, 1942.

Veal, A. J., *Recreation Planning in New Communities: A Review of British Experience*, Research Memorandum 46, Centre for Urban and Regional Studies, University of Birmingham, 1975.

Warren, H. and Davidge, W. R. (eds), *Decentralization of Population and Industry: A New Principle in Town Planning*, P. S. King & Son, 1930.

Warren Spring Laboratory, *Annual Reports*, HMSO.

Warren Spring Laboratory, *National Survey of Air Pollution 1961–71*, 2 vols, HMSO, 1972.

Water Resources Board, *Annual Reports*, HMSO.

Welsh Office, *Cymru: Wales* (annual report by government departments on activities and developments in Wales), HMSO.

Welsh Office, *Welsh House Condition Survey 1968*, HMSO, 1969.

Welsh Office, *Welsh House Condition Survey 1973*, HMSO, 1975.
Wheatley Report: *Report of the Royal Commission on Local Government in Scotland*, (2 vols), Cmnd 4150, HMSO, 1969.
Wilson Report: Committee on the Problem of Noise, *Noise: Final Report*, Cmnd 2056, HMSO, 1963.
Wood, E., *Planning and the Law*, Percival Marshall, 1949.
Worskett, R., *The Character of Towns: An Approach to Conservation*, Architectural Press, 1969.
Wraith, R. E. and Lamb, G. B., *Public Inquiries as an Instrument of Government*, George Allen & Unwin, 1971.

OFFICIAL REGIONAL STUDIES AND PLANS
(HMSO unless otherwise indicated)

Surveys by Central Government Officials
The South East Study 1961–1981 (1964).
The West Midlands: A Regional Study (1965).
The North-West: A Regional Study (1965).
The Problems of Merseyside: An Appendix to the North-West Study (1965).

Reports by Economic Planning Councils
Challenge of the Changing North (1966).
A Review of Yorkshire and Humberside (1966).
The East Midlands Study (1966).
A Strategy for the South-East (1967).
A Region with a Future: A Draft Strategy for the South-West (1967).
The West Midlands: Patterns of Growth (1967).
The North-West of the 1970s (1968).
Halifax and the Calder Valley (1968).
Huddersfield and Colne Valley (1969).
Opportunity in the East Midlands (1969).
Doncaster: An Area Study (1969).
The Plymouth Area Study (1969).
South-East Kent Study (1969).
Yorkshire and Humberside: Regional Strategy (1970).
The West Midlands: An Economic Appraisal (1971).
Strategic Settlement Pattern for the South West (1974).

Command Papers
Central Scotland: A Programme for Development and Growth, Cmnd 2188 (1963).
The North-East: A Programme for Development and Growth, Cmnd 2206 (1963).
The Scottish Economy 1965-70, Cmnd 2864 (1966).
Wales: The Way Ahead, Cmnd 3334 (1969).

Reports of the Central Unit for Environmental Planning
Humberside: A Feasibility Study (1969).
Severnside: A Feasibility Study (1971).

Reports of the South-East Joint Planning Team
Strategic Plan for the South-East (1970).
Studies: Vol. 1: Population and Employment.
   Vol. 2: Social and Environmental Aspects.
   Vol. 3: Transportation.
   Vol. 4: Strategies and Evaluation.
   Vol. 5: Report of Economic Consultants Ltd.

Regional Strategy Team Reports
Strategic Plan for the North West (1974).
Strategic Choice for East Anglia (1974).

Scottish Reports
Lothians Regional Survey and Plan (1966).
Grangemouth-Falkirk Regional Survey and Plan (1968).
The Central Borders: A Plan for Expansion (1968).
Tayside: Potential for Development (1970).
A Strategy for South-West Scotland (1970).
West Central Scotland Plan (1974). (Published by the West Central Scotland Plan Team, 21 Gordon Street, Glasgow G1 3PL.)

Consultants' Reports
Northampton, Bedford and North Bucks Study: An Assessment of inter-Related Growth, 1965.
A New City: A Study of Urban Development in an area including Newbury, Swindon and Didcot, 1966.
A New Town for Mid-Wales – Consultants' Proposals, 1966.
Dawley: Wellington: Oakengates – Consultants' Proposals for Development, 1966.
Expansion of Ipswich Designation Proposals: Consultants' Study of the Town and its Sub-Region, 1966.
Expansion of Northampton – Consultant's Proposals for Designation, 1966.
Expansion of Peterborough – Consultant's Proposals for Designation, 1966.
Expansion of Warrington – Consultant's Proposals for Designation, 1966.
South Hampshire Study: Report on the Feasibility of Major Urban Growth, 3 vols, 1966.
Ashford Study: Consultants' Proposals for Designation, 1967.
Central Lancashire: Study for a City – Consultants' Proposals for Designation, 1967.
Central Lancashire New Town Proposal: Impact on North East Lancashire, 1968.
Expansion of Ipswich: Comparative Costs – A Supplementary Report, 1968.
Llantrisant – Prospects for Urban Growth, 1969.
New Life in Old Towns – Two Pilot Studies on Urban Renewal in Nelson and Rawtenstall, 1971.
Study of the Cambridge Sub-Region, 1974.

DEPARTMENTAL CIRCULARS

Ministry of Town and Country Planning (*HMSO*)
40 (1948), *Survey for Development Plans.*
100 (1950), *Development by Government Departments.*

Ministry of Housing and Local Government (*HMSO*)
49/59, *Purchase Notices.*
58/59, *Delegation of Planning Functions.*
30/60, *Local Employment Act, 1960: Rehabilitation of Derelict, Neglected or Unsightly Land.*
42/60, *Caravan Sites and Control of Development Act, 1960.*
47/63, *Town and Country Planning Act, 1963.*
51/63, *Development near Buildings of Special Architectural or Historical Interest.*
64/65, *Control of Office and Industrial Development Act, 1965.*
17/67, *Rehabilitation of Derelict, Neglected or Unsightly Land: Industrial Development Act, 1966 and Local Government Act, 1966.*

53/67, *Civic Amenities Act, 1967.*
5/68, *The Use Conditions in Planning Permissions.*
44/68, *Countryside Act, 1968.*
49/68, *Caravan Sites Act, 1968.*
61/68, *Town and Country Planning Act, 1968 – Part V: Historic Buildings and Conservation.*
1/69, *Town and Country Planning (Tree Preservation Order) Regulations, 1969.*
15/69, *Town and Country Planning Act, 1968 – Part IV: Acquisition and Disposal of Land.*
26/69, *Purchase Notices.*
63/69, *Housing Act, 1969.*
64/69, *Housing Act, 1969: House Improvement and Repair.*
65/69, *Housing Act 1969: Area Improvement.*
68/69, *Housing Act 1969: Slum Clearance.*
96/69, *Control of Advertisement Regulations.*
16/70, *Mines and Quarries (Tips) Act 1969: Grants to Local Authorities.*
17/70, *Derelict Land.*
46/70, *Town and Country Planning Acts 1962 to 1968: Planning Blight.*
82/70, *Town and Country Planning Act 1968 – Part I: The New Development Plan System of Structure and Local Plans.*

Department of the Environment (HMSO)
3/71, *Industrial Development – Exemption limits for Industrial Development Certificates and Time Limits on Planning Permissions.*
42/71, *The Dangerous Litter Act, 1971.*
44/71, *Town and Country Planning Act 1968 – Part I: The Town and Country Planning (Structure and Local Plans) Regulations 1971.*
60/71, *Town and Country Planning (Minerals) Regulations 1971.*
80/71, *Development by Government Departments.*
12/72, *The Planning of the Undeveloped Coast.*
1/73, *Provision for Sport and Physical Recreation.*
10/73, *Planning and Noise.*
63/73, *Local Government Act 1972: Administration of National Parks.*
104/73, *Local Transport Grants.*
138/73, *Nature Conservancy Council.*
6/74, *Tree Preservation and Planting.*
27/74, *Transport Supplementary Grant: More Details of the New System.*
60/74, *Transport Supplementary Grant: Submissions for 1975/6.*
65/74, *Local Government Act 1972: National Parks.*
76/74, *Local Government Act 1974 – Part III: Local Complaints.*
147/74, *Town and Country Amenities Act 1974.*
13/75, *Housing Act 1974: Renewal Strategies.*
14/75, *Housing Act 1974: Housing Action Areas, Priority Neighbourhoods and General Improvement Areas.*
17/75, *Town and Country Amenities Act 1974.*
77/75, *Clearance of Unfit Houses – Procedural Requirements.*
86/75, *Conservation of Wild Creatures and Wild Plants Act 1975.*
96/75, *The Town and Country Planning (Development Plans) Direction 1975.*
113/75, *Review of the Development Control System.*
121/75, *Community Land – Circular I: General Introduction and Priorities.*

Scottish Development Department (SDD)
49/1971, *Publicity for Planning Proposals.*

52/1971, *The New Development Plan System.*
47/1974, *Regional Transport Planning: Policies and Programmes.*
48/1974, *Public Passenger Transport – The New Role of Local Authorities.*
79/1974, *Housing (Scotland) Act 1974.*
83/1974, *Town and Country Amenities Act 1974.*
 4/1975, *Town and Country Planning – Regional Reports.*
 5/1975, *Regional Transport Planning: Form and Content of Transport Policies and Programmes.*
13/1975, *Regional Roads and Passenger Transport Expenditure: Financial Support.*
14/1975, *Public Inquiry Procedures.*
67/1975, *Housing (Scotland) Act 1974: Houses Below the Tolerable Standard: Housing Action Areas.*
96/1975, *Commission for Local Administration in Scotland.*
100/1975, *Housing Needs and Strategies.*

WHITE PAPERS (HMSO)

Employment Policy, Cmd 6527, 1944.
The Control of Land Use, Cmd 6537, 1944.
Town and Country Planning Bill 1947: Explanatory Memorandum, Cmd 7006, 1947.
Town and Country Planning Act, 1947: Amendment of Financial Provisions, Cmd 8699, 1952.
London – Employment: Housing: Land, Cmd 1952, 1963.
The Land Commission, Cmnd 2771, 1965.
Leisure in the Countryside, Cmnd 2928, 1966.
Transport Policy, Cmnd 3057, 1966.
Town and Country Planning, Cmnd 3333, 1967.
Public Transport and Traffic, Cmnd 3481, 1967.
The Older Houses in Scotland: A Plan for Action, Cmnd 3598, 1968.
Old Houses into New Homes, Cmnd 3602, 1968.
The Protection of the Environment: The Fight Against Pollution, Cmnd 4373, 1970.
The Reorganisation of Central Government, Cmnd 4506, 1970.
Industrial and Regional Development, Cmnd 4942, 1972.
Development and Compensation: Putting People First, Cmnd 5124, 1972.
Homes for People: Scottish Housing Policy in the 1970s, Cmnd 5272, 1973.
Widening the Choice: The Next Steps in Housing, Cmnd 5280, 1973.
Towards Better Homes: Proposals for Dealing with Scotland's Older Housing, Cmnd 5338, 1973.
Better Homes: The Next Priorities, Cmnd 5339, 1973.
Land, Cmnd 5730, 1974.
Development Land Tax, Cmnd 6195, 1975.
Sport and Recreation, Cmnd 6200, 1975:

INDEX

Ministry of Health 21, 26, 33-7
Ministry of Housing and Local Government Chapter III, 116, 228, 229
Ministry of Land and Natural Resources 42
Ministry of Technology 43, 54
Ministry of Town and Country Planning 33-7
Ministry of Transport 26, 43, 44, 52
Ministry of Works and Planning 35
Mobberley 203
Modification Orders 105-7, 113
Motorways 52, 53, 114, 255, 256-7
Mukherjee, S. 60

National Coal Board 114, 170, 172
National Economic Development Council 235-7
National Housing and Town Planning Council 16
National Housing Reform Council 16
National Park Plans 194
National Parks 160, Chapter X
National Parks and Access to the Countryside Act 1949 164, 168, Chapter X
National Parks Commission Chapter X
National Trust 160
Nature Conservancy Council 185, 189-190, 191, 227
Nature Reserves 189-90
Neighbourhood Councils 66
Nettleford, J. S. 18
Newtown (Montgomery) 200
New Towns 24, 25, Chapter XI
New Towns Commission 209-10
Noise 176-7
Noise Advisory Council 177
Non-conforming Uses 106-7
Northampton 201
Northwich 171
Noxious Trades 101

Offa's Dyke Path 187
Office Development – Control of 43, 56-8
Ombudsman 248-50
Opencast Coal Act 1958 173
Operational Land 109
Overspill 30-1, Chapter XI

Parish Councils 66, 67
Parliamentary Commissioner for Administration 248-50

Passenger Transport Authorities 152-3
Paterson Report 71
Pennine Way 187
Peterborough 201
Peterlee 197, 207
Picnic Places 192
Pilcher Report 146
Pilgrim Case 138
Pippard Report 166
Planning Advisory Group 80-2, 114
Planning Blight 113-14, 116, 261
Planning Inquiry Commission 51
Planning Permission: Application for 51, 98, 120-8, 245 et seq.; Conditional 101-4, 113; Deemed 45, 108, 160; Discontinuance 94, 105-7, 157; Modification 105-7, 113; Outline 165; Permitted 101-2, 108; Revocation 105-7, 113; Time Limits 103-4, 108; see also Appeals and Development
Pollution 166-7
Population 15, 32, 213, 228
Port Sunlight 16
Portal, Lord 35
Preservation Orders 161
Priority Neighbourhoods 223
Programme Maps 79; see also Development Plans
Protection of the Environment Bill (1973) 166
Public Health Act 1875 17
Public Inquiries 47, 79, 94, 255-9
Public Participation 95, 123, 125-6, 225-226, Chapter XIV
Purchase Notices 112-14, 116, 163

Ramsay Report 183
Rate Support Grant 54, 156, 168
Recreation Chapter X
Redcliffe-Maud Report 62, 63, 65, 116, 241, 242
Redditch 198
Regional Economic Planning Boards and Councils 43, 82, 230-2
Regional Planning 20, 30, 40-1, 67-9, 82, 91, Chapter XIII
Regional Reports 91
Rehousing 116, 218
Reith Report 196, 204, 205
Reith, Lord 34-5, 40
Restriction of Ribbon Development Act 1935 19
Revocation Orders 94, 105-7, 113
River Authorities 70